Walter Scott at 250

Walter Scott at 250

Looking Forward

Edited by Caroline McCracken-Flesher
and Matthew Wickman

EDINBURGH
University Press

Edinburgh University Press is one of the leading university presses in the UK. We publish academic books and journals in our selected subject areas across the humanities and social sciences, combining cutting-edge scholarship with high editorial and production values to produce academic works of lasting importance. For more information visit our website: edinburghuniversitypress.com

© editorial matter and organisation Caroline McCracken-Flesher and Matthew Wickman, 2021, 2023
© the chapters their several authors, 2021, 2023

Edinburgh University Press Ltd
The Tun – Holyrood Road, 12(2f) Jackson's Entry, Edinburgh EH8 8PJ

First published in hardback by Edinburgh University Press 2021

Typeset in 10.5/13 Bembo by
IDSUK (DataConnection) Ltd

A CIP record for this book is available from the British Library

ISBN 978 1 4744 2986 3 (hardback)
ISBN 978 1 4744 2987 0 (paperback)
ISBN 978 1 4744 2988 7 (webready PDF)
ISBN 978 1 4744 2989 4 (epub)

The right of Caroline McCracken-Flesher and Matthew Wickman to be identified as the Editor of this work has been asserted in accordance with the Copyright, Designs and Patents Act 1988, and the Copyright and Related Rights Regulations 2003 (SI No. 2498).

Contents

Acknowledgements   vii
Notes on Contributors   ix
Abbreviations   xii

Introduction: Walter Scott at 250 – and Counting   1
Caroline McCracken-Flesher and Matthew Wickman

1. Temporality and Historical Fiction Reading in Scott   11
   Ina Ferris

2. 'I bide my time': History and the Future Anterior
   in *The Bride of Lammermoor*   28
   Penny Fielding

3. Scott's Anachronisms   46
   Ian Duncan

4. Scott, the Novel, and Capital in the Nineteenth Century   65
   Anthony Jarrells

5. The General Undertaker: Scott's *Life of Napoleon Buonaparte*
   and the Prehistory of Neoliberalism   83
   Celeste Langan

6. Scott and the Art of Surplusage: Excess in the Narrative Poems   109
   Alison Lumsden

7. Performing History: Theatricality, Gender, the Early Historical
   Novel and Scott   124
   Fiona Price

8. Where We Never Were: Women at Walter Scott's Abbotsford   142
   Caroline McCracken-Flesher

9. Reading Walter Scott in the Anthropocene   161
   Susan Oliver

10. *Redgauntlet*: Speculation in History, Speculation in Nature   181
    Matthew Wickman

Bibliography   198
Index   219

Acknowledgements

As *Walter Scott at 250* shows, good things take time. We began crafting this book in early 2010, when we invited a panel on the subject for the 2011 conference of the Modern Language Association in Los Angeles. Two contributors to this volume, Ian Duncan and Celeste Langan, joined us on that panel. In summer 2011, additional contributors emerged from the University of Wyoming's conference on Walter Scott, where the volume took further shape. A book like this one would be impossible without the large, global community of Scott scholars whose excellent work and generous feedback fuels our collective thinking and extends our conversations. We are grateful to this vast community, comprised of remarkable individuals too numerous to name. To those whose essays are compiled here, we are grateful for your patience and goodwill as well as your considerable intelligence and expertise.

Some individuals and institutions are more directly responsible for this volume and deserve special mention. Our collective work has depended heavily on the achievements of the editors of the Edinburgh Edition of the Waverley Novels (EEWN), and the resources and expertise of the National Library of Scotland and Abbotsford, the Home of Walter Scott. The Institute for Advanced Study in the Humanities (at Edinburgh), the Chawton House Library, the Edinburgh Sir Walter Scott Club and the Clan Scott Society have supported and provided a community for the editors' research and public engagement. Jackie Jones and now Michelle Houston at Edinburgh University Press have been engaged and encouraging editors throughout.

We continue to be grateful for friends and colleagues at the institutions where we work or have worked, and those whose regular conversations or special events geared around Walter Scott have been so instrumental to our thinking: Nick Mason and Paul Westover at BYU; Ali Lumsden,

Cairns Craig, Tim Baker, Catherine Jones and David Duff at the University of Aberdeen; the University of Wyoming in Scotland team, especially Nicole Crawford, Sarah Strauss and Carrick Eggleston; Penny Fielding, Bob Irvine and Peter Garside at the University of Edinburgh; Alan Riach and Murray Pittock at the University of Glasgow; Robert Crawford at St Andrews; Benjamine Toussaint at the Sorbonne; and UW in Scotland friends Naoma Tate, Hilery Lindmier, Fiona Armstrong Lady MacGregor, Sir Malcolm MacGregor and Richard Scott, 10th Duke of Buccleuch. And of course, we are grateful to those closest to home – to Kerry, Hadley and Elena Wickman for accompanying Matt on his adventures on both sides of the Atlantic. Caroline, as ever, thanks Paul and Conor.

Contributors

Ian Duncan is Florence Green Bixby Professor of English at the University of California, Berkeley. His books include *Human Forms: The Novel in the Age of Evolution* (Princeton, 2019), *Scott's Shadow: The Novel in Romantic Edinburgh* (Princeton, 2007), *Modern Romance and Transformations of the Novel: The Gothic, Scott, Dickens* (Cambridge University Press, 1992), *The Edinburgh Companion to James Hogg* (co-editor; Edinburgh University Press, 2012) and *Scotland and the Borders of Romanticism* (co-editor; Cambridge University Press, 2004). He is a general editor of *The Stirling-South Carolina Edition of the Works of James Hogg* (Edinburgh University Press) and *Edinburgh Critical Studies in Romanticism* (Edinburgh University Press).

Ina Ferris, Emeritus Professor of English at the University of Ottawa, has published on the emergence of new novelistic forms, book history, and the making of a reading culture in the Romantic period. Her books include *The Achievement of Literary Authority: Gender, History and the Waverley Novels* (Cornell University Press, 1991), *The Romantic National Tale and the Question of Ireland* (Cambridge University Press, 2002), *Bookish Histories: Books, Literature, and Commercial Modernity, 1700–1900*, co-edited with Paul Keen (Palgrave Macmillan, 2009), and *Book-Men, Book Clubs, and the Romantic Literary Sphere* (Palgrave Macmillan, 2015). She is currently working on linkages between generic innovation and bookishness in the popularisation of knowledge fields in the late eighteenth/early nineteenth centuries.

Penny Fielding is Herbert Grierson Professor of English Literature at the University of Edinburgh and Director of the project for Scottish Writing in the Nineteenth Century. Her most recent publication is *The 1880s*, co-edited with Andrew Taylor (Cambridge University Press, 2019). Previous books include *Scotland and the Fictions of Geography: North Britain 1760–1830* (Cambridge University Press, 2008), *Writing and Orality: Nationality, Culture and Nineteenth-Century Scottish Fiction* (Oxford University Press, 1996), the edited *The Edinburgh Companion to Robert Louis Stevenson*, and an edition of *The Monastery* for the EEWN (Edinburgh University Press, 2000). She is general editor for the New Edinburgh Edition of the Works of Robert Louis Stevenson.

Anthony Jarrells, Associate Professor in the University of South Carolina Department of English, is the author of *Britain's Bloodless Revolutions: 1688 and the Romantic Reform of Literature* (Palgrave Macmillan, 2005). He produced the edition *Blackwood's Magazine, 1817–1825, Vol. 2: Selected Prose* (Pickering and Chatto, 2006). His recent work focuses on regionalism and Romanticism, and his current projects include an edition of John Galt's Scottish stories and a book-length study of the Romantic-period tale. He co-edits the journal *Studies in Scottish Literature*.

Celeste Langan, Associate Professor in the UC Berkeley Department of English, is the author of *Romantic Vagrancy: Wordsworth and the Simulation of Freedom* (Cambridge University Press, 1995), as well as a number of essays in Romantic Media Studies: 'Understanding Media in 1805', 'The Medium of Romantic Poetry' (co-authored with Maureen McLane) and 'Pathologies of Communication from Coleridge to Schreber'. Her chapter for this volume is drawn from research for her current book manuscript, *Post-Napoleonism: Romantic Writing and the Afterlife of Sovereignty*.

Alison Lumsden is Regius Chair in English Literature at the University of Aberdeen. She is Director of the Walter Scott Research Centre and Honorary Librarian at Abbotsford. She was a general editor for the EEWN and is now lead editor for the ten-volume Edinburgh Edition of Walter Scott's Poetry. Her books include *Walter Scott and the Limits of Language* (Edinburgh University Press, 2010). She co-edited the EEWN volumes *The Heart of Mid-Lothian* (with David Hewitt, 2004) and *The Pirate* (with Mark Weinstein, 2000), as well as Scott's *Reliquiae Trotcosiensis* (with Gerard Carruthers, 2004).

Caroline McCracken-Flesher is Professor of English at the University of Wyoming. The past Convenor of the International Association for the Study of Scottish Literatures, she runs the University of Wyoming in Scotland program and directs UW's Center for Global Studies. Her books include *Possible Scotlands: Walter Scott and the Story of Tomorrow* (Oxford University Press, 2005), *The Doctor Dissected: A Cultural Autopsy of the Burke and Hare Novels* (Oxford University Press, 2012), the edited volumes *Culture, Nation and the New Scottish Parliament* (Bucknell University Press, 2007), *Scotland As Science Fiction* (Bucknell University Press, 2012), and *Approaches to Teaching the Works of Robert Louis Stevenson* (Modern Language Association, 2013). Her edition of Stevenson's *Kidnapped* is forthcoming from Edinburgh University Press.

Susan Oliver is Professor of English and deputy Dean of Research at the University of Essex. Her books include *Scott, Byron and the Poetics of Cultural Encounter* (Palgrave Macmillan, 2005) and *Walter Scott and the Greening of Scotland: Emergent Ecologies of a Nation* (forthcoming from Cambridge University Press). She edited the 2017 Yearbook of English Studies (volume 47), titled *Walter Scott: New Interpretations*.

Fiona Price is Professor in Literature at the University of Chichester. She is author of *Reinventing Liberty: Nation, Commerce and the Historical Novel from Walpole to Scott* (Edinburgh University Press, 2016) and *Revolutions in Taste 1773–1818: Women Writers and the Aesthetics of Romanticism* (Routledge, 2009) and editor, with Benjamin Dew, of *Historical Writing in Britain, 1688–1830: Visions of History* (Palgrave Macmillan, 2014). She has edited two historical novels, Jane Porter's *The Scottish Chiefs* (1810; Broadview Press, 2007) and Sarah Green's *Private History of the Court of England* (1808; Pickering and Chatto, 2011). She is currently working on a monograph on the idea of the 'real' in the Romantic-period novel.

Matthew Wickman is Professor of English at Brigham Young University and Founding Director of the BYU Humanities Center. He is the author of *Literature after Euclid: The Geometric Imagination in the Long Scottish Enlightenment* (University of Pennsylvania Press, 2016), *The Ruins of Experience: Scotland's "Romantick" Highlands and the Birth of the Modern Witness* (University of Pennsylvania Press, 2007) and many articles on Scottish literary and intellectual history and in other fields across the interdisciplinary humanities.

Abbreviations

EEWN   Edinburgh Edition of the Waverley Novels. David Hewitt, Series Editor. Edinburgh: Edinburgh University Press, 1993–2012.
Journal   *The Journal of Sir Walter Scott*. W. E. K. Anderson, ed. London: Canongate, 1998.
Life   Lockhart, J. G., *Memoirs of the Life of Sir Walter Scott, Bart*. 7 vols. Edinburgh: Robert Cadell, 1837–8.
Letters   *The Letters of Sir Walter Scott, 1825–6*. H. J. G. Grierson, ed. London: Constable, 1935.
NLS   National Library of Scotland

Introduction: Walter Scott at 250 – and Counting

Caroline McCracken-Flesher and Matthew Wickman

The year 2021 brings the 250th anniversary of Walter Scott's birth. On regular birthdays we look back in celebration and forward in anticipation. For Scott, however, the future might seem decidedly past the possible. There is no going forward, we might presume, for someone dead in 1832. Moreover, Scott's reputation suffered a precipitous decline through the twentieth century. Even during Scott's heyday, as a balladic poet and author of historical romance, he often ran counter to the literary innovations that, looking backward, we consider norms of his era. If poems like *The Lady of the Lake* (1810) challenged the reflectiveness of the Romantic poets with landscapes brought into being by action, they harkened, some thought, to a more demotic but also a less sophisticated theoretical impulse. *Waverley* (1814) made Scott a novelist of times recently past, the realiser of history as stumbling romance. He was touted as 'the Great Unknown', but as much for his popular success as for his literary creativity. Still, Scott was also very modern – sometimes problematically so for a contemporary aesthetic that aimed for 'fit audience . . . though few'.[1] He accomplished sales only to be dreamed of by operationalising the link between publication and printing. Of course, he then gained both contemporary respect and considerable notoriety after financial collapses cascaded outward from his publishing partners' unwise investments – among them, cotton – and carried away both printing and authorial profits.[2] A commercial artist ahead of his time, and peddling the backward gaze, however nobly Scott fought his way forward by refusing bankruptcy and attempting to write his way out of his troubles, the author visibly tripped over the very speculative conditions that allowed his success. Today Scott might stand as a symbol for a populace deluded by 'progress' and disturbingly implicated in commercial and even colonial trade. Such a Scott might be considered 'too well known', then and now. This book recognises that Scott but suggests there is more to know – and that we might not know Sir Walter as well as we thought.

From a critical perspective, Scott's stock sank with his finances, the bank failure indicating that the 'Wizard of the North' had feet of transactional clay. Thomas Carlyle dealt the first major blow in an 1838 review of Lockhart's *Memoirs of the Life of Sir Walter Scott*. Of the author who had struggled to write himself out of financial disgrace, Carlyle observed, 'There is a great discovery still to be made in literature, that of paying literary men by the quantity they *do not* write.'[3] Scott had 'spread himself into breadth and length, into superficiality and saleability'. And Scott declined from George Eliot's 'beloved Walter Scott' into an embarrassment for twentieth-century literateurs.[4] The early century, raised on Scott in schools at home and across the Empire, became disenamoured of his form. E. M. Forster asked 'Who shall tell us a story?' and answered: 'Sir Walter Scott of course.' But this was not a compliment. Scott, Forster thought, had 'a trivial mind and a heavy style. He cannot construct.'[5] F. R. Leavis, tracing a 'Great Tradition of the English Novel', found in it no place for Sir Walter: 'Out of Scott a bad tradition came.'[6] Writing in *The Historical Novel*, outside both Scottish and English traditions, the Hungarian Marxist Georg Lukács for a moment rescued Scott by recognising him as a proponent of complex socialities. In Scotland, however, as the country regained its national ambitions, the author was viewed as retrograde in substance. For J. G. Lockhart, who saw his father-in-law's talents at their cultural apogee when Scott helped to stage George IV's visit to Edinburgh in 1822 as a festival of clans and highland dress, the author too easily frittered away his capabilities in 'celtified pageantry'.[7] In 'Scotland 1941', Edwin Muir lambasted the author as one of the 'mummied housegods in their musty niches, / Burns and Scott, sham bards of a sham nation'.[8] Scott had brought 'spiritual defeat wrapped warm in riches, / No pride but pride of pelf. Long since the young / Fought in great bloody battles to carve out / This towering pulpit of the Golden Calf'. By 1977, Scotland's literary polemicists such as Tom Nairn saw the author's tales as producing 'tartanry', a largely Jacobite but always nostalgic imaginary that actively delimited Scotland's local sensibility and international potentiality.[9] Pursuing his own, cultural perplexes, in 1979 Edward Said was sure this Scott had popularised sentiment internationally. His retrograde writings had helped the west to orientalise the Arab world.[10] Then in 1996, Cairns Craig argued that Scott had placed his country 'out of history', outside modern narratives of progress.[11] George

Eliot, who found it 'a personal grief, a heart-wound [. . . to] hear a depreciatory or slighting word about Scott', would have found this twentieth-century reputation a trial and a distress.[12]

Yet if Scotland courtesy of Scott stood 'beyond history', with Craig's insight came a turn: that impossible beyond increasingly stands revealed as a space of creative and productive imagination.[13] Thus, the 1990s traced Scott's unappreciated impacts. Ian Duncan and Fiona Robertson recognised his contribution to the Gothic and its transformations; Ina Ferris addressed how his work and its reception inevitably and sometimes problematically reworked gendered and generic hierarchies. Assisted by that monumental work, the Edinburgh Edition of the Waverley Novels (1993–2012), with the turn towards the twenty-first century the critical eye recognised an inventive author and complicated person. Scott more and more has been seen as a self-aware, pre-postmodern author, prone to question and disturb form and history, the teller and the romance. Claire Jones has shown how Scott understood the work of memory; Andrew Lincoln pursued Scott's engagement with modernity. As Jerome McGann pointed scholars towards the author's 'Romantic Postmodernity' in 2004, Caroline McCracken-Flesher demonstrated the author's accumulation of competing pasts and the opening up of *Possible Scotlands* through the rewritable tale; Alison Lumsden foregrounded Scott's linguistic inventiveness – his evolving scepticism towards language as communication. Increasingly, that is, we realise that some of Scott's supposed flaws actually stand as critiques of under-interrogated literary and historical canons. Thus Robert Mayer has revealed Scott's ethical, strategic and productive engagement with the press and with fellow writers, particularly women, while numerous scholars are reworking Scott's relation with Romanticism.[14] New vasts of theoretical encounter stand open.[15] More and more, too, we understand that Scott's reputation rises and falls with us. Ian Duncan has recently traced how Scott's literary shadow impacted the work of his contemporaries as they engaged it or raged against it; Ann Rigney has shown how much of Scott we remember through material acts of memory – such as monuments and kitschy mementos – that tell more about how we engage with the past than they do about the author. Scott, and our relation to him, necessarily recedes in the rear view mirror of an advancing present. But objects in the mirror are always closer than they appear. They impinge on us.

In this book we look back only to discover that through Scott we are really seeing sideways, eyeing ourselves, looking forward. As the 'Great Unknown' or the 'Wizard of the North', Scott has been inscribed as a figure of authority and as an inevitable object for resistance. But as the anonymous 'author of Waverley', or the 'eidolon', he has always figured a more pliable, more nimble, and even a strategic possibility. Indeed, if audiences have proved in thrall to a limited idea of the historical author, Scott was in thrall neither to the histories he wrote nor to any idea of himself. Perhaps he had taken a cue from the historic and legendary Thomas the Rhymer, with that poet's tendency to intermittent appearance and belated prophesy. Scott reprised, rewrote or re-echoed True Thomas in poetry and prose from his ballad in *The Minstrelsy of the Scottish Border* (1802) through *The Lay of the Last Minstrel* (1805) with its undead wizard Michael Scott and the late novel, *Castle Dangerous* (1831). In this last, the Rhymer reappears across centuries, purveying and simultaneously calling his information into question with each eruption into an advancing present. Certainly, when Scott anonymously reviewed his *Tales of My Landlord* (1816), he wrote explicitly about history, memory and authorship as different – in terms that might have been familiar to Derrida. 'Probability and perspicuity of narrative are sacrificed with the utmost indifference to the desire of producing effect'; for the reader there is a 'total want of interest [. . . in] the character of the hero'; transatlantic rumour has named an author for the *Tales*, but 'a critic may be excused seizing upon the nearest suspicious person'.[16] The preface to *The Fortunes of Nigel* (1822) went on to spoof the anonymous author as an indeterminate spirit unimpressed by the imperatives of canons and alert to markets and the contingencies of literary and authorial reputations over time.[17] In *The Betrothed* (1825), Scott's personae constitute a joint-stock company, marvel at the production of plots by a steam press, fall at odds with one another, and overtly embrace history – as rewritable fiction.[18]

This Scott consistently challenged both his own plots and also how they are read. Criticised for his supposedly huddled up, unheroic endings, Scott accepted the rebuke and kept right on refusing certainty and entangling his characters in complexity and compromise.[19] Encouraged to pursue major moments and substantial figures, Scott continued to problematise his protagonists, who fall into unexpected and little understood circumstances, and work their way forward not through major heroics but by small, human adjustments in face of complex realities. In *The Heart of Mid-Lothian* (1818) Jeanie Deans, the well-behaved daughter of rigorous patriarchies, reshapes political and personal realities by the simple act of putting one foot in front of another all the way to London – and then she returns home to deal with the local and familial aftermath.

This is the Scott who motivates our consideration at 250; it is this Scott who points towards our possible futures. Scott, although we necessarily look on his times as past, of course experienced them as present. Moreover, those times saw exponential change. From his birth in 1771, Scott's world was challenged not just by literary innovation but by the philosophical, agricultural and industrial disruptions that produced it. The early nineteenth century lurched from change to crisis and crisis to change: revolution in France, the Napoleonic Wars, weavers' marches, medical scandals and advances, global trade, the end of slavery, the movement of masses, financial turbulence. The list goes on. Scott lived a relatively short life, but there was a lot in it. His many roles, too, placed him cheek by jowl with crisis. As a popular author he invested in modern printing, got carried away – as did his print numbers – by the steam press, and suffered the vagaries of both experimental technology and its speculative funding. He was a bourgeois landowner but pursued agricultural improvement beyond his finances. As a national spokesperson he walked the foreign field of Waterloo,[20] wrote a biography of Napoleon and almost had to fight a duel with a disgruntled French general.[21] Serving as President of the Royal Society of Edinburgh he relied upon science, and bought a telescope to observe the comet of 1819,[22] but in 1828–9 found himself mediating the relation between science and the public interest when Dr Knox advanced anatomy by dissecting corpses supplied by the serial murderers Burke and Hare.[23] Scott built a home in the Scottish borders that represented his art, hosted the good and the great, became a model for architects and decorators, and was consequently swarmed by tourists. As chair of the board for the Edinburgh Oil Gas Light company, he made Abbotsford the first house in Scotland to be lit by gas – a light so bright that it dazzled his guests[24] and a fuel source so smoky that he noted concerns for those with 'delicate lungs'.[25] Thoroughly embroiled in his times, Scott stood front and centre to address the challenge of change.

Scott, then, has much to share in the experience, narration, anticipation and response to change as a condition of life – a condition our era, with its existential challenges to climate, to public health, to civilisation, knows only too well.

In the chapters that follow, major scholars in Scott criticism foreground the author as theorist of tomorrow – as the surveyor of the complexities of the present who also gazes, as we do, towards an anxious and hopeful future. Fittingly, one cluster of concentrated attention in the volume addresses the problematics of time – of pasts and futures sedimented in a compact and complex space of reading. Ina Ferris discusses how Scott's novels convey a strong sense of their own medium, forming a conduit that 'announces [their own] presence, make[s themselves] felt'. Scott's characters often travel from one location to another, usually with difficulty; eras, too, pass in Scott's historical novels unevenly, haltingly. His readers thus find themselves navigating what Ferris calls 'intervallic time', experiencing durations between historical epochs that do not open the past as much as unclose it, leave it ajar. In Scott's thick, medial fictions, Ferris shows, something always seems to break down on our journey into modernity. Likewise, Penny Fielding underscores the strangeness of the experience of time in Scott's fiction. Taking up *The Bride of Lammermoor* (1819), Fielding focuses on Scott's appeal to the future anterior, a verb form in which 'the present is not the inevitable telos of the past, nor is it a stable platform from which to predict the future. Rather, the past is a history that we anticipate making sense at some point in the future, while, in the present, we hazard a guess that we will understand the past leading up to a future as yet unknown'. With Ferris, Fielding argues that Scott's work does not provide a straightforward understanding of the past; her term for whatever understanding it does afford is 'knowingness', which is in no way tantamount to certainty.

For both Ferris and Fielding there is something uncanny about our experience of time and history in Scott's fiction, propagating as it does a sense of the unfamiliar that extends into the present. Ian Duncan then shows how Scott converts uncanniness into a methodological principle. This is most evident in Scott's use of anachronism, a narrative technique that 'forges a teleological link between the represented past and the present scene of writing – and, implicitly, of reading'. It does so, moreover, less by illustrating the residues of the past in the present than 'the immanence of the present in the past', the latent seeds of modernity in what the latter supplants. Duncan describes anachronism as a mode of time travel across distinct but suddenly overlapping historical periods, and shows how Scott actually renders the device multiple: an uncanny mode (in *Rob Roy*, [1818]) disrupts our sense of a smoothly successive history, a comic mode (in *Waverley*) melds history into an evocatively eternal present, and a utopian mode (in *Ivanhoe* [1820]) reveals history in exilic form seeking realisation in the present.

That one cluster of critical attention in this book should form around complexities of time and history is probably to be expected given Scott's deserved reputation as a master, if not the inaugurator, of the genre of historical fiction. Another cluster forms around questions of value. Perhaps this should not surprise us given Scott's own force as a virtual industry of authorial invention during the early nineteenth century or the monumental debts he incurred during the financial crisis of 1825–6. But as Anthony Jarrells and Celeste Langan reveal, Scott's sensitivity to matters of value renders him vividly, if a little unsettlingly, instructive in our twenty-first century. Jarrells perceives a correlation between Scott's era and ours in the way that wealth has outpaced growth, fuelling inequality. And so, through readings of *Chronicles of the Canongate* (1827), *Saint Ronan's Well* (1824) and *Rob Roy*, Jarrells shows how Scott addresses tensions between merit and inheritance, with the former often serving as a cover for the latter. If Scott's intuitions reflect our own as we enter the middle decades of the twenty-first century, and if we thus see ourselves reflected in Scott, it is nevertheless remarkable how the judgements rendered in Scott's fictions should have differed in their degree of complexity from other realist novels and political-economic accounts of their own era.

One thing Scott may not have been able to anticipate, but which he nevertheless helps us configure, is the crisis faced by scholars – knowledge workers – in universities. Langan's ingenious insight apprehends Scott as the consummate figure of the indebted author, a forerunner of the situation we face today when debt is no longer sovereign, backed by the state, as much as democratised and thus distributed across the workforce. Not coincidentally, scholars increasingly face situations in which they are 'encouraged to transform themselves into "intrapreneurs", advancing the institution's interests through individual initiative and marketable innovation'; the crisis they face does not concern publishing or perishing so much as demonstrating the economic value of the publishing they do. Scott's life is instructive as he sought to dig himself out of debt after the financial crisis. Scott's *Life of Napoleon* (1827) is especially telling. It 'represents war and commerce, and commerce and writing, as intersecting parts of the same "enterprise"', Napoleon's strategy on the battlefield – overwhelming his opponents through volume of troops – resembling that of Scott and his publisher, Archibald Constable, seeking to overwhelm competitors through the same show of quantitative force: page upon page, volume after volume. Scott would frequently recount in his journal the number of pages he had written that day for *Napoleon*. This eventually had the effect, however, of converting the journal itself into a marketable venture, eradicating the distinction between two experiences of writing, for business and for pleasure. To Scott during this manically productive phase of his life, all writing was reduced to capital. What he illustrates, then, is the emergence of the 'writing industrial complex' so familiar to scholars in today's university culture of neoliberalisation, where scholars write not so much in the fear of getting sacked as facing the threat of extinction.

The idea of returning to Scott, reading him anew, and seeing in his work both new ways of framing traditional topics – time, history, authorship – and a new set of topics altogether is something that characterises all the chapters in this collection. It may especially be the case with a third cluster that coalesces around familiar sites of Scott's work. Alison Lumsden returns us to Scott's poetry, concerning herself with Scott's copious editorial notes. Analyses of *The Lady of the Lake* and *The Minstrelsy of the Scottish Border*, in particular, reveal Scott's habit of compulsively returning to these notes in later editions of his poems, even after the poems were essentially finished and undergoing no further revision. Partly, these notes represent Enlightened addenda to the folk origins of the poems – knowledge work (in Langan's terms) multiplying itself endlessly in the seams of Scott's creative ventures. But as Lumsden shows us, Scott would add supplementary commentary not only on material he had collected but even on his own creative works, sometimes crafting virtual labyrinths of signification out of scenarios he had not found as much as invented. Lumsden's point is that Scott's notes do not document their sources as much as bring into conversation different modes of knowledge: 'written authority, local folklore, literary heritage', and so on. This abundance of epistemic cultures produces a surplus of meanings Scott ultimately did not seek to explain as much as indulge – Maurice Blanchot's *Infinite Conversation* avant la lettre.

For her part, Fiona Price is taken with the surplus inscribed performatively into Scott's work. Scott was known for staging elaborate performances, most notably the national pageant he organised for the visit of George IV to Edinburgh in 1822. But Price turns her attention to two other aspects of performance that inflect Scott's fiction and, more broadly, his historical moment (and ours): the performance of gender and political performance. Scott's contemporaries Ellis Cornelia Knight, Jane West and Jane Porter repeatedly examined public performance in their fiction, focusing on ways to stage or present a nation or self, especially as a female subject. During this period, excessive theatricality was often frowned on in Britain, associated with Catholicism, femininity, and the *ancien régime*. As a result, Scott's own performances, especially in his early novels, present themselves in masculine and Protestant forms. However, in later work like *The Abbot* (1820) or *Kenilworth: A Romance* (1821), Scott's performances become increasingly subtle, rejecting simple binaries (like Jacobin versus Jacobite) in favour of a more layered exhibition of masculine and feminine subject positions. In this way, Scott underscores the never more relevant necessity of self-conscious participation in the body politic.

Caroline McCracken-Flesher explores another performative site of Scott's legacy in turning us to Abbotsford. She argues that visitors to Scott's famous home 'show us something about authors' houses, modernity, access and ourselves that we might carry into our era of intensified celebrity culture'. Visitors, particularly other authors, engage in a kind of authentication project, establishing their own authorial place through imaginative identification with

Scott in his. What these visitors systematically overlook, however, is the lived history of Abbotsford's other residents, especially women. Women, with 'their regular lives and family relationships . . . disrupt the visitors' affecting experience of Abbotsford' and are thus expunged from the record of pilgrimages to the Great Home of the Great Man. This unsettling illustration of how women were marginalised in the formulation of modern ideas of authorship and the creative landscape of the mind nonetheless brings us an opportunity to recognise a more integrated productivity through literature and community in our future.

Attention to landscape brings us to the fourth and final cluster of essays in this volume. Susan Oliver evokes Scott as a writer attuned to environmental concerns, particularly species loss. Scott was a writer keenly aware of landscape – of land as a site of cultural memory – and his work documents the invasion, loss and transformation of Scotland, particularly in the region near his home in the Borders. Oliver provocatively portrays an ecocritical Scott by way of two more familiar categories in the Scottish historical imaginary: 'improvement' and 'the clearances', schemes that introduced science (not to mention sheep) more squarely into Scottish husbandry. Known for their forcible and devastating effects on human populations, improvement and the clearances actually, and drastically, affected a wide range of living things. Oliver shows us how Scott registers these changes in a number of literary works, poems as well as novels.

Finally, Matthew Wickman discusses how Scott implicitly responds to a gauntlet thrown down in environmental scholarship. Amitav Ghosh remarks that the modern novel, which he traces back to Scott, distracts us from addressing problems of greatest magnitude (like the environmental crisis introduced by the Industrial Revolution, of which we are the unhappy, Anthropocenic inheritors).[26] How so? Because modern novels bring the preponderance of attention to individual, rather than species-wide, ecological concerns, fixating on the desire and angst of human subjects. As such, modern novelists, with Scott at their alleged forefront, render unthinkable viable solutions to crises that can only be solved through a collective imaginary. However, the trope of the unthinkable has a longer history in modern thought, and Scott actually provides a model for how to engage the unimaginable. Taking up the theory of speculative realism and turning it to the relationship between history and romance (principal vectors of Scott's historical novels), Wickman discusses how, in *Redgauntlet* (1824), Scott sets romance not against a backdrop of history but against still more romance. The result is not a history that *is* or that *might have been*, but a history that *also is*, a history forever running parallel to itself in multiple array. In this way, Scott demonstrates how to think the unthinkable, a powerful promise for the novel and, more broadly, for our contemporary age.

Our Walter Scott, ourselves: Scott remains so pertinent, so urgent to our present moment. Who was a better reader and writer of the past than Scott? Who better framed it to fit the exigencies of his era and his era's panorama of imagined futures? Scott will still be relevant at 1250; and we would be wise to learn from him if we wish even to speculate on the form future Scott celebrations may take a millennium from now.

Notes

1. Wordsworth, *The Excursion*, xi.
2. Alloway, 'Cadell and the Crash', p. 132.
3. Carlyle, Review, p. 297.
4. George Eliot, Letter to Alexander Main, 9 August 1871, Cross, *Life of George Eliot*, p. 564.
5. Forster, *Aspects of the Novel*, p. 44.
6. Leavis, *The Great Tradition*, p. 14n.
7. Lockhart, *Life*, 5: 204.
8. First published in Edwin Muir, *The Narrow Place* (1943); see Muir, *Complete Poems*, 110.
9. Nairn, *Break-up*, pp. 156–65.
10. Said, *Orientalism*, pp. 60, 102.
11. Craig, *Out of History*, pp. 37–40.
12. Cross, *Life of George Eliot*, p. 564.
13. Craig, *Out of History*, p. 224.
14. See Wickman, *The Ruins of Experience*; McCracken-Flesher, 'Walter Scott's Romanticism'.
15. See Gottlieb, *Walter Scott and Contemporary Theory*.
16. Scott, Review of *Tales of My Landlord*, pp. 431, 480.
17. Scott, 'Introductory Epistle', *The Fortunes of Nigel*, pp. 3–17.
18. Scott, 'Minutes of a General Meeting', *The Betrothed*, pp. 3–11.
19. Walter Scott to Lady Louisa Stuart, 14 November 1816, *Letters* 4: 292–3, 293n. See Lady Louisa's continued critique in Lockhart, *Life*, 4: 177–8.
20. Recounted in Walter Scott, *Paul's Letters to his Kinsfolk* (1816).
21. Baron Gaspard Gourgaud. See *Letters* 10: 270–82, 286–7, 300.
22. Walter Scott to James Veitch, 20 October [1820], *Letters* 6: 277 and n2.
23. See McCracken-Flesher, *The Doctor Dissected*, chapter 2.
24. Bewick, *Life and Letters* 1: 182. Virginia Woolf dwelt upon the effect in 'Gas at Abbotsford'.
25. Copy of a letter to Rev. Joseph Dunn, 25 December 1823, NLS MS 997, f. 73.
26. Ghosh, *The Great Derangement*, p. 7.

1

Temporality and Historical Fiction Reading in Scott

Ina Ferris

Taking up Stendhal's famous metaphor of the novel as a mirror carried along a high road, Hans Ulrich Gumbrecht has retold the history of the European novel as a story of roads: 'the roads of the novel'.[1] Stendhal's trope of moving down a road provides Gumbrecht with a supple heuristic. On the one hand, it allows him to posit a common novelistic structure rooted in the sequential temporality underpinning both narrative and lived experience while, on the other hand, it lets him differentiate novelistic modes on the basis of the various principles by which they connect the events occurring along the road. Thus *Don Quixote*'s realist 'roads of contingency', governed by the principle of probability, stand against both the arbitrary roads of prose romance, where anything can happen, and the overdetermined roads of allegorical narrative, where everything is necessary and meaningful.[2] During the eighteenth and early nineteenth centuries, he argues, the roads of the novel underwent 'de-realisation' as the life of the mind became the touchstone of reality, transforming the novel's roads from sequential patterns displaying normative concepts of identity into sites where protagonists shaped their subjectivities via confrontation with a world of contingent encounters and events. The era's signature genre was the *Bildungsroman*, whose ideal was a world 'that harmoniously fit under the control of the subject's agency'; consequently, it was a novelistic mode that 'had no more use for bumps in its roads'.[3]

Gumbrecht's history concentrates on present-tense genres and finds no room for the 'roads of history', which entered the European novel at much the same time as those of the *Bildungsroman* and which had a great deal of use for those very 'bumps'. On the terrain of historical fiction the roads of the novel become enmeshed in the compound and consequential time of history, the temporal medium through which all questions of formation, whether individual or collective, have to pass.

Matters of temporal orientation (both large and small scale) now assume prominence, along with the more strictly historiographic concern of the relationship between past and present that has garnered most critical attention. And nothing perhaps more sharply separates our current readings of Scott's historical novel from that of his great twentieth-century champion, Georg Lukács than the identification of Scott's paradigmatic status with his production of the past as 'the prehistory of the present'.[4] Today the forward march of history no longer seems quite so self-evident nor the path from then to now so direct as the temporal dimensions that long sustained historical thought rapidly lose purchase. Ours is an era of 'vanishing distance', Chris Lorenz has observed, wherein past and future seem to have collapsed as 'points of orientation', leaving us (in his felicitous phrase) 'unstuck in time'.[5] In an age of such 'vanishing distance' past, present and future occupy the same flat plane, a one-dimensional space whereon we can move smoothly among the terms, encountering no resistance. Time and space, as often remarked, have lost weight. But in the nineteenth-century historical novel they precisely gained weight, and a key dimension of the salience of Scott's fiction in our own day lies in its achievement of such densification by Scott's exploitation of the affordances of his own medium, the printed book and written narrative.

Gumbrecht's trope of the road usefully reminds us that at a concrete level Scott's novels are novels of the road, focused on the experience of moving through ground as much as through the more abstract dimensions we gather under the name of 'history'. On his roads the dimensions of time-space thicken and enact a certain resistance to those who would move through them, thereby moving into the foreground a sense of medium in its older, stronger signification of 'an intervening or intermediate agency or substance'.[6] Defined as an intervening substance rather than simply as a vehicle (a taken-for-granted channel of conduction), a medium announces its presence, makes itself felt. Scott's historical fiction, I want to suggest, turns on this sense of medium, inducing what Kevis Goodman, writing of georgic modes, has called an 'intensified medium-consciousness'.[7] Goodman's phrase incorporates both the early sense of 'medium' as a physical conduit animating organs of sense to make perceptible what is around us (for example air, water, light) and its now primary technological reference to the 'media' of communication. Importantly, Goodman notes, in the eighteenth/early nineteenth century, the common plural was not 'media' but 'mediums', thereby retaining the sense of a plurality of distinct modes of mediation rather than constellating them into a homogenised 'media'. By harnessing both semantic fields, Scott uses his narrative to make palpable the pressure of passage: the movement forward through a space and time. In contrast to its prominent play in Scott's day, however, the question of forward movement retains little traction in current literary-historical thought. Historical time now appears less a straight line than a matrix of involuted dimensions, planar intersections, complex recursions. Spatial models articulating lateral synchronic relations (for example networks, assemblages, ecologies) dominate our critical landscape. Linearity has come to seem dull at best, suspect at worst. And yet it remains the case that lived historical time *is* linear, and so too is the time of reading.

Histories and historical models may not necessarily take linear form, but time's arrow moves in one direction, and sequence remains the baseline of historical thinking about past events and experiences: what Reinhart Koselleck calls the 'unalterable before and after of events that are actually past'.[8] The time of reading is similarly linear and constrained. At the level of the page our eyes move across the lines from left to right; at the level of the sentence we establish semantic order through phonetic sequence and rules of syntax; at the level of the narrative we connect events in anticipation of an ending that will bring the whole 'into line'. Our eyes may flick back and forth as we construe a series of words into a meaningful sentence, and readers habitually flip back to earlier pages of a book to jog memory or establish the sequence of events or (more rarely) jump ahead. But as the common habit of referring to going 'back' or skipping 'ahead' when reading indicates, the experience of reading is essentially governed by a sense of the line. Where 'the viewing eye is free to rove over an image as it will', John Durham Peters observes, 'the reading eye must track a text largely in serial order'.[9] Within and around the line in both historical life and reading life, there is room for manoeuvre but always within bounds, and for Christina Lupton the printed book serves as a pre-eminent material emblem of this condition. The bound volume contains a foreseeable sequence of events; the pages allow readers to skip, mark up, reread, and so on.[10] We can move around in different ways and at difference tempos but, as Mark Currie emphasises, the relation between text and reader in narrative forms represents a 'tensed' conception of time (a view of sequence in terms of past, present and future) that remains a constant.[11] As with historical sequence, it constitutes the baseline of reading. Scott's historical novel takes off from this baseline, paying particular attention to the pragmatic-performative axis of narrative. In doing so it brings material text, material world and the dynamics of reading into conjunctions that bore on his own present's sense of its temporality and continue to resonate in an age bound, as Alan Liu puts it, 'to an ever more expansive, yet also vanishingly thin, present – a razor's slice of *now*'.[12]

Positioning Readers

I begin with Scott's location of his readers. Historical fiction differs in general from other modes of fiction reading in that it makes inescapable an awareness of the reader's own status as a historical being in a way other forms of fiction do not. Novels of manners, for example, assume a shared contemporaneity between readers and the fictional world; gothic novels move them into conventionalised story time no matter their ostensible historical setting; national tales, despite drawing heavily on historical material, address readers in their role as contemporary national subjects. Novel reading was proverbially the domain of the 'ordinary class of readers' entrenched in present time, and Scott makes these readers and their temporal orientation the explicit starting point of his venture into historical fiction. The subtitle of *Waverley*, "*Tis Sixty Years Since*', immediately positions readers in the time of 'now', and its celebrated first chapter underscores the point by interpolating them as participants in a shared modern culture of literacy. Importantly, however, the chapter does not leave them there for long nor, on the other hand, does it move them directly into the time of 'the last generation' it identifies as the novel's historical setting. Rather, the chapter shuttles readers back and forth between the present day and different eras of the past (medieval, early modern, eighteenth century). Notably, it does so via the metonym of dress, evoking distinct eras (including the era of the present) through signature fashions: the 'steel corslet' of the fifteenth century, the 'brocaded coat' of the eighteenth, the 'blue frock and white dimity waistcoat of the present day'.[13] Implicating readers as bodies as well as minds in this way, the move launches them not into any particular time but simply into historical passage, something Scott underlines in the 1829 'Magnum' edition where he appends a note mock-lamenting that the attire accounted 'respectable and gentlemanlike in 1805' has already become 'antiquated'.[14] As Timothy Campbell points out, fashion's sequences comprise simply a series: recurring but arbitrary change. For this reason they neither readily fold into the enduring patterns that sustain historical understanding nor offer a connecting tissue between past and present.[15] What they do enable in Scott, however, Campbell notes, is the creation of a doubled horizon which opens 'as much onto the material habits of his modern readers as onto the psychology of his characters'.[16] Identifying a similarly doubled aperture in Scott's historical novels from a different angle, Devin Griffiths argues that by setting past and present alongside one another in complex analogic relation, Scott turns his novels into 'zones of contact that operate at the border between past and present'.[17] Building on Scott's own analogy in *Ivanhoe* between translation and the task of the historical novelist, Griffiths astutely notes that such translation is not simply a linguistic matter of converting idioms between past and present but crucially involves 'a form of physical translation (moving character, narrator, and reader across historical borders)'.[18] On his reading, then, both past as representational object and reader as inhabitant of the present move around in the space between them, neither remaining quite still but the two also never converging.

Griffiths's border space and Campbell's doubled horizon may also be understood as a kind of time, an intervallic time: neither past nor present but acutely aware of both modalities. The *OED* defines interval as 'a space of time intervening between two points in time': it is thus at once a measure of the distance between two points, allowing them to be marked off (in this sense it is a space), and a pause in a forward movement that will resume (the temporal inflection most pertinent for my purposes). In the suspended time of the interval, what came before and what will come after remain in view or, more accurately, in mind. This intervallic vantage point underwrites Scott's key tactic as a historical novelist: an 'unclosing' of the past. Although we rarely encounter the term today, it was in common use in the early and mid-nineteenth century and it shows up in a range of literary contexts, from George Crabbe's late eighteenth-century poem, *The Library*, where an ancient book lies with 'close-press'd leaves, unclosed for many an age' (a passage Scott quotes in *Guy Mannering*) to Charlotte Brontë's focus on a door 'unclosing' at the end of *Jane Eyre* which triggers a decisive turn in the fortunes of Jane and Rochester.[19] As the example of Brontë suggests, to choose 'unclosing' over 'opening' is to effect a subtle but decisive shift of attention, for it brings into view the fact that something (an object, idea, event) has been closed. The term, holding within itself the dialectically related states of open and closed, thus centres on the interim when a referent is neither open nor closed. And it charges this interim with verbal force by throwing emphasis on the action of making a change in the condition of being closed. To 'unclose' something, that is, is to respond to its prior condition of being closed (past and present tenses held in tandem), whereas to 'open' something is to point to its future condition of being open (present and future tenses here held in tandem). Applied to the historical novel, unclosing offers an opening *of* the past – paths into the past – rather than necessarily an opening *up* of the past. This is worth stressing, for if there are multiple pathways into the past, it nonetheless remains a determinate zone. As

Christian Thorne wryly notes, 'it doesn't matter how many times you reread *Waverley*, the Highlanders aren't going to win this time'.[20]

For the historical novel to unclose means to decompose what has been composed. Disaggregation and dilation are the primary techniques, bringing into view the degree to which particular pasts have become stabilised in and for a particular present. *Ivanhoe*, Scott's most self-conscious foray into historical fiction, is exemplary. Its 'Dedicatory Epistle' constitutes an extended reflection on and defence of the historical novel, concluding with his much discussed translation model of the genre. But it opens on a more concrete note where narrative pragmatics rather than narrative's representational axis come into sharp view. Laurence Templeton, putative author, rehearses a debate between himself and the antiquary Dr Dryasdust on whether an English writer could do for English readers what the Waverley Novels had done for Scottish readers. Dryasdust vehemently denies the possibility, detailing various obstacles. To clinch his case he invokes 'the circumstances in which the English reader is placed'. As explanatory gloss, he posits an English reader of the 'ordinary class of readers' who may be 'prepared to believe' anything of the Scots since he has either never been to Scotland or has visited only on a summer tour, 'eating bad dinners, sleeping on truckle beds, stalking from desolation to desolation'. Once ensconced in his own 'snug parlour' by 'an English fireside', however, this same reader is much less disposed to believe 'his own ancestors led a very different life from himself'.[21] He does not, that is, recognise that he inhabits a historical and not an absolute present, and *Ivanhoe* takes up the challenge presented by such a reader, deploying a disaggregating, kaleidoscopic technique to shake loose the categories into which the medieval past has been congealed. Working with conventional medieval types, tropes and themes, Scott juggles them about: multiplying plots, re-inflecting standard figurations, recasting set topoi from unconventional angles (the siege, for instance, or the tournament). But his most far-reaching move comes at the very start in a disassembling of the national language itself. In the dialogue between the swineherd Gurth and the jester Wamba in the opening pages, the latter strips language down to the minimal semantic unit of the word. To exhibit the asymmetry of power between Saxon and Norman, he launches into an etymological riff on the names of farm animals, pointing out, for example, that the creature attended by 'a Saxon slave' is designated by the Saxon 'swine' but when transformed into a dish for Norman nobles in the castle turns into the Norman 'pork'.[22] The words Wamba cites (he adds ox/beef, calf/veal to the list) are commonly accepted as English, then and now, and his riff impresses on current English speakers the hybrid origins of what Scott pointedly identifies as 'our present English language'. At the same time, it also functions to remind the 'general reader' (who, Scott says, 'might be apt to forget') that the Anglo-Saxons persisted as 'a separate people' many generations after the Conquest.[23] Underscoring the status of 'our' language as at once historically sedimented and politically charged, the novel's opening chapter sets the stage for directing attention to what Janet Sorensen calls the 'long uneasy process of becoming English'.[24]

Scott's dilation of the past from the point of present reading in this way thus makes visible what has been smoothed out or over in the historical past. Equally, it directs attention to its compaction (not quite the same thing). Compaction is inevitable over the course of time, a function of temporal distance. As time moves ever forward from points in the past, the area between a past moment and the present moment increasingly narrows. But this funnel effect, Scott recognised, was not only the work of time; it was also a function of the channels of transmission of the past. And in a period that saw an explosion of both historical publications and popular interest in the historical past, those channels seemed to be assuming ever more truncated form. Commenting on the distillation of the past in a reflective, bookish moment in *Rob Roy*, Frank Osbaldistone records this process. As he looks at the bookshelves in the library at Osbaldistone Hall, 'bent beneath the weight of the ponderous folios so dear to the seventeenth century', he muses that from those ponderous folios 'we have distilled matter for our quartos and octavos, and which . . . may, should our sons be yet more frivolous than ourselves, be still farther reduced into duodecimos and pamphlets'.[25] The 'matter' of the past, as well as 'matter' from the past, was being increasingly pressed into smaller and smaller print formats; reading into ever-lighter, abbreviated modes. To counter this vector of reduction the Waverley Novels harnessed the weight and length of the book, the density of lines of prose on a page. Scott himself may have been an eminently modern author – fully engaged in the literary market, writing much and writing fast – but what he wrote deliberately demanded slow reading. Deceleration is not simply a by-product of the thickness of a prose that blocks speedy reading in the first place but is built into Scott's narrative as an endogenous function. It is telling, for instance, that he not only ignored criticism of the dilatory opening chapters of *Waverley* (pronounced by Francis Jeffrey the 'worst part of the book by far') but added a note to the 'Magnum' edition drawing explicit attention both to their critical censure and to his own resistance to making any changes.[26] The key is that slowness registers palpability – *something* slows us down – and Scott utilises the book as 'a slow form of exchange', along with the sequentiality of narrative and of reading, to endow with a certain substantiality not only the time of the past but also the reader's own time-space.[27]

Slow Reading/Slow Going

Thinking about the time-space of narrative, Gérard Genette observes that written narrative, 'produced in time, like everything else . . . exists in space and as space, and the time needed for "consuming" it is the time needed for *crossing* or *traversing* it, like a road or a field'.[28] By italicising 'crossing' and 'traversing' in this way, Genette infuses the long-standing trope of reading as journeying not just with a material but with a kinetic charge: reading as a literal movement over a material medium. So too does Scott when he recharges the same venerable metaphor in his well-known address to readers early in *Waverley*. Directing himself to novel readers seeking only 'amusement' (notably 'fair readers'), he begs their pardon for boring them with old-fashioned politics, explaining that his narrative vehicle is no 'flying chariot drawn by hippogriffs, or moved by enchantment' but 'a humble English post-chaise, drawn upon four wheels, and keeping his Majesty's high-way'.[29] A conventional enough gesture of realist dissociation from romance, the passage becomes something more when Scott goes on to elaborate his conceit. Up to this point, attention has been directed to the post-chaise as analogue for the novel itself and its adherence to the norms of a familiar world (hence a trope of authorship), but Scott now shifts to the road to bring the act of reading into more direct view. Telling readers they may leave at 'the next halt' if they wish, he warns those who choose to stay that they 'will be occasionally exposed to the dulness inseparable from heavy roads, steep hills, sloughs, and other terrestrial retardations' along the way.[30] By dwelling on the contours of the ground (dips, hills, dense surfaces), the passage spotlights constraints on forward movement, those 'terrestrial retardations' that determine the rate of motion. Impeded movement is the passage's leitmotif, and pace – the slow and uneven pace of hindered passage – emerges as the signature of Waverley reading.

Impeded movement punctuates the Waverley Novels at the level of both discourse and story. Recurring scenes of difficult traversal in the story world intersect with narrative's deceleration through extensive descriptive interludes in a reciprocity of slow going and slow reading. Commenting on the pacing of narrative in Scott, Franco Moretti posits a sharp opposition between description and narration ('in order to describe, one must stop narrating') and laments that despite there being exciting stories to tell in *Waverley*, Scott nonetheless 'manages to *slow down* the narrative, multiplying its moments of pause'. In these moments of pause, he argues, Scott literally finds 'the "time" to develop a new analytical-impersonal style', and in the process he establishes a 'new type of description' that will weigh down the realist novel for the rest of the century.[31] The descriptive mode Moretti has in mind is thick, visual, proto-sociological description of customs and objects that invokes a specific historical-social world. His objection is that such precise embedding locks persons into an already-made world and blocks the flow of events that makes narrative the bearer of history's meaning. But if Scott's novels abound in this kind of description – as they notoriously do – it is not their only descriptive mode. Scenes of traversal (walking, riding, marching), more particularly those of difficult traversal, activate a kinesthetic descriptive mode that embeds persons in a rather different order. Here bodies on the move take centre stage, confirming Yoon Sun Lee's observation that Scott had a keen but under-acknowledged interest in the sensation of motion. As she points out, landscape in the Waverley Novels is typically described in terms of bodily sensations: spaces are 'rough or smooth, broken or steep; there are always sudden turns, drops, and swerves'.[32] Consider Edward Waverley's long walk into the Highlands, for example. Scott devotes a great deal of space to describing this trek, an excursion Waverley undertakes casually enough out of 'curiosity' to see a people he can hardly believe continue to exist in 'the otherwise well-ordered island of Great Britain'.[33] But from the start the journey proves more strenuous than he anticipated: he finds himself toiling up a 'steep and rugged' path to a mountain pass; negotiating a precipitous descent to a narrow glen; trying to find purchase on 'a black bog, of tremendous extent, full of large pit-holes . . . traversed with great difficulty'. The path itself, 'rough, broken, and in many places quaggy and unsound', forces Waverley and his companions to half walk, half wade as they make their way across.[34] The episode interweaves different determinations of time, notably the historical and national registers manifest in the contest of male prowess between the Englishman Waverley and the Highlander Evan Dhu, but topography dominates and with it the physical effort of moving forward on inhospitable ground. Hence what impresses most strongly on Waverley (and the reader) is less his formation as a historical, social or national being than the constraints to which he is subject as a corporeal being negotiating a material environment. Embedding the protagonist in a natural order understood as ahistorical (if not necessarily unaffected by history), description effects a certain stripping down of the civilised subject of modernity to rudimentary bodily elements. In encountering so recalcitrant a medium that does not allow him easy passage, Waverley becomes unsettled, his confidence in his own centrality undermined. Nor is it ever fully restored even when more familiar historical-social parameters resume their accustomed place in the novel's foreground by the novel's end.

In contrast to the world in Gumbrecht's *Bildungsroman*, then, the world of the historical novel does not readily fit 'under the control of the subject's agency'.[35] Its roads are abrasive, their traversal an encounter with resistant or indifferent elemental forces of earth, air, water as much as with the more abstract play of historical forces. Scott's scenes of 'terrestrial retardation' typically feature characters who go out to take a 'look' or simply seek to pass through a terrain only to encounter, as does Waverley, an unexpectedly rough going. Plans and calculations go awry. Thus the young Guy Mannering, whose crossing of 'a wide black morass' in Scotland on horseback opens Volume 1 of Scott's second novel, is on his way to the village where he plans to stop overnight but is overtaken by darkness, becomes disoriented and ends up on the wrong road.[36] Similarly, Harry Bertram, whose walk to Scotland features in the opening of Volume 2 of the same novel, plans to cross the Waste of Cumberland in daylight but is overtaken by darkness, compelled to slow his 'round pace' and carefully negotiate an irregular path and highly 'broken ground'.[37] Nor is such blocking of human intent confined to those on unfamiliar ground. In *The Antiquary* Sir Arthur Wardour and his daughter, Isabella, take a familiar path, choosing to walk home via the 'easy curving line' along the sands rather than the straighter path of the high road because it offers 'pleasanter passage', but they too end up in unexpected difficulties, trapped by a sudden storm.[38] Indeed, *The Antiquary*'s storm scene pushes terrestrial retardation to a limit. Initially, the pair is forced from smooth passage ('the pleasant footing afforded by the moist hard sand') to 'a rougher path', but finally they are blocked from any passage whatsoever, 'pent between . . . a raging tide and an insurmountable precipice' with no way up or down.[39] More radically than Edward Waverley, they are reduced to creaturely status, along with Lovel (who has lifted them out of immediate but not ultimate danger) and Edie Ochiltree (who had come in vain to warn them). Scott describes the quartet as 'four shivering beings, who now, like the sea-fowl around them, clung there in hopes of some shelter from the devouring element which raged beneath'.[40] Eventually local ingenuity, traditional knowledge and communal effort secure a full rescue, but not before Meiklebackit repeats the narrator's reductive gesture, referring to the four figures 'sitting down yonder like hoodie-craws in a mist'.[41]

Narrative theorists tend to class descriptive interludes like these as narrative 'fillers' – 'what happens *between* a turning point and the next'[42] – but Scott's scenes of impeded passage are not static set pieces nor simply levers of transition.[43] Possessing performative and thematic energy, they typically target a certain heedlessness in modern minds absorbed in and by their own inventions. At particular issue are the limits of rational calculation and projection as subjects continually overestimate their own powers and underestimate those of the terrain. When Sir Arthur and Isabella decide on the route over the sands, they do take the movement of the tide into account, but when they notice the tide is not as far out 'as they had computed', they remain unworried. Probability is on their side: there are 'seldom ten days in the year' that do not allow a 'dry passage'.[44] Even as Isabella becomes uneasy at the rising sea and wind, Sir Arthur 'did not see, or would not acknowledge, any signs of immediate storm'.[45] Whether wilfully or not, his reliance on calculation at the expense of input from his senses blinds him to the forces at work around him to which he as a corporeal creature is subject. Sir Arthur, that is, fails to be attentive to a key medium of his existence.

The question of attention is very much at stake in such interludes. It is not incidental that Scott interrupts his account of Harry Bertram's walk into Scotland with a slighting reference to Dr Johnson's conviction that 'life had few things better than the excitation produced by being whirled rapidly along in a post-chaise'.[46] Targeting the 'excitation' of such rapid passing over and through a ground, Scott's descriptive interludes slow down characters and reader alike to promote heightened attention to material forces operative in our daily existence but generally overlooked or discounted. Pauses in the action, temporal intervals, a braking of reading – through such tactics Scott incorporates into his historical novel 'a poetics of the interval', to appropriate Lily Gurton-Wachter's phrase in her discussion of Wordsworth. Wordsworth like Scott attaches enhanced receptivity to the suspension of the interval, but by contrast, as Gurton-Wachter shows, he valorises not heightened attention but precisely its lapse or slackening ('what happens during the intervals *between* acts of attention'), for it is precisely when the organs of attention are not 'braced' that new or unexpected perceptions appear.[47] Intent on unsettling habitual perception, both writers undertake such unsettling through a swerve away from the mind's concentration on its own powers. In Scott, however, this swerve hinges on the body and the experience of the resistance of an exteriority, while in Wordsworth it pivots on the working of involuntary mental processes and their assimilation of an exteriority. Wordsworth's poetry, that is, is governed by the problem of consciousness, Scott's historical novel by the problem of passage. What does the gesture of moving forward mean or do? Through what dimension and with what consequences? Raising such questions, the Waverley Novels deploy different registers of forward movement: the directed movement of progress, the sheer movement of process, the simple motion of bodies. And it is through articulation of these registers that they effect an intervention in the experience of time-space in their own period that very much bears on that of our own.

Weighting Progress

Koselleck reminds us that progress became a modern concept 'when it shed or forgot its natural background meaning of stepping through space' to assume ever higher levels of generality.[48] Scott's historical novel is a potent reminder of this detachment. Its narrative typically overlays three tracks of forward movement: the slowed down time of the printed book (the humble English post-chaise moving on an uneven road); the speeded-up global time of progress (mail coaches hurtling down the road); and the organic time of human and animal steps as bodies propel themselves across space from point A to point B. The plots of the novels play out between the abstract modern inflection of progress (progress with a capital P) and its original experiential inflection of stepping forward. Connected to both dimensions but converging with neither is the slow time of the book and reading. Through this temporal structure the fictions set out to restore density and depth both to the thinned out past and to a thinning out present. Ultimately at issue, however, I want to suggest, is less the sense of time than that of space. Slow reading in Scott seems to me best understood as a tactic chiefly aimed at the attenuation of space under the conditions of modern technology and acceleration. Here I take my cue from Zygmunt Bauman's account of the relationship of time and space as experiential categories in 'liquid modernity'.[49] Taking value as a function of the effort required to attain an objective, Bauman points out that time has long served to bestow value on space. He explains: as a measure of the effort needed to span a certain distance ('how long to get from here to there?'), time is a gauge of the resistance of space and hence a determination of its value. For centuries, he notes, the answer to the question, 'how long to get from here to there?', was reckoned by the power of human or animal muscle ('wetware'), but with the invention of ever more efficient external aids to moving us through space, time became increasingly manipulable and spatial distance more elastic. In the age of software capitalism, traversing space takes 'no time' at all. With time no longer a factor in the event, then, the difference between 'far away' and 'here' is cancelled. We typically think about this condition as the annihilation of time – 'acceleration' is the theme of our own time – but for Bauman this is a crucial misrecognition. At a more fundamental level, he contends, what we are experiencing is the new irrelevance of space: 'since all parts of space can be reached in the same time-span (that is, in "no time"), no part of space is privileged, none has "special value"'.[50]

Bauman's argument throws an important light on the recurrence of scenes of impeded passage in the Waverley Novels and on Scott's insistence on proximity and the resistance of space. While his own era was some distance from the full-blown 'irrelevance' Bauman attributes to our own, it was highly conscious of how speeded-up forms of communication and transport were overriding the particular configurations that make for place (that is, the parts of space bearing 'special value'). 'Ideas are communicated by the press, like the electric fluid along the wire', reported the *New Monthly Magazine* in 1820, while the mail coaches speeding through the countryside, famously recalled in De Quincey's 'The English Mail Coach', quickly became a standard period trope for the centralising and homogenising impetus of modern improvement.[51] Coaches are everywhere in the Waverly novels but assume prominence in the narrative frames, those sites where the novels look sideways to the present rather than backward to the past. Nowhere more evocatively than in Peter Pattieson's frame in *The Heart of Mid-Lothian* with its declarative opening line: 'The times have changed in nothing more . . . than in the rapid conveyance of intelligence and communication betwixt one part of Scotland and another'.[52] In reducing the distance between 'one part . . . and another', rapidity evens out their value, nor do the mail coaches spend much time in either spot or along the way. In his own village, he remarks, seven coaches now 'thunder through the streets each day', replacing the sole 'miserable horse-cart' that used to carry the mail 'with difficulty' a generation ago.

Gathering up the motifs encompassed by Scott's trope of 'terrestrial retardations', *Mid-Lothian*'s frame is emblematic of the project of his fiction as a whole. Divided into two parts, the frame raises both the question of passage and that of story-making. Following Pattieson's remark on 'the rapid conveyance of intelligence', he first reflects on the problem of heedless passage, juxtaposing two types of coaches: the thundering modern coach roaring through his village and the 'slow and safe motion' of the obsolete Fly-coaches of the previous era.[53] Imaging the end of each type, he moves into the forefront the relationship between vehicles of transport and the medium through which they travel. In an attunement of rhythm between coach and medium, the old coaches 'used to settle quietly down, like a ship scuttled and left to sink by the gradual influx of the waters' whereas modern coaches, maladjusted to their medium, find themselves 'hurled against breakers' where they are 'smashed to pieces'. To bring home the point, Pattieson provides a local anecdote of having witnessed the crash of a speeding coach. He focalises this anecdote through glimpses of the coach's 'appearance and disappearance at intervals'[54] on the undulating road as he walked along to meet it (the two rates of motion set in pointed contrast). Shifting the scene, the second part of the frame is located in the village inn where three of the passengers thrown out of the coach when it crashed are forced to stay overnight. Joining the stranded passengers, Pattieson spends the evening listening to their exchange of tales, one of which he later dilates into the four-volume novel we are about to read. Ruth Livesey highlights this sequence as a central instance of the way interrupted modern mobility operates as narrative catalyst in Scott's fiction. As she points out, coaches in Scott have a disconcerting habit of running late, overturning or being otherwise delayed, ejecting their passengers from the space of modern transport and national homogeneous time as a result. Thus ejected, the passengers (stand-ins for readers) encounter heterogeneous localities and temporalities, and from these 'side-steps from even temporality' emerge the novels we read.[55] Livesey's is a compelling argument and *Mid-Lothian*'s frame clearly is a premier instance. At the same time, however, the frame enacts a critical divergence from the model it inhabits. Ejection in this case does not initiate modern passengers into the zone of local time and local story. Not only do the stranded men engage in modern urban banter about novel reading versus 'real records'[56] of human vagaries but, more important, the tales they tell pertain to an urban site familiar in different ways to each of them (a barrister, a solicitor, a discharged debtor): Edinburgh's prison, the Tolbooth. After exchanging their tales of the prison, they resume their journey to the city the next morning, and we hear no more of them. The storytelling interlude produced by enforced delay has thus served to give depth to the city-space they already inhabit. Their anecdotes of the prison are explicitly cast as the story of a building, an official and impersonal site which they animate through their tales ('how many hearts have throbbed within these walls' [16]). What has counted, then, is not so much encountering a different temporality than simply encountering a resistance to simple passage, which has afforded the time for reflection on the place to which they were always going and to which they keep going. Here the coach time of modern mobility and the traditional time of story are not cordoned off from each other but operate in interactive relation.

The notion of interaction is vital to the narrative form and technique of Scott's historical novel. Working out of and with the doubled aperture of intervallic time, his novels open onto both past and present without either collapsing the two onto the same temporal plane or distributing them on non-intersecting parallel lines. Past and present stand in asymmetric but interactive relation. If the Waverley Novels imbued the past with unprecedented vividness in their day, bringing it 'before our eyes' as contemporaries attested, this vivacity depended in no small part on awareness that their own eyes inhabited another age.[57] Advocating the promotion of such an awareness in postmodern historicism, Alan Liu urges a tactic of conscious anachronism in the choice of medium so as to convey the historical past as a 'compound' of proximity and distance: 'It's like holding a microphone up to the far past.'[58] His striking image of the microphone is deliberately jarring – a 'listening' to the past that is also its alienation – but Liu, like Scott, is looking for medial interactions that will put into play a doubled historical aperture. And it's precisely to the historicism of the age of Scott that he turns for a 'critical complement' to the age of social computing with its ideal of 'connecting everyone to everyone in a single shared now'.[59] In such an age, he suggests, 'there is a case to be made for preserving the older sense of history (complete with its temporal grammar and narratology)'.[60] Liu's own essay, mingling the lexicon of information theory with ancient tropes of earth and voice, takes narrative form as it tracks what amounts to 'stages' in the story of 'keepers of transmission', from the age of 'the ancestors' to the age of 'real time' media. Perhaps, he opines, the keepers of transmission, 'remediated as historical print authors and documents' in the nineteenth century can be 'remediated yet again for the age of social computing'. What matters for Liu, as for Scott, is hindering the easy passage which flattens out both past and present. Restoring density and dimension by keeping to history's road but ensuring there remain 'bumps' along the way, the Waverley Novels retain a salutary force.

Notes

1. Gumbrecht, 'The Roads of the Novel'; Stendhal, *Le Rouge et le Noir* (1830).
2. Gumbrecht, p. 623.
3. Ibid. p. 632.
4. Lukács, *The Historical Novel*, p. 57.
5. Lorenz, 'Unstuck in Time', pp. 90, 92.
6. Williams, *Keywords*, p. 203.

7. Goodman, *Georgic Modernity and British Romanticism*, p. 108.
8. Koselleck, *The Practice of Conceptual History*, p. 108.
9. Peters, *The Marvelous Clouds*, p. 294.
10. Lupton, 'Contingency, Codex'.
11. Currie, *About Time*, p. 16.
12. Liu, 'Friending the Past', p. 1.
13. Scott, *Waverley*, p. 5.
14. Alexander, *Introductions and Notes From The Magnum Opus*, p. 65.
15. Campbell, *Historical Style*, pp. 203–18.
16. Ibid. p. 208.
17. Griffiths, *The Age of Analogy*, p. 89.
18. Ibid. p. 115.
19. For Scott's quotation of the lines from Crabbe, see *Guy Mannering*, p. 109.
20. Christian Thorne, 'In Saecula Saeculorum', p. 266.
21. Scott, *Ivanhoe*, p. 7.
22. Ibid. p. 21.
23. Ibid. p. 17.
24. Janet Sorensen, *Strange Vernaculars*, p. 198.
25. Scott, *Rob Roy*, p. 81.
26. [Francis Jeffrey], 'Waverley – A Novel', p. 242; for Scott's note see Lamont's edition of *Waverley*, p. 390.
27. The quoted phrase is from Carla Hesse, 'Books in Time', p. 27.
28. Genette, *Narrative Discourse*, p. 34.
29. Scott, *Waverley*, p. 26.
30. Ibid.
31. Moretti, 'Serious Century', pp. 389, 376.
32. Lee, 'Vection, Vertigo, and the Historical Novel', p. 195.
33. Scott, *Waverley*, p. 78.
34. Ibid. pp. 81–2.
35. Gumbrecht, 'The Roads of the Novel', p. 632.
36. Scott, *Guy Mannering*, p. 3.
37. Ibid. p. 125.
38. Scott, *The Antiquary*, pp. 56, 53.
39. Ibid. p. 57.
40. Ibid. p. 59.
41. Scott, *The Antiquary*, p. 62. Such scenes underline Matthew Wickman's point that Scott thinks by way of 'an ecology of relations', *Literature after Euclid*, p. 56.
42. Moretti, 'Serious Century', p. 367.
43. For a very different understanding of description by a narrative theorist, however, see Mieke Bal, 'Over-Writing as Un-writing', pp. 571–610.
44. Scott, *The Antiquary*, p. 54.
45. Ibid. p. 55.
46. Scott, *Guy Mannering*, p. 118.

47. Gurton-Wachter, *Watchwords*, p. 86.
48. Koselleck, *The Practice of Conceptual History*, p. 221.
49. Bauman, *Liquid Modernity*, pp. 110–23.
50. Ibid. p. 118.
51. 'On Reading and Readers', p. 533.
52. Scott, *The Heart of Mid-Lothian*, p. 7.
53. Ibid. pp. 7, 8.
54. Ibid. p. 9.
55. Livesey, *Writing the Stage Coach Nation*.
56. Scott, *The Heart of Mid-Lothian*, p. 15.
57. I elaborate this point in '"Before Our Eyes"'.
58. Alan Liu, *Local Transcendence*, p. 25. Celeste Langan has drawn attention to Scott's understanding of print and orality as mutually constitutive media in his poetry, 'Understanding Media in 1805'.
59. Alan Liu, 'Friending the Past', p. 22.
60. Ibid. p. 25.

2

'I bide my time': History and the Future Anterior in *The Bride of Lammermoor*

Penny Fielding

The Bride of Lammermoor appeared at an uncertain time, published during the tumultuous political events of the summer of 1819 that were memorialised most prominently in the shocking reverberations of Peterloo.[1] We are familiar with these events as a crisis in political representation, but it was also a disruption in time: the inevitability of progress, the teleology of Enlightenment, the expansion of the public sphere were all challenged by radical protest and ensuing restrictions on the press. This rupture or temporal dislocation in the flow of history was not just a challenge to Whig historicism – we can also trace it in the response of radical sympathisers as well as in the reaction of the Tory Walter Scott.

Shelley's political poems of this year, 'The Masque of Anarchy', 'England in 1819' and 'Ode to the West Wind', all propose a future that is expected, even though we cannot tell what form it will take. It is a 'glorious Phantom' or 'The trumpet of a prophecy' of which we cannot yet see the shape or hear the language.[2] The present moment is grasped through an intimation of its future and will gain meaning from it, but that future as yet cannot be narrated. At the same time, Scott provided his own ironic vision of the temporal situation of 1819 in his anti-radical letters, collected as *The Visionary*, in which the dream of reform has become a nightmare. The fictive narrator of these letters sends to the editor of the *Edinburgh Weekly Journal* a sequence of three dream visions in which radicals, abetted by the Whigs, have destroyed the industrial and agricultural progress of the nation with their revolutionary sympathies. The letter writer can imagine only an uncertain future: 'Happy is he who at the present unpleasant crisis can substitute sleep and dreams for the gloomy moments of the waking day, and the still more dismal anticipations of what may arrive to-morrow.'[3] Insofar as the present moment can be experienced at all, it consists of a state of crisis, oscillating between sleeping and waking, and infused with an anxious anticipation of the future.

The Bride of Lammermoor, then, marks a time in which the course of history was not easily predictable, and, unsurprisingly, its sense of historical time exposes the complexity and strangeness of time. History in the novel is far from linear, rarely proceeding forward with any kind of causality or expectation. So far from what we think of as Enlightenment historiography, or a stadial development passing uniformly from one stage to the next in any given eventuality, *The Bride* exposes fissures in this model. The novel's temporal formations (or malformations) have already been figured in interesting ways. Ina Ferris focuses on Edgar Ravenswood to explore the idea of the 'remnant', a figure (or sometimes an object) that circulates through Scottish literature of our period. The remnant is both an obsolete figure from the past and one who clearly lives and functions in the present, and the effect is to render the present ghostly and unsubstantial and to 'block the abstracting moves through which bridging narratives and categories recuperate and consolidate what has been left behind'.[4] Luke Terlaak Poot analyses Scott's use of 'momentaneousness' – cliffhangers and supercharged moments – to think about how the conditions of reading generate the novel's 'disruptive experience of historical time'.[5] And, in a formulation that will be particularly relevant to my own argument, Olga Volkova, in a study of Scott and Gogol, points to a crucial tactic in *The Bride of Lammermoor*: 'while using distance to order various pasts along a single diachronic axis, the novel also undermines linearity by conflating past, present and future; by turning time into an expressly discursive category'.[6] In this chapter, I want to advance these ideas and to think about the temporality of *The Bride* both generally and specifically. In abstract terms, the novel poses a significant challenge to historical sequence. Even under 'normal' Scottish Enlightenment conditions, the course of progress folds stages in on each other. The feudal society of the Ravenswoods gives way virtually overnight to an advanced (and already corrupt) professional political rule without the intervening stages of agricultural progress. But this is really a clue to a temporality far removed from the teleology of Enlightenments as *The Bride* attempts to explain time; to hold moments of time in one place; to unscramble past, present and future, or to decode linear time. All of these temporal structures fail because the novel is not underpinned by any predictable chronological sequence.

Instead, *The Bride* leans towards the tense of the future anterior – that which will have been. In the future anterior the present is not the inevitable telos of the past, nor is it a stable platform from which to predict the future. Rather, the past is a history that we anticipate will make sense at some point in the future, while, in the present, we hazard a guess that we will understand the past to be leading up to a future as yet unknown. Points at which we seek to identify past events and objects, or explain them through causality or context, give way to a recognition that the past is incomplete – indeed it cannot be completed in the present but must remain unconceivable. Although the doubtful present of 1819 gives us a way to think about *The Bride of Lammermoor*, I will resist the trap set by the novel itself of exegesis through historical context. It is precisely the attempt to understand its own present that the novel undermines. Instead, I want to think about its narrative in more formal or generic terms. Or to be more precise: in order to admit historicism into this analysis I want to consider how Scott starts with an awareness of the narrative structures available to him, rather than positing an extra-narrative position from which the past can be judged. In what follows, I will consider first the strange temporality of the novel, and then explore how it asks the reader to acknowledge this strangeness by confronting the disruption of officially sanctioned narrative forms.

The Time of *The Bride of Lammermoor*

Time, in *The Bride of Lammermoor*, is out of joint. Nothing seems to happen in sequence, past and future fail to anchor an unstable present between them, and history obdurately refuses to reveal its direction. The novel reaches towards a future that never arrives, gestures towards a past that seems unwilling to perform its function as history, and inhabits a present troubled by both of these. Things seem to happen outside their expected or sequential order. In the frame narration Dick Tinto 'began to paint before he had any notion of drawing'.[7] In the body of the novel, Edgar Ravenswood witnesses the wraith of old Alice Gray before knowing that she is actually dead. When Lady Ashton retrospectively uses the excuse of Lucy and Edgar's betrothal for dismissing Edgar, Lord Ashton comments 'It is a cause . . . which has emerged since the effect has taken place; for, if it exists at all, I am sure she knew nothing of it when her letter to Ravenswood was written.'[8] 'Before' and 'after' are terms that prove difficult to tie down either temporally or historically. Scott, famously, could not decide whether the events of the novel should take place before or after the 1707 Acts of Union, and a decade after the first publication he moved the dates forward for the Magnum Opus edition of 1829–30.[9]

The novel's disruption of historical sequence is embedded in the experience of reading it. Its first move is to lull us into a false sense of security. If we were to start reading the novel at chapter two, the opening of the historical story, we would not at first detect anything unusual in its historicism as it seems to begin confidently enough, staking its claim to act as a historical record. The chapter offers a historical and geographical panorama in which time and place work together to unlock the heuristic force of change. The landscape bears the signs not only of local history, but also of national narratives. The 'visible' ruins of Ravenswood Castle are absorbed into the local families' history, which 'was frequently involved in that of Scotland itself, in whose annals their feats are recorded'.[10] The chapter mixes tenses to encourage us to see the past as instructive for our understanding of the present and of the current of history in general. In the following extract 'they' refers to the public, who could historically, and still can, read history in terms of political partisanship and consequent change:

> They said that the Lord Keeper . . . had, previous to the final purchase of the estate of Ravenswood, been concerned in extensive pecuniary transactions with the former proprietor; and, rather intimating what was probable than affirming anything positively, they asked which party was likely to have the advantage in stating and enforcing the claims arising out of these complicated affairs, and more than hinted the advantages which the cool lawyer and able politician must necessarily possess over the hot, fiery, and imprudent character, whom he had involved in legal toils and pecuniary snares.[11]

The public voice of the early eighteenth century, encapsulated in this impersonal 'they', enfolds individual 'character' within a universal enquiry into historical process – a process which 'must necessarily' take place. And if any doubts remain about the universality of this process, the next paragraph addresses 'the character of the times' (following James VI of Scotland's leaving the Scottish Court to become James I of Britain) as a form of absentee landlordism that we might use to read other historical situations:

> The evils attending upon this system of government, resembled those which afflict the tenants of an Irish estate, owned by an absentee. There was no supereminent power, claiming and possessing a general interest with the community at large, to whom the oppressed might appeal from subordinate tyranny, either for justice or for mercy.[12]

We see here the extent to which the novel goes to set up a form of historicism in which all the pieces – temporal and spatial – seem to fit together.

Historical distance does not even trace the epistemic difference in public opinion, but rather confirms that history runs in measurable patterns that confirm certain fundamental cognitive facilities. That is, historical distance is not a product of the early nineteenth century, but is shored up by a *longue durée* of modernity from which a detached, objective perspective is possible. Difference may point to historical specificities, but the possibility of historical difference itself remains constant. There is always a place from which historical change can be viewed and assessed.

Behind the opening scene-setting lies a historicism bound up in a concept of law that underpins a key stratum of Enlightenment philosophy that we can trace in Montesquieu's *De L'Esprit des Lois*. For Montesquieu, history and law are intricately involved with each other, and both are fundamental to the possibility of societal change. The legal constitution of government and the laws that a people acknowledge are co-dependent:

> Law in general is human reason, insofar as it governs all the peoples of the earth; and the political and civil laws of each nation should be only the particular cases to which human reason is applied.
>
> Laws should be so appropriate to the people for whom they are made that it is very unlikely that the laws of one nation can suit another.
>
> Laws must relate to the nature and the principle of the government that is established or that one wants to establish, whether those laws form it, as do politic laws, or maintain it, as do civil laws.[13]

Here the very diversity of forms of government can be understood as historical principle. Regional differences give rise to different laws, but it is social groupings and their acquiescence or resistance to government that allow those laws to take hold. Laws should be calibrated according to 'the way of life of the peoples, be they plowmen, huntsmen, or herdsmen; they should relate to the degree of liberty which the constitution can sustain'.[14] That is, if a system of government is properly adapted to the way its people live, their social habits and their geographical needs, the system will constitute itself through laws that those people will accept. As Scott puts it, an individual monarch, however personally corrupt, will succeed if he is 'rigourous' in respecting the formal 'administration of justice' that his public requires.[15]

Yet this is *not* the historical underpinning of *The Bride of Lammermoor*. Scott has introduced his Montesquieu-like analysis to challenge the reader's faith in history and to indicate that Scotland *cannot* be easily read through a mirrored structure of law and governance. Rather than exhibiting the rule of laws that are themselves produced by social forces, history has been interrupted by a single event. Scott notes that 'It is very different when the powers of sovereignty are delegated to the head of an aristocratic faction, rivalled and pressed closely in the race of ambition by an adverse leader.'[16] Rather than 'the law' emerging as a constant underlying principle, history is now subject to the unregulated influences of singular 'laws'. In a phrase the novel repeats – 'Show me the man and I will show you the law' – Enlightenment causality is turned on its head. Montesquieu's configuration of powerful rulers who are produced by their geographical or historical circumstances is here rendered as an indeterminate historical condition in which the subject, so far from arising from environmental circumstances, manipulates the multiple historical currents that present themselves.

The Bride of Lammermoor refuses to adhere to the historical temporality of Enlightenment or of causal, sequential history altogether. It introduces such modes only to interrogate them or to undermine the reader's dependence on them. On the one hand, and with a certain grim historical/dramatic irony, is Edgar Ravenswood. Ravenswood, despite his family's being assigned in the second chapter to the passing of feudalism, has a strikingly modern outlook on history. He is twice described by the adjectives 'stirring' and 'active',[17] implying a man not driven by events but able to intervene in the world. He himself has a remarkably positive view of historical futurity and the possible perfectibility of society. He is optimistic that the corruption of politics through party partiality will wither away with modernity, as we see in the following conversation with Bucklaw about the popular use of cant terms for Royalists and Covenanters:

> 'I hope to see the day when justice shall be open to Whig and Tory, and when these nick-names shall only be used among coffee-house politicians, as slut and jade are among apple-women, as cant terms of idle spite and rancour.'
>
> 'That will not be in our days, Master – the iron has entered too deeply into our sides and our souls.'
>
> 'It will be, however, one day,' replied the Master; 'men will not always start at these nicknames as at a trumpet-sound – as social life is better protected, its comforts will become too dear to be hazarded without some better reasons than speculative politics'.[18]

The 'one day' to which the Master refers may have resonated among the novel's 1819 readers as their own present – a triumph of 'social life' over the cultural conditions in which the novel was itself published. As Ian

Duncan has shown, early nineteenth-century Edinburgh fostered a culture in which a republic of letters guaranteed an apparent impartiality through a literary-legislative coterie that moved debate from party faction to abstract considerations of value.[19] Yet, as I mentioned at the start of this chapter, the present of 1819 had thrown progressive history out of joint, and the novel refuses to identify this progressive movement. The apparently forward-looking Edgar is also vacillating and hesitant, as if stuck in a present that cannot be clearly shaped by past or future. He changes his plan to join the exiled Stuart court in France, and when Bucklaw asks him why, he simply replies: 'Because I had changed my mind . . . and renounced my enterprize, at least for the present.'[20] There is no temporal structure that can explain or justify his decision.

Taken at face value, Edgar's view of progress offers a reassuring vision of gradual political improvement, but, as we have seen, the time of *The Bride of Lammermoor* does not admit such an easy conclusion. As the novel unfolds, Edgar starts to equate the law with another form of modernity – a system of technical manoeuvres that supervene upon the empirical passage of time. His own historicism cannot accommodate the change from ancient feudal rights to a present that seems to squeeze out considerations of time altogether. He describes to William Ashton the legal means by which the Ravenswoods have been dispossessed:

> the lands of Ravenswood which you now occupy were granted to my remote ancestor for services done with his sword against the English invaders. How they have glided from us by a train of proceedings that seem to be neither sale, nor mortgage, nor adjudication for debt, but a non-descript and entangled mixture of all these rights . . . all this you understand better than me.[21]

Edgar does not simply confront one historical force, feudalism, giving way to another, bourgeois professionalism. Rather, a time that was causal and predictable has been supplanted by events that seem to have happened without it being apparent how this has taken place. Edgar is aware that historical events have happened, and are still happening, but they are not shaped nor explained by historical experience and he can find no platform from which to view them.

This is the form of time that informs *The Bride of Lammermoor* and makes it such a strange historical novel – one that works against stadial or sequential forms of historical time. Scott invites us explicitly to consider these problems in a synechdocal example. The ancient motto of the Ravenswoods is 'I bide my time'. The family legend refers to an imagined event in the past: the story runs that Sir Malise Ravenswood, temporarily dispossessed of his castle by a rival chieftain, insinuated himself into a feast at the castle disguised as an attendant. The motto was coined when Sir Malise placed a bull's head, as a symbol of death, on the table, uttered the words of the motto, and 'The explosion of the conspiracy took place upon the signal.'[22] The castle was retaken and passed back into the Ravenswood family.

At first glance the motto seems to anchor the Ravenswoods within an expected historical sequence. According to this structure, the iconic event acts causally to shape the historical future. But the motto raises more questions than it answers. What does it mean to 'bide' or await one's own time? What is the time that is proper to oneself? The motto suggests a pattern of formal iteration – all Ravenswoods bide their time, as it is a structure of historical inevitability. But on the other hand, that seeming inevitability is undermined by a much less predictable temporal structure. The motto implies that there is a right time for events to occur, but in fact this time can only begin to be understood when the event *has* occurred. That is, the singular time, proper to the individual subject, is really a narrative position, or something that can only be understood in retrospect and as a process of repetition that will change its meaning in different contexts. After all, the next entry of a bull in the fortunes of the Ravenswood family is the moment when Edgar saves Lucy from one by shooting it as it charges her.[23] Is this an example of biding one's time? But, if so, what does it mean? That the 'real' meaning of the motto pointed to this moment all along? Or that the motto in fact points to an unspecified future that can *only* be understood provisionally and in retrospect. The first and second bull-related incidents appear to form a narrative of fatal determinism, but only after the second has taken place.

The paradoxical temporality of biding one's time prompts us to think about the wider structure of the *The Bride*'s historicity. We assume that the historical novel is a way of measuring the distance between our present and the past. That past may be complex, multiple, even unpredictable, but it remains mensurable in a stable way – the same form of historicist measurement that allows Georg Lukács to write *The Historical Novel*. What the historical novel does *not* do, according to Lukács, is to encourage us to read novels to discover alternative ways of thinking about time. Time in *The Bride of Lammermoor* comingles the Lukácsian structure of the historical – the idea that the past shows us how we have arrived at our present – with the very different temporality of biding one's time, in which an anticipated present can only be 'known' – that is to say narrated – in the future.

The grammatical tense of this temporal epistemology is the future anterior. When we talk of the future, we do not know what will happen, only that something will have happened. The future will always be belated, because its meaning will always be delayed as an act of interpretation, but this future is also retroactive in that it determines the narrative of the past that leads up to it. That is to say, we know that our present will be read in light of the future, but we cannot tell what relation it will have to that future moment. We can never establish the 'right time' to act in *The Bride*'s peculiar logic of biding one's time. The present is not a stable position from which to narrate the past but is simply unknowable, or at best a projection about what may at a later date be articulated, even if that date will not mark a defined end. This is an anxious prospect as it demands the continual deferring of an assessment of what it means to be at any point in history. And thus an Enlightenment model of history is radically undermined: not only is modernity impossible as a telos, but it is itself founded on impossibility.

The Ravenswood motto is subject to the future anterior. Time, here, is something to be awaited if it is to become proper to the speaker or the subject. If I bide *my* time I am anticipating a future that will provide *me* with a coherent narrative, but if I am biding *time*, rather than anticipating a specific event or outcome, then what I am really committed to is a structure of indeterminate temporality – there will be events that can be narrated in the future, but time itself is something that I am perpetually awaiting with no guarantee of fruition. These alternative temporalities are introduced early in the second chapter when Edgar's recently deceased father is referred to as 'the last proprietor of Ravenswood Castle'.[24] This makes perfect sense to us if we read the novel as linear history. From our reading present we know that the Ravenswoods never reclaim their ancient patrimony, so Lord Ravenswood was indeed the last proprietor of the castle. But the fate of the family is also bound up in another kind of lastness. Caleb Balderstone, the old Ravenswood retainer, recites a rhyme that has clung to the family through generations:

> When the last Laird of Ravenswood to Ravenswood shall ride,
> And woo a dead maiden to be his bride,
> He shall stable his steed in the Kelpie's flow,
> And his name shall be lost for evermoe![25]

The narrator's 'last proprietor of Ravenswood' and 'the last Laird of Ravenswood' from this rhyme are not just two different people, they are two different temporal positions. They are two different understandings of lastness – one that belongs to sequential history (the past) and the other to the future anterior. Edgar *will have been* the last Laird at a point beyond the utterance of the rhyme in the present, but that point cannot be known in advance. And the rhyme itself articulates this unspeakable future as its passage into declared history is equally unutterable: the last Laird's name will be eternally lost.

The Bride of Lammermoor is haunted by this temporal grammar. The Ravenswood curse is not so much on the family, as on the family's temporal condition. Caleb Balderstone ascribes its origins to the untraceable, legendary time of the ballad-figure Thomas the Rhymer: 'Thomas the Rhymer, whose tongue couldna lie, spoke the word of your house that will e'en prove ower true if you go to Ravenswood this day – O that it should e'er have been fulfilled in my time!'[26] Caleb can only articulate the curse – the passage of historical time – in the future anterior. For him, its force lies in the temporality of an event that has not yet taken place but can only be grasped at in terms of a future position from which it might be narrated: 'that it should . . . have been', it will always be yet to come. The prophecy emanates from an indistinct past that has no single origin as it is not certain when it was first pronounced, and it is a past that has no clear determining effect on the present. Neither does the prophecy, despite its oracular cast, encompass the future. We can only know who the subject of the first line is after that person is dead and has become the *last* Laird – in effect, we cannot understand to what the prophecy refers until we can determine its relevance after the event. But what *is* the event? We don't witness Edgar riding into the morass called 'the Kelpie's flow'; all that remains to suggest that he has done so is an image – the synechdocal feather that Caleb retrieves. So the prophecy also prophesies something that works against the possibility of determining its meaning at all. The 'last Laird' is not named in the rhyme and the prophecy itself asserts that 'his name shall be lost for evermoe'. Even in the act of determining meaning after the fact, we cannot fix that meaning in the record of history. Insofar as the prophecy is accurate, it succeeds only in prophesying its own lack of determining power. This is a time that can be interpreted fictively but not causally. Lucy is obviously not literally a dead maiden at the time she is wooed by Edgar but she is already dead in another sense, or, rather, she is both living and dead. Lucy's 'death' in the rhyme inhabits the future anterior. Rather than the expected form of the prophecy ('She will die') the rhyme refuses to occupy a linear structure – the past from which it originates is indeterminate, the future in which it will have taken place cannot be known. As the novel's titular character, Lucy should be the bearer of history. But, like Edgar, her historical temporality is complex. The novel is the future anterior of a history that is always already dead. As the subject of history, Lucy is dead, but her past remains to be narrated in the future of the novel. But, equally, her death, as an event, can never be put to rest in a completed past. It is a condition of the future anterior, which, as Samuel Weber puts it, is 'a "time" which can never be entirely remembered, since it will never have fully taken place'.[27] Lucy's death will never be 'over' in the sense that it will never be inscribed in a historical sequence that can fully tell her story. The past is always still to come if it is to be figured in an act of narration.

The Time of the Tale

If the historical temporality of *The Bride of Lammermoor* seems unfathomable, that may be in part a condition of the way in which we seek to understand it as a Waverley novel. The future anterior sits with difficulty within the narrative time of the historical novel. But if we relax the generic structures of the novel, and allow in other forms of storytelling, then the narrative picture changes. Scott's own definition of the novel, here opposed to the romance, stresses both temporal sequence and a narrative perspective rooted in the present day: 'the events are accommodated to the ordinary train of human events, and the modern state of society'.[28] The temporal structure of a romance like *The Bride* is strange and out of the normal order of events. It calls upon the supernatural to disrupt the expected sequence of historicism. But in another way, the novel's temporality is a familiar one, found commonly in the period in the form not of the novel, and not only, in Scott's terms, in the romance, but in the tale – a genre much less concerned with standing outside the contours of history.

If we read *The Bride of Lammermoor* in terms of storytelling, then its seemingly strange time becomes less of an abstruse theoretical formulation and more of an everyday condition of temporality as we experience it. As we have seen, the novel continually throws its readers off historical balance. There is no place to stand within the novel's narrative from which the past can be subject to scrutiny. This is true not only for conjectural history, but also for antiquarianism, which in *The Bride* fails to render time sequential or rational. Antiquarianism reaches into the past to pull its objects and stories into the empirical present. In Scotland in particular, this means the everyday past as it was lived, and the record of that past in the form of songs, ballads, stories, customs and beliefs. *The Bride of Lammermoor* works by opening up a space for such emanations of the past and then alienating them from any position by which they might be explained. Here is the way the narrator configures Lucy's response to the doom-laden stories of Alsie Gourlay and the prophecy recited by Caleb Balderstone:

> Lucy might have despised these tales, if they had been related concerning another family, or if her situation had been less despondent. But circumstanced as she was, the idea that an evil fate hung over her attachment, became predominant over her other feelings, and the gloom of superstition darkened a mind, already sufficiently weakened by sorrow, distress, uncertainty, and an oppressive sense of desertion and isolation.[29]

That is, Lucy cannot see herself as a subject apart from the tales that seem to enfold her life within them. The bourgeois, professional family into which she was born exists in a form outside herself: 'in her exterior relations to things of this world, Lucy willingly received the ruling impulse from those around her'.[30] She can insert herself affectively into the subjects of antiquarian study – 'Her secret delight was in the old legendary tales of ardent devotion and unalterable affection' – but she cannot stand outside them.

Lucy inhabits these 'legendary tales' as an inner world; she is unable to adopt the controlling position of the antiquarian. Her father objects that she 'make[s] it a point of conscience to record the special history of every boor about the castle'.[31] 'Special' here means particular, personal or singular, but the note of patronising sarcasm from Lord Ashton banishes such individual accounts from official history. The rest of the exchange makes this clear as Lucy appeals to oral history and Ashton rejects its authority:

> 'I am not quite so faithful a chronicler, my dear father; but I believe that Norman once served here while a boy, and before he went to Ledington, whence you hired him. But if you want to know any thing of the former family, old Alice is the best authority.'
>
> 'And what should I have to do with them, pray, Lucy,' said her father, 'or with their history or accomplishments?'[32]

Antiquarianism is a way of doubling history. In one sense it enfolds the past into the present by making it immediate, haptic and experiential. The objects of the past can be held in one's hands and the songs and stories of the past can be at once read or heard. On the other hand, it creates a distance between those objects and texts and the subject who receives them, now to be called 'the antiquarian'. Antiquarianism nominates the historian as the custodian of the past experiences of others. But what happens when these custodial forms come up against narratives that challenge their claim to empiricism? In order to understand how the generic interplay of novel and tale works in *The Bride of Lammermoor*, I want to compare it with a short example from the contemporaneous author most interested in the role of the story in the lives of individuals and socials groups – James Hogg.

Many of Hogg's stories are about how people experience psychological states in time. These people are not generally the custodians of these events and experiences – that is, antiquarians – but those to whom such events occur. Sometimes these stories have antiquarian frame narrators, but these people are generally left baffled by the stories they transmit. Their role is to pass on stories they have heard but without much attempt at historical context or explanation. Generally Hogg's frame narrators point out that the story has no clear external logic and cannot be explained by rational means. Indeed Hogg's stories are typically unconcerned with sequential time. Ghosts return to make legal claims in the present; the future is foretold; geographical distance is superseded by temporal simultaneity as characters appear in different places at the same time.[33] The time that haunts *The Bride of Lammermoor* is a very common one in Hogg's stories, but I will take a single example that shows how the temporality of the future anterior is woven into the lives of characters in a way that cannot be incorporated into official historical modes.

'The Fords of Callum' is about an 'event' that never quite takes shape *as* an event that can be mapped or be understood in time. Like *The Bride of Lammermoor*, it features the premonitions of people who may or may not be dead, and supernatural occurrences that do not respect common notions of temporality, or challenge normative ideas of sequence and causality in which one thing must happen after another. These premonitions may, like ghosts, come to bear witness from the past in a way that obliterates our usual sense of the passage of time – they irrupt directly from the past into the present with no signs of historical change or process to link these temporal conditions.

The present moment in any Hogg story is always complex and shifting between past and future iterations. In 'The Fords of Callum' Janet and Wat Douglas have three daughters living away from home, one of whom, Annie, is especially beautiful. Wat announces a sudden terrible dread that 'there's some heavy judgment guan to happen to us very soon'.[34] Wat and Janet cast around in the past for an explanation – Wat asks Janet if she has 'been guilty of ony great sin lately?'[35] and when she says that she has not, he wonders if it might be Annie who is guilty of some transgression. But reaching into the past only produces another sense of the future, and one edged about with mystery. Janet replies: 'There is something about her that I can never comprehend. I had some heavy, heavy dreams about her afore she was born. I think always there is something to happen to her.'[36] That night, the couple hear a voice that they believe to be Annie's that asks: 'Is Wat Douglas away to the Fords o' Callum?'[37] Janet observes that this is a strange way for Annie to name her father, and says that he is here in bed. The voice fades out of hearing with the words: 'Then it is ower late now.' Wat then reveals that Annie had appeared to him the previous night and told him to go to the Fords of Callum. He also says that a 'secret'[38] that cannot be told passed between them.

The phrase 'ower late' underscores the strange temporal arrangement of the story. It is too late to prevent something that is about to happen – the present is already haunted by the future. But the present is also belated, haunted by a past that could not be understood *in* the past. And the persistent belief, shared by Janet and Wat, that something that cannot be as yet understood is about to happen points to the recognition of the provisionality of past experience. That is, the acknowledgement that not only the understanding of these events, but also the way in which they are remembered and re-experienced, is subject to revision in the future. The suggestion that Wat is not in fact Annie's father is a buried secret not to be explained in the present in a sequence of cause and effect, and a traumatic experience that cannot be articulated.

We are left not with a simple past but with another instance of the future anterior. As we have seen, the future anterior is a way of thinking about a present that cannot be known at the time it is lived. It is not simply a prediction of the future, but of something that will have to be narrated in the future. So the future anterior is also a way of thinking about language, and in using Annie's disembodied voice as the story's pivot, Hogg directs our attention towards the temporality of utterances. Once something is spoken it is already over, or past, and we are already moving into the future, which, of course, cannot be known. We know that there is always something about to happen but that we must defer knowledge of it until we are in a position to narrate it. In Hogg things are always either too early or too late and in the case of 'The Fords of Callum' they appear to be both.

The story here shifts from being largely a dialogue focalised on Janet and Wat to a story narrated from the outside by the narrator. He tells us that they hurry to the Fords of Callum where they find Annie's corpse, which is wearing unusually fine clothes. A doctor is summoned and the narrator points out that it's a little odd that no one asks what Wat and Janet are doing there. Janet is distraught but Wat seems to be coping. But when they take the body home these roles are reversed and Wat dies before the funeral can take place. His place is taken by a mysterious gentleman who the narrator tells us was later thought to be the Duke of Queensberry. These events *should* have a logical connection with what has gone before, but their relations are not knowable rationally and they fail to explain the mysterious apparitions of the first part. What the second half of the story describes is a series of unresolved problems and possible interpretations, from which a *number* of persuasive stories about Annie's death might be told. Why does the narrator insist on the strangeness of Janet and Wat's arrival? Why does Wat seem fine at first but then die when the body is retrieved? Who is the mysterious gentleman and what was his relation to Annie? These narrative possibilities work like the future anterior – they are what will have been in relation to a present that could not be understood at the time but had to defer its meaning. Because that meaning did not already exist, the future can only be narrated in retrospect (a future past), and as is the case with all utterances, those narrations have a provisional, contextual relation to what went before.

The story ends by a swift reversal to a more immediately recognisable form of history, and the process of dating: 'as this unaccountable incident is well known to have happened when the late Mr George Brown of Callum was a bridegroom, it settles the time to have been about sixty-six years ago'.[39] With perhaps a passing hint at the subtitle of *Waverley* – *'Tis Sixty Years Since* – the story offers what is both the most comprehensible but least adequate of endings, undermining history as such and replacing it with an experiential time in which the possibility of recorded history seems like an intrusion or a rupture.

This short excursion into Hogg brings us back to the kind of novel *The Bride of Lammermoor* is. The novel is not only about how history is understood but also about how it is experienced and how assumptions about history are underpinned by the temporal position of the subject which may or may not conform to external historical contours. The fate of Annie is deeply affecting for her parents, but the story refuses to explain it in external, historical terms as if grief does not configure itself to the patterns of history. Similarly, *The Bride* explores the possibility that history is not something given, but an epistemological-temporal structure that depends on continual reinterpretation of the past imbricated in conjectures about the future. We are invited to acknowledge that the novel contains an affective relationship between Edgar and Lucy but are not invited to share in an official record of this. Edgar vanishes into the Kelpie's flow and Lucy into madness. The novel explicitly tells us that their personal names – the sign of their subjectivity – cannot enter into the structure of repetition that history requires. Edgar's name is 'lost for evermoe'. The title of the novel is not *Lucy Ashton* but *The Bride of Lammermoor*, and Edgar struggles with the idea of reiterating her name, telling a confused Caleb Balderston: '*She*, Lucy Ashton – would you kill me, old man, by forcing me to repeat her name?'[40] Neither of the lovers can be absorbed into official history, a condition the novel reserves for Lady Ashton: 'A splendid marble monument records her name, titles, and virtues, while her victims remain undistinguished by tomb or epitaph.'[41]

We are used to thinking of the Waverley Novels as the dominant tradition in Scottish historical fiction, with Hogg as a playful, subversive counterweight to the force of the historical novel. But if we rethink the generic field as heterogeneous, one that folds in different forms of temporality rather than plotting moments of time along a course, we can understand *The Bride of Lammermoor* better. This is not because the tale can offer a resolution to the characters' troubles but precisely because it cannot. Rather, the temporal structure of the tale acknowledges experiential time that slips the narrative of the historical novel. In one of the best discussions of *The Bride of Lammermoor*, Andrew Lincoln identifies 'the psychological disruptions entailed in the historical disembedding of identity'.[42] Lincoln reads this process through a tension between the romance of feminine sensibility and a new political rationality that underscores the failure of sentiment to effect social change. And we can also map this doubled consciousness in another generic sense – the temporal experiences of the tale sit uneasily within the novel and cannot be assimilated by it. We are reminded by this relation that *The Bride of Lammermoor* and 'The Fords of Callum' share a subtitle: they are both an 'Ower True Tale'. Exactly what this means is hard to pin down. The colloquial meaning of 'only too true' has a complex structure that approaches something like 'that which appears to be true in retrospect' or 'that in which we recognise a truth'. In each case, 'truth' corresponds to something that we might call 'knowingness' – a grasping at a truth that seems to be promised by past experience, but that cannot fully be articulated, or, like the future anterior, depends at the point of telling on an intimation.

The novel after all invites us from its beginning into a temporal conundrum that we cannot readily solve. The first chapter of the historical story, that seems to trace Enlightenment historicism, is not the first chapter of the novel, which in fact begins in the present. Dick Tinto, describing the sketch that may or may not be the origin of the novel, says that from it we can divine 'not only the history of the past lives of the personages represented, and the nature of the business on which they are immediately engaged' but that it also 'lifts even the veil of futurity, and affords a shrewd guess at their future fortunes'.[43] But to lift the veil of futurity and to guess at the future are actually in opposition with each other, undermining Tinto's nonchalant belief that history is freely available in whatever direction you look for it. The *Bride of Lammermoor* traces a future anterior history that *bides its time*, unable to say when that time will be realised in an event or an outcome – we cannot understand the novel as history without also understanding its complex temporality.

Notes

1. Scott wrote *The Bride of Lammermoor* between early September 1818 and late April/early May of 1819. The way Scott turns this time into new categories of history has been noted by James Chandler, who asks us to 'take the events of 1707 as having constituted the status quo for the British Parliament of 1819' and points to the relation of the novel's setting against the Acts of Union to the sudden and accelerating crisis of parliamentary representation that culminated in August of that year with Peterloo (Chandler, *England in 1819*, p. 342).
2. P. B. Shelley, *The Major Works*, pp. 446 and 414.
3. Scott, *The Visionary*, p. 41.
4. Ferris, '"On the Borders of Oblivion"', pp. 478–9.
5. Poot, 'Scott's Momentaneousness'; also p. 295.
6. Volkova, 'On *Scott's Russian Shadow*', p. 151.
7. Scott, *The Bride of Lammermoor*, p. 5.
8. Ibid. p. 187.
9. See Peter Garside, 'Union and *The Bride of Lammermoor*'; and Jane Millgate, 'Text and Context'. The Edinburgh Edition from which I quote uses the first edition as copy text.
10. Scott, *Bride*, pp. 14–15.
11. Ibid. p. 16.
12. Ibid. p. 16.
13. Charles Louis de Secondat de Montesquieu, *The Spirit of the Laws*, p. 8.
14. Ibid. p. 9.
15. Scott, *Bride*, p. 16.
16. Ibid. p. 16.
17. Ibid. pp. 71, 123.
18. Ibid. pp. 73–4.
19. Duncan, *Scott's Shadow*.
20. Scott, *Bride*, p. 57.
21. Ibid. pp. 128–9.

22. Ibid. p. 24.
23. See Poot, 'Scott's Momentaneousness', pp. 303–6 for an important reading of this episode.
24. Scott, *Bride*, p. 15.
25. Ibid. p. 139.
26. Ibid.
27. Weber, *Return to Freud*, p. 7. Weber draws on the most important theoretical formulation of the future anterior by Jacques Lacan as a condition of the unconscious in psychoanalysis: 'What is realised in my history is not the past definite of what was, since it is no more, or even the present perfect of what has been in what I am, but the future anterior of what I shall have been for what I am in the process of becoming.' *Ecrits: A Selection*, trans. Alan Sheridan (London: Tavistock, 1977), p. 86.
28. Scott, 'Essay on Romance', *The Miscellaneous Prose Works of Sir Walter Scott* 6: 156.
29. Scott, *Bride*, p. 240.
30. Ibid. p. 25.
31. Ibid. p. 29.
32. Ibid.
33. For a fuller study of Hogg's temporalities, see Fielding, '"That roaming meteor world"'.
34. Hogg, 'The Fords of Callum', p. 188.
35. Ibid. p. 189.
36. Ibid.
37. Ibid. p. 190.
38. Ibid. p. 191.
39. Ibid. p. 196.
40. Scott, *Bride*, p. 266.
41. Ibid. p. 269.
42. Lincoln, *Walter Scott and Modernity*, p. 189.
43. Scott, *Bride*, p. 13.

3

Scott's Anachronisms

Ian Duncan

Jane Austen's Scottish Novel

Why are there so many Scottish names in *Persuasion*? Jane Austen's precisely drawn southwest English topography swarms with them: Elliot, Dalrymple, Grierson, Hamilton, Maclean, Mackenzie, Wallis (Wallace) – even Musgrove, strictly speaking an English name, hails from the Debatable Land. Mackenzie is the gardener at Kellynch Hall, in Somersetshire. If the historical 'flow of Scottish gardeners to England' between the sixteenth and nineteenth centuries can account for his presence there[1] – like that of Andrew Fairservice on the Osbaldistone estate in Walter Scott's *Rob Roy*, published in the same month as *Persuasion* (December 1817) – the other names remain cryptic: out of place. They can all be found, however, in a book published a dozen years earlier, Scott's *Minstrelsy of the Scottish Border* (1802–3), which features the great border clan of the Elliots alongside their one-time rivals, the Scotts.[2]

We would be committing an anachronism if we identified the genealogy-obsessed 'Sir Walter' of Austen's opening pages with Scott, since the latter's baronetcy was not published until 1820, five years after the time of writing and three years after Austen's death. Anachronism feels alien to Austen's scrupulous precision about date as well as place throughout *Persuasion* – whereas, we shall see, the case is different with the great historical novelist. Scott's shadow falls elsewhere in *Persuasion*. In the episode at Lyme, Anne Elliot and Captain Benwick discuss the merits of 'Mr. Scott and Lord Byron', the most famous poets of the day.[3] They make no mention of the new novel that was captivating thousands of readers, the author of *Persuasion* among them, in the autumn of 1814. 'Walter Scott has no business to write novels, especially good ones', Jane Austen wrote to her niece Anna on 28 September: 'It is not fair. He has fame and profit enough as a poet, and should not be taking the bread out of other people's mouths. I do not like him, & do not mean to like Waverley if I can help it – but fear I must.'⁴ Austen issued her complaint eleven weeks after the publication of *Waverley* (in early July) and six weeks before the conversation between Anne and Benwick is supposed to take place (in mid-November). *Persuasion* opens in 'the summer of 1814',⁵ around the peace treaty of 30 June, and closes on the eve of Napoleon's escape from Elba the following March, by which time *Waverley* had gone into a fourth edition. Austen's careful calibration of her story with the chronology of public history – exceptional among her novels – thus spans the appearance and first impact of Scott's novel, even as *Waverley*, like Napoleon, goes unmentioned in her text. (The only contemporary historical persons to be named in *Persuasion* are the poets, Lord Byron and Mr Scott.) Rather than a feature of the historical scene represented in *Persuasion*, *Waverley* constitutes its literary horizon: a model for the interweaving of fictional private histories with a larger national history.⁶

Jane Austen quietly acknowledges that horizon early in *Persuasion*, in the backstory of Anne Elliot's broken engagement. The 'little history of sorrowful interest'⁷ closes with a delicate echo of a key passage in *Waverley*:

> She had been forced into prudence in her youth, she learned romance as she grew older – the natural sequel of an unnatural beginning . . . With all these circumstances, recollections and feelings, she could not hear that Captain Wentworth's sister was likely to live at Kellynch, without a revival of former pain; and many a stroll and many a sigh were necessary to dispel the agitation of the idea.⁸

An analogous summary of the protagonist's history, also rehearsing his meditative, melancholy stroll and sigh, occurs towards the end of Scott's novel:

> These reveries he was permitted to enjoy, undisturbed by any queries or interruption; and it was in many a winter walk by the shores of Ulswater, that he acquired a more complete mastery of a spirit tamed by adversity, than his former experience had given him; and that he felt himself entitled to say firmly, though perhaps with a sigh, that the romance of his life was ended, and that its real history had now commenced.⁹

Anne's turn to 'romance' is characterised as the poignant consequence of an interrupted development, 'the natural sequel of an unnatural beginning', whereas Edward Waverley follows the normative – 'natural' – path of a renunciation of romance, the genre of youthful illusion and aesthetic signpost of a deviation from 'real history', which marks his entry into adulthood. Austen's reversal of the conventional sequence highlights an affinity with Scott's art rather than a repudiation of it. Both *Waverley* and *Persuasion* close not with an emergence from romance but with a modified triumph of it, in which a happy marriage, typifying a new historical order, compensates hero and heroine for the disappointments they have endured. Anne's belated union with Wentworth repairs her broken history, while Waverley's accession to 'domestic felicity . . . even to the height of romance'[10] follows his all but miraculous delivery from the juridical consequences of treason. As well as providing Austen with a formal precedent for the synthesis of national with fictitious history, then, *Waverley* offers romance as a principle of grace – or exceptional good fortune – for the novel's protagonist, who enjoys the special protection of literary convention.

Recent criticism gives us several accounts of *Persuasion* as Jane Austen's exercise in the historical novel, brought to bear on a nearer (and greater) crisis than Scott's 'sixty years since'. Anne Frey argues that the novel's much-remarked transfer of prestige from the landed gentry to the navy tracks the ascendancy of a new idea of the nation, based on a professional civilian and military state apparatus, consolidated at the end of the Napoleonic Wars.[11] Historically this idea of a new Great Britain, superseding traditional territorial allegiances, took hold in eighteenth-century Scotland, where it constituted the governmental model of the nation-state to which Scots could look for integration after the 1707 Acts of Union. To read *Persuasion* in this light is indeed to read it as an honorary Waverley Novel, since it rehearses a version of the national story promoted in Scott's historical fiction, according to a tradition of commentary that takes its cue from Benedict Anderson's *Imagined Communities*.[12] Anderson argues that the novel imaginatively realises the nation-state by synchronising its dispersed constituencies into a standardised common time, the 'homogeneous, empty time' of national modernity. That synchronisation conscripts not only the various peoples represented in the novel (English, Lowland Scots, Highlanders) but, crucially, the reading subject, who occupies the novel's historical endpoint, modern civil society.[13] We begin to see what Austen might have meant by overwriting Regency Somersetshire and Dorsetshire with an onomastics of the Scottish Border. The proliferation of Scots names shadows forth the imminent Britishing of this southwest corner of Old England, a backward zone in need of modern nationalisation – much as Scott's and Austen's contemporary Maria Edgeworth had drawn on Scottish Enlightenment tenets of improvement to evoke a future for Ireland within Great Britain in her 1809 novel *Ennui*.[14]

Persuasion registers time out of joint as a moral rather than a sociological or anthropological predicament – although Anne's reflection on the 'total change of conversation, opinion, and ideas' as she travels from Kellynch to 'the little social commonwealth' of Uppercross plays with the anthropological theme.[15] Austen's novels 'keep time', Deidre Lynch argues, with the pace and rhythm of everyday life, coordinated in *Persuasion* with the larger arc of national history, to secure a habitable dimension of human time for nineteenth-century readers, 'the feel of duration' as a 'feeling at home'.[16] Developing this line of enquiry, Yoon Sun Lee reads both Scott's and Austen's novels as 'scale-making projects', 'concerned with imposing measures on lived experience to enable its abstraction'.[17] Austen's 'minute synchronizations point toward the time of globalizing modernity, the world of "objects in motion", put into motion for the sake of profit and pleasure', whereas Scott 'describes the intersection of differently scaled temporalities' in which 'movement is time and time, movement', and 'direction or destination seem to matter less than movement's varied, idiosyncratic speeds, rhythms, paces, and modes'.[18] These temporalities remain heterogeneous, interlayered, fluid and mobile in relation to each other, Lee shows, even when a national crisis (rebellion or civil war) appears to regiment them into a single event – a revelation of 'history' as such, breaking the textures of everyday life.

The Necessary Anachronism

Lee's essay, introducing the question of scale as a collocation of variable relations of time and space, complicates the idea of modern national time as a synchronisation of heterogeneous local temporalities, and attends to the subtlety of Scott's as well as Austen's meditation on 'pace and synchronicity'.[19] Lee and Lynch refer their arguments to critical principles of the 'contemporaneity of the non-contemporaneous' and 'uneven development', dialectical preconditions for the conception of historical modernity as a tropism towards temporal standardisation, developed in the twentieth century by Ernst Bloch and Reinhart Koselleck from Marxist historical analysis.[20] These principles have roots, in turn, in the philosophical history of the Scottish Enlightenment, and Scott gives them explicit articulation in the last chapter of *Waverley*, the 'Postscript, which should have been a Preface'. (The title designates a chronological disruption, to which I shall return.) James Chandler has discussed 'the emergence of a new conception of anachronism, now understood as a measurable form of dislocation', through the logic of uneven development, and its foundation of a distinctively modern – Romantic – sense of history.[21] This conception of anachronism has been influential in Scott studies thanks to Georg Lukács, whose account of the 'necessary anachronism' as a key technique of Romantic historicism in *The Historical Novel* Chandler summarises along with Lukács's source, Hegel in the *Aesthetics*. The necessary anachronism (Lukács paraphrases Hegel) 'can emerge organically from historical material, if the past portrayed is clearly recognized and experienced by contemporary writers as the *necessary prehistory* of the present'.[22] Anachronism, in other words, forges a teleological link between the represented past and the present scene of writing – and, implicitly, of reading – by disclosing the present's immanence in the past.

In fact two vectors or operations of anachronism work together in *Waverley*: one that discovers the past in the present, and one that retrieves the present in the past. For the first, Scott's novel reanimates a social formation, Highland clan society, which is manifest as archaic or primitive within the novel's represented world – Scotland in 1745 – as well as in the view of modern readers. To southern eyes the clansmen appear as savage remnants or revenants, 'as if an invasion of African negroes, or Esquimaux Indians, had issued forth from the northern mountains of their own native country'.[23] Anachronism discloses the Highlanders as lost in history, out of time, figured (via the logic of uneven development) as radically out of place.

The hero of the novel, Waverley himself, bears the opposite temporal charge. Characterised by modern liberal habits of sympathy and taste, he is a proxy for the reader, dropped into the scenery of sixty years (actually seventy years) since. His time travelling enables ours. These two modes of anachronism collaborate dialectically. The intrusion of the modern visitor – an army officer playing the role of gentleman tourist – forecasts the clans' demise, while their archaic appearance confirms the ascendancy of his, in other words our, modern sensibility. Waverley himself, in short, is the vehicle of the necessary anachronism. Our recognition of the past as prehistory of the present takes place through Scott's 'more or less mediocre, average' hero, who serves as a neutral lens through which we view contending historical forces as well as an anchor for our sympathetic attachment.[24] He personifies the historical novel's mediation between its represented past scenery and the present scene of reading. In Matthew Wickman's summary of the 'algebraic' logic of this mediation, 'romance is the product of the sympathetic attachment of reader to character and of character to history'.[25] Romance, designating the character's and through his our own aesthetic attunement to the 'scenic impulse' ('He had now time to give himself up to the full romance of his situation'[26]), makes Waverley an early receptor of what Fredric Jameson calls 'affect', one of his 'antinomies of realism': 'the impersonal consciousness of an eternal or existential present', floating loose from the chronological order of narration or *récit*, which constitutes, antithetically, the 'time of the preterite, of events completed, over and done with, events that have entered history once and for all'.[27]

Crucially, Waverley's anachronistic function absorbs the historical present of the novel's time of writing into the 'eternal or existential present' of the time of reading. Scott date-stamps the frame of his story, 'this present 1st November, 1805',[28] but the date (supposed epitome of historical fact) is a fiction, since it cannot correspond to the present of any reader of *Waverley* – and, as Peter Garside has established, Scott almost certainly did not write these words in 1805.[29] Narration and reading join in a perpetual present tense, renewed every time we open the book. The novel redeems its protagonist's untimely relation to the scenes through which he moves with a domestication in modern civil society which is realised by ourselves, in the act of reading, more than it is by him – and hence the novel's objective status as 'romance', a work of fiction.

The price of that redemption is the hero's conversion from narrative subject to descriptive object in the last scene of the novel, as he is relegated, literally, to the décor of private life. The much-commented-on painting of Waverley, transfixed in the landscape of his adventure, offers an emblematic summation of the necessary anachronism. It reverses a Gothic trope of haunting as frame-breaking, established in Horace Walpole's *The Castle of Otranto*, in which the unquiet dead step out of the canvas to admonish the errant living.[30] Here we read the opposite motion: Waverley's absorption into the ecphrastic frame consigns him to a fictitious past (in which romance absorbs history) as a sign that we, viewers and readers, are taking his place, occupants of the tale's historical horizon – a horizon that would remain asymptotic were it not for our reading. 'What characterizes modern manners for Scott', writes Chandler, 'is the closing of the gap between the actual state of things and the manner of their self-representation. The literary form that corresponds to and participates in the modern system of manners is what Scott alternatively called the modern romance and "the novel".'[31]

This closing of the gap between historical scene and novelistic representation is secured by a displacement of the breach to another – extradiegetic – formal level. The narrator takes over the trope of frame-breaking as a narrative and rhetorical gesture: a metalepsis, in Gérard Genette's terminology, or parabasis, in Friedrich Schlegel's.[32] 'Anachronism is produced in representational art and narrative through the overlap of multiple temporal frames', writes Justin Sider – and through the breach across them.³³ As (Schlegel insists) the formal sign of irony or self-reflexivity, the parabasis marks the contemporaneity of Scott's novel with our reading of it:

> Raeburn himself, (whose Highland Chiefs do all but walk out of the canvas) could not have done more justice to the subject; and the ardent, fiery, and impetuous character of the unfortunate Chief of Glennaquoich was finely contrasted with the contemplative, fanciful, and enthusiastic expression of his happier friend.³⁴

Sir Henry Raeburn is, for formal purposes, our contemporary, since his art, with Scott's, belongs to (indeed constitutes) our existential present. This emphasis on the formal mediation of the work of art, via the trope of ecphrasis, would appear to confirm Sider's account of anachronism as 'a kind of remainder', which '[draws] attention to literary form as the medium of representation' in order to disclose its failure 'to be absorbed entirely into the scene it represents'.³⁵ Scott's ecphrasis functions, in this light, as a sort of meta-anachronism, calling attention to the novel's work of mediation in the translation between painting and literary description.

Sider's analysis marches with recent critical accounts that favour anachronism's affordances of 'untimeliness and temporal heterogeneity', disruptions of a linear, unified, progressive history. In Jeremy Tambling's appraisal, anachronism 'counters a reading where events happen within a definable historical framework, with "before" and "after", cause and effect'.³⁶ And Mary Mullen argues that Edgeworth's Irish writings invoke 'anachronistic pasts' in order to 'refuse the assumed futurity that useful history naturalizes, allowing history's heterogeneity – the way it resists generalization and ordered chronologies – to imagine [alternative] political possibilities'.³⁷ These accounts, compelling in themselves, are at odds, however, with the function of the necessary anachronism as described by Hegel and Lukács. Rather than a technique of estrangement, in their account, anachronism makes the past familiar – it makes us at home in history. Securing readers' recognition of their own historical condition as present – latent, incipient or emergent – in the represented scene, anachronism (paradoxically) synchronises past and present. The teleological guarantee of progress from then to now, it makes the past knowable, sympathetically available, imaginatively habitable – ours. 'History is only ours', writes Hegel, 'when it belongs to the nation to which we belong, or when we can look at the present in general as a consequence of a chain of events in which the characters or deeds represented form an essential link'.³⁸ Anachronism maintains this link by revealing 'the higher interests of our spirit and will, what is in itself human and powerful, the true depths of the heart', within 'what is strange and external in a past period', i.e., the contingent, transient forms of historical difference:³⁹

> In that event the work of art speaks to our true self and becomes our own property. For even if the material with its superficial form is taken from ages past long, long ago, its abiding basis is that human element of the spirit which as such is what truly abides and is powerful, and its effect can never fail, since *this* objective basis constitutes the content and fulfillment of our own inner life.⁴⁰

The human spirit, timeless and universal, constitutes the profound continuity between – and secret identity of – past and present.

Lukács characterises his historicism in Hegelian terms, as an allegiance to 'a new humanism, a new concept of progress', articulated now however by revolutionary leaps forward. Yet his recasting of the necessary anachronism admits a potentially radical principle of contingency and heterogeneity into the chain of historical causality. The artist or writer who would make history ours, Lukács writes, should

> allow those tendencies which were alive and active in the past and which in historical reality have led up to the present (but whose later significance contemporaries naturally could not see) to emerge with that emphasis which they possess in objective, historical terms for the product of this past, namely, the present.⁴¹

The anachronism, that is, discloses those tendencies that have issued in our present condition: it interprets what was historically contingent at the time, since other tendencies and potentials were also active in the past, as historically necessary for us now, since those particular tendencies have produced our present. The present wears the guise of historical necessity because it happens to be what happened. If, for Hegel, artistic objectivity designates the abiding human spirit, for Lukács it designates only the positive causality of circumstances and events.

The Chief With his Tail On

Scott presents an anthropological rationale for the necessary anachronism in the opening, introductory chapter of *Waverley*. Among the historical novel's innovations is its representation of historical process as a wholesale transformation of human life, visible in the variability of social forms – manners, customs, costumes – across time and space. The novelist regulates this potentially infinite field of variation by charging his story with 'those passions common to men in all stages of society ... which have alike agitated the human heart, whether it throbbed under the steel corslet of the fifteenth century, the brocaded coat of the eighteenth, or the blue frock and white dimity waistcoat of the present day'.[42] A universal human nature, expressive in the passions of historical agents, stabilises the flux of historical forms. Scott asserts the immanence of this universal principle in his novel: 'It is from the great book of Nature, the same through a thousand editions, whether of black letter or wire-wove and hot-pressed, that I have venturously essayed to read a chapter to the public.'[43] But the renovation of an ancient metaphor reopens the difference it seeks to absorb. The book of nature is at once a virtual entity, a text, and a material one, an edition; it consists of a universal code and an historically contingent mode of production – paper manufacture and printing.[44] Scott closes these differences, as I have suggested, by synchronising his historical act of narration with our iterative act of reading: 'I have venturously essayed to *read* a chapter to the public'. Elegant as it is, evoking the existential or eternal present of the work of art, the formulation defers rather than resolves the anthropological question of the relation between a universal human nature and the historical variables of culture.

That relation is a crux of late Enlightenment projects of philosophical history and anthropology, flourishing in Scotland, which provided a scientific foundation for Scott's historicism. Against Jean-Jacques Rousseau's contention (in his *Discourse on the Origins of Inequality Among Men*) that society is an artificial invention, alienating human life from human nature, Adam Ferguson, the philosophical historian closest to Scott's practice, defended the premise of an original social instinct, such that historical progress – the formation of more complex states of society – entails a realisation rather than a betrayal of human nature.[45] Nevertheless, for Ferguson too, nature and history eventually break apart, as those typically modern phenomena, the imperial enlargement of the state and the division of labour, 'dismember the human character'.[46] In a striking inversion of the necessary anachronism, Ferguson imagines the reaction of a visitor to modern commercial society from an earlier historical situation – like the insurgent Highlanders, compared to 'an invasion of African negroes, or Esquimaux Indians', in *Waverley*:

The savage, who knows no distinction but that of his merit, of his sex, or of his species, and to whom his community is the sovereign object of affection, is astonished to find, that in a scene of this nature, his being a man does not qualify him for any station whatever: he flies to the woods with amazement, distaste, and aversion.[47]

Waverley does not fail to register the unsettled, contentious status of 'the great book of Nature' in the occasional glimpses it affords of a radical – anthropological rather than merely historical – human difference. 'Ah! if you Saxon Duinhé-wassal (English gentleman) saw but the chief himself with his tail on!' boasts Evan Dhu Maccombich, as he takes Waverley to meet Fergus Mac-Ivor.[48] The allusion to the scandalous evolutionist hypothesis of Lord Monboddo ('that there are men with tails, such as the ancients gave to their satyrs, is a fact so well attested that I think it cannot be doubted'[49]) quickly resolves into a comic misprision:

'With his tail on?' echoed Edward in some surprise.
    'Yes – that is, with all his usual followers, when he visits those of the same rank'.[50]

The milder anachronism, an encounter with an earlier state of society, replaces the violent one, the eruption of a prehistoric, pre-human, simian ancestor – and its breach of the universal nature that anchors the novel's historicism.

Scott's 'Postscript' invokes a universal logic of stadial progress, drawn from Enlightenment historiography, and at the same time highlights a melancholic loss of distinctive forms of human life. Civil war has accelerated two centuries of historical change into two generations, issuing in a manifest cultural extinction:

This race [of Jacobites] has now almost entirely vanished from the land, and with it, doubtless, much absurd political prejudice; but, also, many living examples of singular and disinterested attachment to the principles of loyalty . . . and of old Scottish faith, hospitality, worth, and honour.[51]

Again we glimpse the afterglow of a more drastic difference than of costumes and manners. Scotland sixty years since yields a temporary, provisional dispensation, as the title of this closing chapter tells us. 'A Postscript, which should have been a Preface' makes explicit the circular logic of historical retrospection, which views its own situation as the destined outcome of a tangle of contending causes – the logic, in short, of the necessary anachronism.

It seems that sixty years, the outer span of living memory, together with the regional geography of a small nation (Scotland), defines the range within which Hegel's 'human spirit' can be secured. Subsequent novels stretch the *Waverley* chronotope, the spatiotemporal continuum of the prehistory of the present, beyond its breaking point – and with it the lifeline of national history and its corollary, a universal human nature. Historical difference swells more decisively into anthropological difference in Scott's revision of the anachronistic Gael and the romantic historicism of *Waverley* in *Rob Roy*. 'I am a man', announces the mysterious Highlander who keeps crossing the protagonist's path: 'He that is without name, without friends, without coin, without country, is still at least a man; and he that has a' these is no more'.[52] Like Ferguson's savage, Rob Roy is the last fully human being, the complete yet fugitive embodiment of what it means to be a man, on the brink of the new historical regime of civil society and the division of labour. At the same time, Scott's descriptions exhibit him as a weird, prehistoric, 'half-goblin half-human' creature, one that bears an uncanny resemblance to the figure proposed by Rousseau, Monboddo and (more recently) Jean-Baptiste Lamarck as a type or ancestor of 'natural man' – an orang-outang.[53]

Time's Exiles

Rob Roy, primitive man, secret sharer of our existential present, embodies the principle of anachronism as a natural surplus or vital excess (literally: in the novel's descriptions, he has *too much* body) in relation to a progressive history that cannot contain him. The patriarch of the superseded historical regime in the novel, the elderly Jacobite Sir Frederick Vernon, personifies the antithetical principle, a spectral half-life that tries and fails to re-enter the stream of history. Scott marks him with the Gothic trope of frame-breaking, discussed above:

> Diana Vernon stood before me, resting on the arm of a figure so strongly resembling that of the portrait so often mentioned, that I looked hastily at the frame, expecting to see it empty. My first idea was, either that I was gone suddenly distracted, or that the spirits of the dead had arisen and been placed before me.[54]

Symptomatically, the apparition infects the first-person narrator, who occupies a 'distracted', untimely relation to his own story, as though Frank Osbaldistone's assumption of the first-person mode of memoir – tortuously rehearsed in the opening pages – has emptied the 'Waverley hero' role of teleological confidence. He 'cannot quite make sense of his own life', as Jane Millgate comments, even in the act of narrating it; his bid for authorial agency fails to coincide with our time of reading, making his story ours to interpret more than it is his.[55] The Jacobites of *Rob Roy*, and the narrator himself, are adrift from the futurity (our present) implicit in Frank's affective attunement to scene and atmosphere.

Elsewhere, in moral rather than anthropological mode, Scott shifts the valence of the anachronism the hero's sensibility bears. Henry Morton in *Old Mortality* and Edgar Ravenswood in *The Bride of Lammermoor* inhabit what Ina Ferris calls 'the time of the remnant', characterised by 'a suspension of connection and continuity that generates a curiously insubstantial existence in the present'.[56] At odds with their historical moment, returning belatedly to Scotland – like ghosts of themselves – after a critical absence, both characters struggle to reclaim the hero's function as avatar of the necessary anachronism. 'I hope to see the day when justice shall be open to Whig and Tory, and when these nicknames shall only be used among coffee-house politicians', cries Ravenswood: '[As] social life is better protected, its comforts will become too dear to be hazarded without some better reasons than speculative politics'.[57] Ravenswood's attempt to produce the prehistory of the present through a speech act – prophecy – bears a double pathos: beset by 'temporal dislocations, false starts, and unfortunate coincidences', he will not live to see a realisation of his 'anachronistic vision of progress', while his author, at the time of writing (1819), views a bitter resurgence of 'speculative politics' in national life, splintering the neo-Moderate consensus of the years of wartime patriotism.[58] In contrast to Waverley, Ferris writes, Ravenswood's 'passivity signals less the prudential reflex of modernity's civil hero than a disconnection from historical time altogether'.[59] He and Morton are exiles in time as well as in space.

In *Ivanhoe*, published six months after *The Bride of Lammermoor*, Scott widens the gap of temporal distance and historical difference by an order of magnitude – from sixty to 600 years since. This drastic chronological separation of past from present entails a structural redistribution of the necessary anachronism across the novel's character system, in which Scott develops the antithetical valence to 'remnant time' by amplifying the prophetic and utopian harmonic of Ravenswood's cry for a post-political civil society.

Scott signals a rebooting of his historicist project in the 'Dedicatory Epistle', where, as Lukács and Chandler note, he articulates the Hegelian idea of anachronism through the trope of translation: 'It is necessary, for exciting interest of any kind, that the subject assumed should be, as it were, translated into the manners as well as the language of the age we live in.'[60] Scott revisits the anthropological crux outlined in *Waverley*:

> What I have applied to language, is still more justly applicable to sentiments and manners. The passions, the sources from which these must spring in all their modifications, are generally the same in all ranks and conditions, all countries and ages; and it follows, as a matter of course, that the opinions, habits of thinking, and actions, however influenced by the peculiar state of society, must still, upon the whole, bear a strong resemblance to each other. Our ancestors were not more distinct from us, surely, than Jews are from Christians.[61]

The story that follows turns this last proposition into a vexed question: How distinct are Jews from Christians? The equivalent differences Scott invokes – between our ancestors and us, between Jews and Christians – are resolved in the pre-scientific history of humanity authorised by scripture, according to which Christianity digests its Judaic heritage. The Old Testament remakes the Hebrew Bible, and with it the Jewish faith and people, as the original necessary anachronism by recasting it as Christian prehistory. This version of universal history, with its anthropological subtext, underwrites the story of national formation prefigured in *Ivanhoe*, in which conquering Normans and colonised Saxons are assimilated into a future English homeland, guaranteed by the sacrificial exclusion of the Jews and their designation as anachronistic remainder.

This resolution does not quite take hold, however. The novel's eponymous hero recovers his inheritance and claims a bride, but the sovereign who authorises this settlement, Richard Coeur-de-Lion, realises – the narrator interjects – 'the brilliant, but useless character, of a knight of romance':

> his reign was like the course of a brilliant and rapid meteor, which shoots along the face of heaven, shedding around an unnecessary and portentous light, which is instantly swallowed up by universal darkness; his feats of chivalry furnishing themes for bards and minstrels, but affording none of those solid benefits to his country on which history loves to pause, and hold up as an example to posterity.[62]

The allusion to the close of Pope's *Dunciad* ('universal darkness swallows all') sharpens the warning note. The last lines of the novel frame the domestic settlement with a reminder of Richard's wasteful premature death – the opposite of a redemptive sacrifice: 'With the life of that generous, but rash and romantic monarch, perished all the projects which [Ivanhoe's] ambition and his generosity had formed.'[63] Reasserting a modal distinction between 'real history' and the 'romance' announced on the title page, Scott severs the novel's resolution from its proximate historical future.

The Jews, European history's tragic strangers, represent a more intractable disruption of the official story of national foundation based on a reconciliation of alien peoples into a common humanity.[64] Rebecca, the most admirable character in *Ivanhoe*, embodies Christian and chivalric virtues of honour, fidelity, charity and courage – the official virtues of the English nation-in-waiting – more reliably than any of the novel's knights and clerics, including Wilfred of Ivanhoe himself. Where Ivanhoe remains ideologically locked in his historical epoch – sharing the anti-Semitism of his fellow Christians, defending the extravagant codes of chivalry – Rebecca pleads ardently, in the great debate between them at the centre of the novel, for what modern readers are trained to recognise as humane principles. 'In the dialectic between past and present values', writes Alide Cagidemetrio, 'Rebecca consistently embodies contemporary England much more than does the novel's canonic mediator, Ivanhoe.'[65] She herself proclaims, 'I am of England, Sir Knight, and speak the English tongue, although my dress and my lineage belong to another climate.'[66] More human than 'our ancestors', Rebecca, not Ivanhoe, is the bearer of the necessary anachronism.

Historical necessity (what happens to have happened) excludes Rebecca from the future national community convened in the closing chapters, and banishes her to the prehistory of an unrealised present. The exclusion triggers the most outrageous of the anachronisms in *Ivanhoe* (a novel notorious for its anachronisms), as Rebecca and her father prepare for an exile that will transport them not just in space but in time: 300 years into the future, to the court of 'Mohammed Boabdil, King of Grenada – thither we go, secure of peace and protection, for the payment of such ransom as the Moslem exact from our people'.[67] Abu Abdullah Muhammad XII, the last Nasrid Sultan of Granada, surrendered his kingdom to the Catholic monarchs Ferdinand and Isabella in 1492; with the *Reconquista* came the final expulsion of Jews and Muslims who were not Christian converts from the Iberian Peninsula. (One of the signs of Rebecca's moral integrity is her persistent refusal of conversion.) Scott's anachronism reminds us that further cycles of dispossession await Rebecca and her people, a fate his readers should have recognised as reaching into their own historical present.[68] Through Rebecca we view a categorically different history from the official English destiny of reconciliation and settlement that *Ivanhoe* is usually taken to be promoting. Scott's heroine gestures towards an unfinished, unsettled history of worldwide dispossession and vagrancy, which is at the same time the medium of utopian aspiration and humanist hope. Rebecca personifies the (Hegelian) ideal of a universal spirit which cannot be housed within a merely national history, since the bonds of custom and sympathy that secure the imagined community are also, as her case reveals, bonds of bigotry and xenophobia.

Ivanhoe stages not just a modal turn but an ideological crisis in Scott's 'classical form of the historical novel', in which its key technique, the necessary anachronism, splits apart the utopian prospect of a fully human civil society (romance) from the diminished achievement of a domestic national order (real history). The cost of the latter is the designation of some human beings (Jews, migrants) as permanent outcasts – as not fully human. The close of the novel poses a hard question to readers about the adequacy of their modern social and political order to the ethical values supposed to sustain it.

'The Present Time. Ourselves'[69]

Where critics and theorists have emphasised a single mode or function of anachronism, this essay has sketched three variants at work in the novels Scott wrote between 1814 and 1819. The novels negotiate a crux of the historical anthropology they inherit from the Enlightenment 'science of man', in which anachronism expresses a disjunction between human nature (universal) and human history (variable). Rather than merely reproducing the disjunction, as a symptomatic contradiction, Scott activates anachronism's multiple valences across the constituent domains – moral, political and anthropological – of his novels' historicism. In *Waverley* the Hegelian-Lukácsian 'necessary anachronism', in a comic operation, brings history home to the 'eternal or existential present' – underwritten by a universal human nature – of the time of narration and reading. Subsequent novels (*Old Mortality*, *Rob Roy*, *The Bride of Lammermoor*) experiment with an ironic or uncanny mode which releases anachronism's alienating, dislocating force: deranging the alignment of a uniform progressive history upon a universal humanity, casting characters adrift in history, unsettling our time of reading. *Ivanhoe* radicalises this exilic tropism for a critical and utopian mode of anachronism which dramatises the separation of a spiritually evolved humanity from its historical homeland, and throws the ethical burden of realisation upon us, the novel's readers. Our reading – our existential present – is split between the historical reality of domestic settlement and a romance desire which, severed from that reality, unspools into utopian longing.

Persuasion, with which this chapter began, allows us to compare the 'ceremonies of closure'[70] that synchronise the protagonist's marriage with national history in both Scott's and Austen's novels. We saw that Waverley, avatar of the necessary anachronism, disappears from our time of reading as he is folded into it, absorbed into the décor of historical romance. No longer a character, a proxy for the reading subject, he inhabits our own reality as an aesthetic object – a figure in a scenic description. In an inverse operation, Austen redeems Anne Elliot's predicament of untimeliness ('the natural sequel of an unnatural beginning'), but withholds that redemptive synchronisation from the reader. Scott's ending may tell us why.

Persuasion makes love the all-but-miraculous instrument of 'simultaneity': in Deidre Lynch's phrase, 'love is the perfect timing that would ensure that her eyes would meet his in a crowded room'.[71] Much of what happens between Anne and Wentworth throughout the novel consists of little accidents that keep bringing them together, but not quite, and parting them again. Famously, the revelation that makes them present to each other is routed through a sequence of lapses and indirections. Anne's declaration of her feelings is mediated through her debate with Captain Harville (the theme of which is the discrepancy between men's and women's time), which Wentworth overhears while he is writing a letter; he breaks that one off to write another, to Anne, which he leaves behind for her to read after he has left the room. When Anne and Wentworth at last catch up with one another, it is in a public space – which yet affords them (for the first time in the novel) a moment of privacy, marked by a discreet narrative withdrawal:

> There they returned again into the past, more exquisitely happy, perhaps, in their re-union, than when it had been first projected . . . And there, as they slowly paced the gradual ascent, heedless of every group around them, seeing neither sauntering politicians, bustling housekeepers, flirting girls, nor nursery-maids and children, they could indulge in those retrospections and acknowledgements, and especially in those explanations of what had directly preceded the present moment, which were so poignant and so ceaseless in interest. All the little variations of the last week were gone through; and of yesterday and today there could scarcely be an end.[72]

The reader also, excluded from a direct representation of what Anne and Wentworth are saying to each other, becomes part of that crowd of which the lovers remain blissfully unaware. This is more than tact on the narrator's part. The lovers withdraw from the present to realise their reunion in an interplay between retrospection and anticipation in which they read and reread each other's story, reclaiming it as a story that belongs to them both, enjoying an ecstatic temporal fullness: 'of yesterday and today there could scarcely be an end'. But we are left outside, hence one of the well-noted effects of reading Austen: the impulsion to read again, at once a moral imperative and a spontaneous desire. The close of the novel sentences us to a perpetual rereading in which we are always seeking to catch up with the lovers' rapturous synchrony, to enter a world – and a time – that will never quite be ours. *Waverley*, in contrast, flattens its protagonist, emptying him of subjective, inhabited time, as our present, heavy with the burden of history, rolls over him. This is the ontological cost – the character's life for ours – of the necessary anachronism: the reason (no doubt) why Austen must sequester her characters in an eternal present apart from us.

Notes

1. See Craig, *Intending Scotland*, pp. 30–1.
2. Margaret Doody notes the Scottish provenance of Elliot, Dalrymple, Wallis/Wallace, Grierson and Mackenzie, but does not comment on their possible provenance in Scott's *Minstrelsy*; *Jane Austen's Names*, pp. 175–8.
3. Austen, *Persuasion*, pp. 84, 90. Future references to James Kinsley's 2004 Oxford edition will be given in the text.
4. Austen, *Jane Austen's Letters*, p. 277.
5. Austen, *Persuasion*, p. 13.
6. Jane Millgate argues that Scott's first three novels – *Waverley*, *Guy Mannering* and *The Antiquary* – inform Austen's 'heightened sensitivity to the temporal dimension of the lives of [her] characters'; Millgate, '*Persuasion* and the Presence of Scott'.
7. Austen, *Persuasion*, p. 28.
8. Ibid. p. 30.
9. Scott, *Waverley*, p. 301.
10. Ibid. p. 143.
11. Frey, *British State Romanticism*, pp. 116–39. See also Jocelyn Harris, *A Revolution Almost Beyond Expression*, pp. 109–18; Favret, *War at a Distance*, pp. 161–72.
12. See for example Deidre Lynch, 'Austen Extended', pp. 237, 248. See also Lynch's introduction to *Persuasion*, ed. Kinsley.
13. Anderson, *Imagined Communities*, pp. 22–36.

14. See Duncan, *Scott's Shadow*, pp. 75–8.
15. Austen, *Persuasion*, pp. 38–9.
16. Lynch, 'Austen Extended', pp. 235–65.
17. Lee, 'Austen's Scale-Making', p. 172.
18. Ibid. pp. 176, 181–2.
19. Lynch, 'Austen Extended', p. 248. See also Matthew Wickman's discussion of the fluxional – variable, curved, mobile – rather than geometrically fixed relations of space and time in Scott's fiction: 'the condensation of time . . . the way [the novel] folds eras one over the other'; *Literature after Euclid*, pp. 58–92 (65).
20. See Bloch, 'Nonsynchronism'; Koselleck, *Futures Past*.
21. Chandler, *England in 1819*, p. 107.
22. Lukács, *The Historical Novel*, p. 61.
23. Scott, *Waverley*, p. 229.
24. Ibid. p. 33.
25. Wickman, *Literature after Euclid*, p. 69.
26. Scott, *Waverley*, p. 84.
27. Jameson, *The Antinomies of Realism*, pp. 25, 18. On Jameson's antinomies and *Waverley* see Duncan, 'History and the Novel after Lukács'.
28. Scott, *Waverley*, p. 4.
29. See Garside, 'Essay on the Text', in *Waverley*, pp. 367–70.
30. See Fiona Robertson, *Legitimate Histories*, pp. 266–7.
31. Chandler, *England in 1819*, p. 145.
32. Genette, *Narrative Discourse*, pp. 234–9; on Schlegel, see Handwerk, 'Romantic Irony', pp. 210–17.
33. Sider, '"Modern-Antiques"', p. 458.
34. Scott, *Waverley*, p. 361.
35. Ibid. pp. 458–9.
36. Tambling, *On Anachronism*, p. 4.
37. Mullen, 'Anachronistic Aesthetics', p. 235.
38. Hegel, *Aesthetics*, I: 272.
39. Ibid. I: 272.
40. Ibid. I: 278.
41. Lukács, *The Historical Novel*, pp. 61–2.
42. Scott, *Waverley*, p. 5.
43. Ibid. p. 6.
44. 'Wire-wove and hot-pressed' refers to the Fourdrinier paper-making machine, operative in Scotland by 1811. See Bill Bell, *The Edinburgh History of the Book in Scotland*, 3: 22. See also Garside's note, *Waverley*, pp. 526–7.
45. On Rousseau, Ferguson and the 'natural history of man' see Duncan, *Human Forms*, pp. 34–44.
46. Ferguson, *An Essay on the History of Civil Society*, p. 218.
47. Ibid. p. 173.
48. Scott, *Waverley*, p. 81.

49. Monboddo, *Of the Origins and Progress of Language*, 1: 262–6 n. (262).
50. Scott, *Waverley*, p. 81.
51. Ibid. p. 363.
52. Scott, *Rob Roy*, p. 170.
53. For a fuller discussion see Duncan, *Scott's Shadow*, pp. 111–13; *Human Forms*, pp. 71–5, 102–6.
54. Scott, *Rob Roy*, p. 329.
55. Millgate, *Walter Scott*, p. 150.
56. Ferris, 'On the Borders of Oblivion', p. 475.
57. Scott, *The Bride of Lammermoor*, pp. 73–4.
58. Poot, 'Scott's Momentaneousness', pp. 299, 301.
59. Ferris, 'On the Borders of Oblivion', p. 482. Compare Padma Rangarajan's account of characters in Scott's *Chronicles of the Canongate* (1827) as 'temporal exiles, their presents so consumed by what has come before that they have no place in what is to be'; 'History's Rank Stew', p. 64.
60. Scott, *Ivanhoe*, p. 9.
61. Ibid. p. 10.
62. Ibid. p. 365.
63. Ibid. p. 401.
64. See Simpson, *Romanticism and the Question of the Stranger*, pp. 98–101, 107–8.
65. Cagidimetrio, 'A Plea for Fictional Histories', p. 19.
66. Scott, *Ivanhoe*, p. 235.
67. Ibid. p. 399.
68. See Ragussis, *Figures of Conversion*, pp. 89–93, 116–26.
69. Woolf, *Between the Acts*, p. 121.
70. Lynch, 'Austen Extended', p. 260.
71. Ibid. p. 250.
72. Austen, *Persuasion*, p. 194.

4

Scott, the Novel, and Capital in the Nineteenth Century

Anthony Jarrells

First published in France in 2013, Thomas Piketty's bestselling *Capital in the Twenty-First Century* analyses the 'deep structure' of contemporary economic inequality by drawing on statistical data and historical sources that go back as far as the eighteenth century.[1] As reviewers were quick to highlight, prominent among these sources are the nineteenth-century novels of Honoré de Balzac and Jane Austen.[2] In such literary works, writes Piketty, 'the effects of inequality' are rendered with 'a verisimilitude and evocative power that no statistical or theoretical analysis can match'.[3] So, for instance, Austen's fiction is employed to show the stability of wealth in the pre-inflation age of the late eighteenth and early nineteenth centuries, a time when the rate of return on capital – land, say – was so taken for granted that it did not need to be mentioned (it was about 5 per cent), and when average income remained consistent enough over years that a person's estate could communicate clear and 'concrete realities' to readers across the nineteenth century.[4] Austen would have known, says Piketty, that 'to live comfortably and elegantly, secure proper transportation and clothing, eat well, and find amusement and a necessary minimum of domestic servants, one needed . . . at least twenty to thirty times' the average per capita income, which was about thirty pounds per year.[5] In *Sense and Sensibility*, Elinor and Marianne Dashwood each have to get by on roughly four times the average per capita income. Thus, theirs would be understood to be a precarious existence, teetering on the edge of the clearly delineated social group whose values, both economic and moral, structure Austen's novelistic universe.

A second reason that Balzac and Austen feature so centrally in Piketty's account is because, in his view, capital in the twenty-first century is starting to look eerily familiar to capital in the era brought so fully to life in their novels. In both periods inherited wealth outpaces economic growth, and in both periods, too, the values which nominally govern democratic society suffer as a result. 'When the rate of return on capital exceeds the rate of growth of output and income, as it did in the nineteenth century and seems likely to do again in the twenty-first', Piketty writes, 'capitalism automatically generates arbitrary and unsustainable inequalities that radically undermine the meritocratic values on which democratic societies are based'.[6] What are these meritocratic values? For Piketty, they equate with 'study, work, and talent' and are closely connected to institutions and conditions that reward 'the diffusion of knowledge'.[7] These 'forces of convergence', as he calls them, were effective for much of the twentieth century at holding in check the 'forces of divergence' – for instance, the concentration and lopsided distribution of inherited wealth – that long have worked to separate the very rich from the rest of the population.[8] Starting at the end of the 1970s, however, these forces themselves were checked, allowing wealth to regain the upper hand on work and returning us to nineteenth-century levels of inequality. In Piketty's view, 'inherited wealth comes close to being as decisive at the beginning of the twenty-first century as it was in the age of Balzac's *Père Goriot*', a novel set in 1819.[9] But were not such forces of convergence also at work in the nineteenth century? And do the novels of the period not also point to economic growth that was both tied to the diffusion of knowledge and presented a clear challenge to the dominance of inherited wealth?

The answer to both questions is 'yes', although a view of the novel that extends beyond the realist plots of Balzac and Austen is helpful for grasping the extent of the work/wealth tension that characterised capital in the nineteenth century. It is curious, in fact, that in foregrounding the work of Austen and Balzac, Piketty, the bestselling economist who writes about novels, leaves out Walter Scott, the bestselling novelist who writes about economics – or rather, about what used to be called 'political economy', a disciplinary designation alluded to in more than a few reviews of Piketty's work.[10] Scott's 'speculations' on 'the happiness and improvement of political society', as Dugald Stewart described the field, also span centuries, and as scholars from Duncan Forbes to Alexander Dick have demonstrated, show him to be both an attentive student of Stewart, his teacher at Edinburgh University, and of Scottish Enlightenment philosophy more generally.[11] Piketty's choice of Austen and Balzac is not likely to raise eyebrows among the general readers and fellow economists who made his book such a hit. Both, of course, are well-known, canonical authors and the reputation of Austen in particular continues to grow in the twenty-first century. But for scholars of the novel, and especially for those who agree with Georg Lukács that Scott's 'ability to translate . . . new elements of economic and social change into human fates' made Balzac's achievements in the form possible in the first place, the pairing feels slightly off, even after admitting that Scott's reputation as a major literary figure is much diminished compared with what it was in the nineteenth century.[12]

In what follows, I imagine what it would look like if Scott had been included in Piketty's account. What kind of evidence about capitalism do Scott's novels provide? How and where does this evidence add to, differ from, or even contradict the evidence that Piketty finds in the novels of Austen and Balzac? And perhaps more generally, what is the value of evidence found in nineteenth-century novels for scholars working in the twenty-first century, whether in the social sciences or the humanities? For quite some time now Scott's novels have disrupted canonical histories of the Romantic period and of the novel more generally. It is my contention that the evidence they provide of capital in the nineteenth century is similarly disruptive to Piketty's account of work and wealth today. To read Scott's fiction as it might have featured in Piketty's book is to understand anew that it offers one of the best accounts available of how the 'concrete realities' of value observable in Austen and Balzac are themselves part of a massive but quiet restructuring of values more generally. Foremost among these values is meritocracy itself, a discourse that Piketty says 'plays no part' in the justification of what he describes as early nineteenth-century ownership societies but which Scott's novels show as not only already available in the period, but also useful for justifying the very capitalism of the nineteenth century that Piketty fears we are returning to today.[13]

Scott's Present

Rarely does Scott explicitly engage 'the age of Balzac's *Père Goriot*' in his fiction. But in the couple of instances when he does so it is interesting to note the economic particulars that he stresses. The framing narrative of one such instance, *Chronicles of the Canongate* (1827), is set in 1826, the year of the financial crash that left Scott bankrupt. When the narrative commences, the book's authorial persona and collector of tales, Chrystal Croftangry, has squandered his fortune, sought refuge in the 'asylum for civil debt' provided by the Canongate, remade himself abroad and returned to settle again in Scotland.[14] Before ultimately deciding to take up quarters in his former neighbourhood of the

Canongate, Chrystal considers the possibility of repurchasing the family property that he 'fooled away' in his youth.[15] The estate, it turns out, is on the market, and in a newspaper sent to him by his agent Chrystal reads an advertisement in which is 'set forth the advantages of the soil, situation, natural beauties, and capabilities of improvement, not forgetting its being a freehold estate, with the particular polypus capacity of being sliced up into two, three, or, with a little assistance, four freehold qualifications'.[16] 'The upset price at which "the said lands and barony and others" were to be exposed', Chrystal explains, 'was thirty years' purchase of the proven rental, which was about a third more than the property had fetched at the last sale'.[17] His curiosity piqued, Chrystal decides to revisit his old family home.

The earlier sale price of the estate, twenty times the proven yearly rental, reflects the 5 per cent return on land that Piketty highlights in his discussions of nineteenth-century novels. The new sale price, reflecting a return of only 3 per cent, is likely attributable to what Chrystal characterises as the 'improvable character of the land' and its capacity to be divided into multiple estates, an allusion to the party politics of the region and to the agricultural revolution that was transforming rural Scotland more generally.[18] 'The sheer scale and speed of social and economic change in the Scottish countryside in this period', writes T. M. Devine, made the country 'unique in a European context at this time'.[19] Agricultural improvements in turn justified the 'larger rent rolls' that Devine says became 'essential to service the new levels of conspicuous consumption' and which in turn effected the era's 'Revolution in Manners', something that Austen's novels provide an especially detailed account of and that Chrystal himself hints at when he describes his estate as 'affording the rude materials out of which a certain inferior race of creatures, called tenants, were bound to produce . . . a certain return called rent, which was destined to supply my expenses'.[20] Not content with two or three hundred pounds a year when he could have 'as many thousands', Chrystal ends up losing both his home and, thinking later of the improvements he might have made to it, 'something I could call business'.[21] Now, despite the 'fatigue' and 'labour' that he endured in making himself economically independent again, Chrystal cannot afford to buy back the family property, at least not without help from a fellow client who desires to purchase the estate as 'merely an investment'.[22] So instead he returns to the Canongate and, like Scott himself did, makes literature his business.

Saint Ronan's Well (1824) also highlights Scotland's 'rapid' increase in 'wealth and cultivation' and includes a passing reference to rents having 'doubled, trebled, quadrupled' since the American war.[23] The only one of Scott's novels to be set in the nineteenth century – roughly, between the years 1809 and 1812 – *Saint Ronan's Well* is filled with the kinds of details about finance and fashion that Piketty finds everywhere in Austen. There are complaints about 'nabob' wealth raising the price of food staples, mentions of stock, capital, bills of exchange and branches of the national bank, and descriptions of 'three per cents', or consolidated annuities issued by the government to manage the national debt, as 'the goose which lays the golden egg'.[24] *Saint Ronan's Well* was a deliberate departure from the historical novels that made Scott the bestselling fiction writer of the day. As Scott himself explains in the Introduction to the Magnum Opus edition of 1832, his aim was to 'give an imitation of the shifting manners of our own time' and thus to adopt a 'style of composition' that brought him onto the terrain of 'formidable competitors' such as Austen, Maria Edgeworth, Susan Ferrier and Charlotte Smith.[25] With its central conflict involving a disputed title, its many domestic scenes and its failed marriage plot, *Saint Ronan's Well* does indeed encroach upon Austen's terrain. But the novel's two most interesting characters, perhaps because both are throwbacks of a sort, feel like they would be much more at home in one of Scott's historical romances than in any of Austen's realist plots. Still, they are not any less revealing of present concerns for this. Meg Dods, for instance, is an 'old world landlady' who runs an inn on the site of the deserted Mowbray family mansion. Her parents, who managed the inn before her, acquired the inn and some of the surrounding property, making Meg 'a considerable heiress' despite her being a working woman.[26] Thanks to a nearby spa catering to fashionable types and to Meg's unwillingness in the face of such competition to raise prices above what they were in her father's time, the inn can hardly be said to be a thriving business. But as Scott notes, 'although her inn had decayed in custom, her land had risen in value in a degree which more than compensated the balance on the wrong side of her book'.[27]

What makes Meg 'old world', as Scott describes her, is not her low prices or even her increasingly valuable land. Rather, it is her contempt for new world commerce – the professionals and 'shop folk' who 'sell trash and trumpery at three prices' – and her abiding respect for old world authority.[28] As Fiona Price argues, Meg is a 'keeper of feudal loyalty'.[29] But she is not only that – not all old world, so to speak. On the one hand, as Miranda Burgess suggests, Meg is 'a paradoxical *blend* of commercial acumen and nostalgia for the landlord class'.[30] On the other, she exhibits a trait that Harold Perkin identifies as essential to the very modern, professional society that was starting to take shape in the nineteenth century and that Meg herself deplores: her success seems to be earned through merit.[31] Meg is successful because of the increasing value of her inherited land, yet she continues to work hard in 'her profession', earning points for character in the process.[32] This particular blend, of feudal loyalty stemming from inheritance and modern, professional merit, is not as paradoxical as it might at first seem. As Perkin himself argues, '[a]s long as professional men [sic] were comparatively few and depended on the rich and powerful for their incomes' – as they would have done in the days before a fully-fledged professional society took shape – 'they tended to temper their social ideal to the values of their wealthy clients'.[33] I am not arguing here that Meg is already, in 1809, an exemplar of a class that Perkin suggests formed only in the wake of industrial change, starting in the 1880s. But even though Scott does not emphasise it in his descriptions, dialogue or chapter headings, his old world landlady also exhibits a defining trait of this new world professional society, the contours of which would have been especially evident to Scott, a man whose own baronial estate was financed by his successes as a commercial author.[34]

What Burgess describes as the paradoxical blend of the aristocratic and the commercial is shared by another of the novel's curious, throwback characters: the merchant capitalist Peregrine Touchwood. Touchwood, like Chrystal, has made his fortune abroad; he was, in fact, disinherited because he 'loved to make money as an honest merchant, [rather] than to throw it away as an idle gentleman'.[35] Having changed his name from Scrogie to Touchwood on account of a godfather and partner in his grandfather's firm 'who admired [his] spirit in sticking by commerce', Touchwood circulates anonymously among the inhabitants of Saint Ronan's.[36] Despite his success in the market, however, Touchwood has nothing positive to say about the rapidity of change brought about by commerce. When he first appears in the novel, at the start of volume two, he is hailed by Scott as a 'praiser of past times'.[37] He has come to Mr Bindloose, who keeps a branch of one of the 'lately established' national banks, to cash a Bank of England bill.[38] After a testy discussion about premiums, pars and rates of exchange, the conversation turns to the region's economic progress of late. Extolling the positive virtues of this progress, Bindloose exclaims, '[y]ou do not seem much pleased with our improvements, sir'.[39] Touchwood, in response, suggests that rapid change threatens the character and stability of the country. '[T]here have been more changes in this poor nook of yours within the last forty years, than in the great empires of the East for the space of four thousand', he quips:

I left your peasantry as poor as rats indeed, but honest and industrious, enduring their lot in this world with firmness, and looking forward to the next with hope – Now they are mere eye-servants – looking at their watches, forsooth, every ten minutes, least they should work for their master half an instant after loosing-time – And then, instead of studying the Bible on the weekdays, to kittle the clergyman with doubted points of controversy on the Sabbath, they glean all their theology from Tom Paine and Voltaire.[40]

The lairds of the region fare little better in Touchwood's tirade and Meg, who has been listening to the conversation, chimes in to say, 'Weel I wot the gentleman speaks truth.'[41]

Where the banker's account, expectedly, lays its stress on gain and value, Touchwood and Dods, despite having fortunes that have grown dramatically in value in the previous forty years, counter with a stress on values and loss. This is not merely nostalgia for the good old things. It is also, I want to suggest, a justification for what Bertolt Brecht called the bad new ones, including the commercial economy that was transforming old world value into new world wealth. To return for a moment to Piketty, his reading of nineteenth-century fiction sees the confusion between values and value being resolved quite clearly in favour of the latter: this is what Vautrin, the charismatic villain of *Père Goriot*, teaches Rastignac: that 'social success can[not] be achieved through study, talent, and effort'.[42] Scott's own life story might be enlisted to counter the lesson taught by Vautrin, as it was precisely through study, talent and effort that the professional man of letters became the Laird of Abbotsford. And like Scott himself, many of his characters also achieve success through study and effort, even if such success is stumbled into more by accident – or the currents of history – than by initial talent. At the same time, however, Scott connects this success achieved through work back to property and rank, justifying the latter, we might say, in the process. Although Chrystal's case does not quite fit this rule, as the fortune he makes abroad is not enough to repurchase his family property, John Mowbray's does: the Laird of Saint Ronan's can be understood to have earned his hereditary right through work and effort after failing to do so through scheming and play.

Early in *Saint Ronan's Well*, when Mowbray is struggling with a bout of conscience while considering his plan to sell off his sister's three per cents, he exclaims, 'I will not pillage her, come on't what will. I will rather go a volunteer to the continent, and die like a gentleman.'[43] Mowbray does in fact go after his sister's capital. But he also, in the end, goes to the continent – first as a volunteer, after not dying as a gentleman in a duel with Valentine Bulmer, and then as a commissioned lieutenant. The conclusion of the novel highlights the change in character effected by Mowbray's turn in the army: 'nothing could be more strikingly different than was the conduct of the young Laird of Saint Ronan's', writes Scott. 'The former, as we know, was gay, venturous, and prodigal' – that is, he was everything that Touchwood excoriates the landed class for being.[44] '[T]he latter', Scott continues, 'lived on his pay, and even within it – denied himself comforts, and often decencies, when doing so could save a guinea'.[45] Such a transformation of character might be chalked up to the familiar figure of the rich man turned miser. But Scott suggests, too, that Mowbray has earned the reward of a settled life and estate: 'most people', he explains, 'think that Mowbray of Saint Ronan's will be at last [Touchwood's] heir', especially now that the intended recipient, Francis Tyrrel, a commercial artist and, of late, 'nobleman of fortune', runs off to join a Moravian mission.[46] As in *Guy Mannering* (1815), it is capital from abroad that shores up the estate at home. And as in that novel, too, the rightful heir of the estate can be said to have earned – or merited – his hereditary right through work. It may be true, as Alexander Welsh argues, that property in the Waverley Novels is 'restored or bequeathed but not earned'.[47] But if Harry Bertram and John Mowbray do not literally purchase their properties through commercial or professional earnings they do, through their labours, come to merit, and thus perhaps to more fully secure, what is by rights already theirs. For Scott, it seems, earning and purchasing are not always the same thing.

Scott and the Past

The tension between wealth and work that is evident – just – in those few fictional works that Scott set in the present is even more pronounced in the historical novels that made Scott's a household name in the period and that inspired the totalising view of society that would distinguish the realist aesthetic of writers such as Balzac.[48] With their settings in the distant rather than the recent past, these novels are less about the minutiae of economic life in Regency-era Britain than they are about modernisation, progress and the transition from one kind of society (feudal, or clan-based) to another (commercial, or what Piketty calls 'ownership society'). What is made visible in Scott's novels, as Fredric Jameson argues, is 'the process whereby the definitive establishment of a properly capitalist mode of production . . . reprograms and utterly restructures the values, life rhythms, cultural habits, and temporal sense of its subjects'.[49] Capitalism, as both Jameson and Piketty suggest, may have been definitively established by this period. But the values in question had not yet caught up to, so to speak, nor found their equilibrium with, the new conception of value that this capitalist mode of production brought with it. Such is one way of explaining the confusion of temporal sense that Scott's historical novels, with their long view of the present, capture so effectively.

Perhaps the clearest example of the tension between inherited wealth and success through work being resolved by folding the latter into the former is *Rob Roy* (1818), one of Scott's most explicitly commercial-themed novels. As Ian Duncan suggests, although the novel is set in 1715, Nicol Jarvie, the novel's 'spokesman' for commercial modernity, provides a perspective on economic growth that was only made possible much later, at the 'very site from which Jarvie, quasi-prophetically, speaks: Glasgow', and in the work of Adam Smith, a writer who, in the 1760s – the time that the novel's hero, Frank Osbaldistone, looks back from – 'is delivering the university lectures on jurisprudence out of which will emerge *The Wealth of Nations*'.[50] By the time of *Rob Roy*'s publication, there was growing antipathy to Smith's classical account of economics, itself a critique of the mercantilism of the earlier eighteenth century. William Wordsworth's exclamation in his sonnet, 'The world is too much with us', that he would rather return to a 'creed outworn' than accept the idea that 'getting and spending' amount to a higher expression of human nature is one example.[51] And what Andrew Lincoln describes as Scott's own 'anxieties' about the 'abominable manufacturing districts of Scotland', which were a product of the 'extension of commerce' celebrated at the end of *Waverley* and of Smith's grounding principle in the *Wealth of Nations*, the division of labour, is another.[52] But if there is a critique in the novel of a new, classical conception of value, one that pits honour against credit and that sees in 'mechanical persons and . . . pursuits' a highly efficient means of destroying the organic – whether it be community, the environment or seemingly timeless masculine values – there is also an attempt to smooth over the divisions of an emerging world system and to link its successes to what Smith, in his other great philosophical work of the period, *The Theory of Moral Sentiments* (1759), characterised as 'merit', or actions and behaviours deserving of reward.[53]

Take the character of Jarvie himself, for instance, a merchant and magistrate whose growing 'wealth, honour, and credit' earn him 'the highest civic honours in his native city', Glasgow.[54] Jarvie is also, as Duncan reminds us, a 'proprietor of slaves' who boasts about having coffee from 'a snug planation of his own . . . in the island of Jamaica' and limes from a 'little farm' in the

West Indies.[55] When we first meet him, Jarvie has come to the cell where Owen, the head clerk of the counting house run by Frank's father, has been imprisoned for debt. It is just past midnight, and Jarvie, after complaining about having 'amaist broken the Lord's day', states that it is his 'rule never to think of warldly business on the Sabbath'.[56] Ironically, Jarvie's statement about keeping his religious and commercial duties separate has the effect of assuring the reader that the two are in fact compatible – flip sides, we might say, of the coin that is his good character. And apart from owning slaves – something that in 1715 would not necessarily point to a moral failing – Jarvie is indeed presented as a good, if also a comic, character, a man who explains to Owen that while he 'understands business' and 'can win my crowns, and keep my crowns, and count my crowns, wi' ony body in the Saut-Market', he is also 'an honest civil gentleman' who is 'willing to do justice to all men', something he proves by standing as surety for the friendless Englishman.[57] Witnessing the scene, in addition to Frank, is the Highlander, Rob Roy, a 'reiving villain' and 'disloyal traitor', in Jarvie's words, but also someone the otherwise dutiful magistrate agrees to turn a blind eye to, either because the two men have the same gentle blood flowing in their veins or because Rob owes Jarvie a thousand pounds Scots.[58] Probably it is both.

For Jarvie is nothing if not practical, finding in figures 'the only true demonstrable root of human knowledge'. Armed with his calculations, Jarvie can make short work of ledgers, ably determine the best source for coffee and limes, and prove the 'possibility' of draining a picturesque lake while gliding across it.[59] He also, after calculating the population of Highland men of arms-bearing age and then figuring in the rate of unemployment, can state with confidence the likelihood of uprising in the Highlands, sounding not unlike Scott's contemporary, Thomas Malthus, in the process. But Jarvie proves himself to be generous as well as calculating, and his respect for hard work, the church, patriarchal authority and family ties makes him a prototype of sorts for the twenty-first-century 'family-values' capitalist, a man who can participate in an economy that degrades human beings and the environment without seeing either as constituting a stain on his good name. Fearing for the future of his distant kinsman Rob's two sons, for instance, and hoping to provide for their education, Jarvie offers to take them on as apprentices in his trading house. Rob, whose experiences have taught him to despise the economy of post-1707 Scotland, rejects the offer outright, though he acknowledges Jarvie's kind intentions. When Rob then moves to discharge his debt, Jarvie returns a portion, as Rob himself is reported to have been in the habit of doing, so that Rob's wife might have a new gown and his sons anything they like 'except gunpowder'.[60] Once back home, after rising to his civic honours, Jarvie 'promote[s]' his housekeeper, Mattie, 'from her wheel by the kitchen fire, to the upper end of his table, in the character of Mrs Jarvie'.[61] Whether this is 'owing to her descent' – it turns out that she is 'kin' to the 'Laird o' Limmerfield' – or her 'good gifts' as a servant, Frank says, 'I do not presume to decide'.[62] Again, probably it is both.

Frank, in contrast, is not nearly as practical-minded, although he too is rewarded in the end with a gifted and high-born wife, a woman already deceased by the time of Frank's narration. While Jarvie is busy calculating the economic benefits of draining a Highland loch, Frank is enjoying the scenery and imagining living out his days as a hermit on one of its secluded islands. And when Jarvie sets out the causes and probability of uprising in Scotland, Frank listens on, baffled as to how his family's finances can have anything to do with it. Such a response is hardly surprising given that Frank's story commences with him expressing his 'aversion to mercantile business' and rejecting his father's beloved 'profession'.[63] What interests him instead, he suggests, are study and literature. As a result of his rejection, Frank is disowned by his father and replaced in the family firm by his cousin, Rashleigh. At Osbaldistone Hall, the family seat that Frank's father himself was long ago disinherited from, and Frank's new place of abode, little goes on aside from sport, drinking and general idiocy. But a plot is set in motion and Frank, in attempting to clear his own name, is led to the point where he must, despite his 'dislike of the commercial profession', 'aid ... in the management of [his] father's affairs'.[64] This is what takes him from Northumbria to Glasgow and on to the Highlands, just then poised on the brink of uprising. By the time of the actual rebellion, Frank has practically become a partner in his father's firm. Before obtaining a commission at his father's expense to fight on the side of the government, he joins with bankers and 'eminent' merchants – the 'monied interest', he calls them – in thwarting a Jacobite conspiracy to deplete the national funds.[65] Using the family's finances to 'support the credit of the government', Frank and his father manage to find purchasers, including themselves, 'for a quantity of the national stock, which was suddenly flung into the market at a depreciated price'.[66] Doing so averts the crisis and keeps the government financially afloat. It also adds to the family fortune. When all is settled, Frank's father commends him for 'joining him with heart and hand in his commercial labours' and agrees that having 'worked at the desk' to please him, Frank should now 'wive to please [him]self'.[67]

Many readers of the novel have noted Frank's seeming lack of awareness, in the end, of any larger meaning in his narrative, a lack which mirrors his inability to cognitively map his position in a global economy where the goings-on of his father's counting-house in London can somehow be tied up with a multi-nation uprising at the seeming-other end of the world. Still, in rejecting commerce for study and then in stumbling into an adventure that takes him close to the heart of the rebellion, Frank not only ends up restoring both the credit and the finances of his father's firm, helping in the process to save the nation from Jacobitism, but he also becomes the sole heir of the very estate that his father was long ago disinherited from. Sir Hildebrand's will, says Frank's father, had 'repaired the disgrace' of his own disinheritance by making Frank rather than Rashleigh the sole heir, a substitution that has the effect of bringing Frank home, so to speak, by reversing his earlier replacement in the firm.[68] Thanks to Sir Hildebrand's 'carelessness' and to the 'expense and debauchery' of his useless sons, the estate has been 'reduced to almost nothing'.[69] But the commercial wealth that Frank has helped to secure is brought in to cover expenses. Frank's father's firm, we recall, was able to secure a quantity of national stock – at depreciated prices – following the Jacobite attempt to provoke a run on the funds. This stock having now appreciated considerably, Frank's father is able to 'convert a great share of the large profits which accrued from the rapid rise of the funds upon the suppression of the rebellion' in order to pay off 'certain large mortgages, affecting Osbaldistone Hall' and to settle them on Frank.[70] This is a remarkable turn in the narrative: Frank's father, a lifelong commercial trader, finally experiences 'the perils of commerce' and converts his money from moveable forms, which now appear to be unstable and open to manipulation by anti-government forces, to the more permanent form of property – in this case, the very property whose earlier loss occasioned the professionalism and hard work that gained him 'heaps of wealth' in the first place.[71]

In his own way, Frank, like his father, also finds 'success through work', gaining the favour of his uncle and, eventually, the money that secures his right to the family estate.[72] Although he never comes close to being the gambler or schemer that John Mowbray is for much of *Saint Ronan's Well* – clearly it is the Osbaldistone sons, not Frank, who are debauched – he does, like Mowbray, come to earn the property that will settle him for life. He does so in part, again like Mowbray, by securing the interest of a merchant capitalist (his own father) who, despite his success in the market, fears the possibility of a link between economic growth and political instability. To go back to the Welsh argument cited above, property in *Rob Roy* is bequeathed, restored and earned.[73] There is much more that could be said here regarding Scott's personal feelings about property and the role that his own profession, writing, played in making him the 'laird of Abbotsford'. But thinking only in terms of his fiction, it is clear that there is confusion and perhaps a good deal of anxiety on Scott's part about how and whether merit should coincide with wealth. On the one hand, study, work and talent are rewarded with property, as is the case in *Rob Roy*, *Saint Ronan's Well*, *Guy Mannering* and even, in a sense, *The Heart of Mid-Lothian* (1818), in which the efforts of Jeanie Deans merit a house on the estate of the Duke of Argyle. Chrystal is the exception that proves the rule here, as his example shows that labour and effort can recover economic independence but not forfeited property. On the other hand, though, the same pattern in Scott's novels suggests that property itself can serve to secure and stabilise the very gains of a commercial society, which, in addition to rewarding merit, also threaten to reduce all value to contingency.[74]

In the Balzac example highlighted by Piketty, merit and inheritance represent two options in an either/or choice: to have the satisfaction of the former is to lose the rewards of the latter. But Frank's success does not exclude him from the fortune and leisure of inherited wealth. Instead, it entitles him to both, along with the possibility of pursuing the plan of writing and study that he was disowned for adopting in the first place. Austen is more nuanced in her portrayal of the relationship between merit and inheritance. In *Persuasion* (1818), for instance, as Anne Elliot is preparing to visit her former home, now occupied by Admiral and Mrs Croft, she is warned by her friend Lady Russell that the visit is likely to be painful for her given her family's recent displacement due to financial duress. But unlike her father, her sister and even Lady Russell herself, Anne does not see the Crofts as undeserving interlopers. As Austen writes,

> she had in fact so high an opinion of the Crofts, and considered her father so very fortunate in his tenants, felt the parish to be so sure of a good example, and the poor of the best attention and relief, that however sorry and ashamed for the necessity of the removal, she could not but in conscience feel that they were gone who deserved not to stay, and that Kellynch-hall had passed into better hands than its owners.[75]

To Anne, the Crofts and their profession – the navy – exemplify the traditional values of the aristocracy better than the aristocratic class itself does. Austen, in her final novel, appears to justify the professionalism of modern, commercial society by tying it to aristocratic values of old. But Scott, as the examples above suggest, does something like the opposite: in his fiction, a new vocabulary of professional merit is used as a cover for the continuing power of inheritance.

Scott and Today

The idea of using merit as a cover for the gains of inherited wealth is unlikely to register as a radical one these days. Piketty himself highlights 'the role of meritocratic beliefs in justifying inequality in modern societies'.[76] And more recent treatments of the subject, such as Matthew Stewart's June 2018 cover story in *The Atlantic* and Daniel Markovits's 2019 book *The Meritocracy Trap*, go even farther in suggesting that in places like the US the meritocratic class has become a new aristocracy.[77] But to see such an idea as it begins to take shape in Scott's fiction is to understand not only that it was indeed quite radical at the time – new enough, in fact, that characters like Touchwood and Meg can often seem to confuse worth and worthiness – but also that an emerging discourse of merit was already a feature of capital in the nineteenth century. This will not surprise readers of Adam Smith, perhaps the more conspicuously absent figure in Piketty's book. Smith's early account of sympathy and of the ways that our passions, in meriting praise or blame from those around us, prove that we are naturally social creatures has never quite squared with his later celebration of individual self-interest and the human propensity to get and spend. Scott, of course, does not solve the so-called Adam Smith problem, which continues to stump economists and philosophers alike. But there is something both unique and fascinating in his attempt to resolve at the level of the historical novel's form what must have felt to him, on a personal level, to be a major tension in the society he lived in. His training in political economy, a subject that was soon to be separated from the moral philosophy curriculum that it was still a part of in Scott's university years, would not have helped him much. As Amartya Sen, who describes Smith's *The Theory of Moral Sentiments* as the first 'systematic' analysis of what we now term 'meritocracy', explains, merit is 'dependent on the preferred view of a good society', and while such a society was the explicit aim of eighteenth-century political economy, neither Smith nor Scott would have seen inequality as being incompatible with the good.[78]

It may be the case that we see things differently today and that inequality is no longer compatible with our collective sense of a good or a just society – although the sense of urgency that Piketty says he felt in publishing his massive account of inequality's deep structure suggests that this is not entirely the case. In addition, growing scepticism today regarding the benefits of living in a meritocratic world should remind us that the choice between work and wealth, or meriting and inheriting, is in many ways a false one as the economic structures that condition our social existence are unevenly weighted from the start. This is perhaps where the novel can come in, and a book such as Piketty's is helpful in providing an opening. Piketty is not the only social scientist of late to bring older literary sources to bear on big questions concerning the present. Jedediah Purdy's *After Nature*, in which Purdy looks carefully at the works of Rousseau and Wordsworth to better understand changing attitudes to the environment and to argue for a new 'politics for the Anthropocene', is another recent example.[79] In the ambitious spirit of eighteenth-century political economy, both books ask pointed questions about the kind of society – or democracy – we want to live in, and both books draw on a combination of social scientific data and literary sources to supply thoughtful if perhaps sometimes overly-optimistic answers. Indeed, Piketty's most recent book, *Capital and Ideology*, is explicit in assigning a positive role to the 'a priori plausible ideas and discourses describing how society should be structured'.[80] But do not humanities scholars, too, have something to add to the discussion, drawing as they can on a wider field of literary sources and the many nuanced accounts of such sources that comprise their respective fields of scholarship? Thinking of Piketty's work, for example, might we ask how and whether an historical account of the deep structure of values can complement his own long history of value? And does not the question itself point to the possibility of both a useful and a genuine interdisciplinarity?

Any such account of values, certainly as they have changed and developed in the modern, capitalist west, would have to include Scott. As with the novels of Balzac and Austen, Scott's fiction can be mined for the evidence it provides of how much things cost, what the rates of return were at the time, and how the plasticity of property is ever evolving. And like the novels of Balzac and Austen, Scott's fiction can also be considered as an instrument, of sorts, for telling us what it feels like to live in a capitalist society whose contours suggest a complex and often unfair set of economic structures. But if Scott's novelistic portrayal of capital in the nineteenth century reveals something richer and more complicated than both the realist novels and the political-economic accounts of his day, it is because his fictions adopt a 'totalising' view not just of 'above and below', as Lukács argued, but also of before and during, as Piketty does as well in his study.[81] What such a view reveals is that while capitalism may have succeeded in avoiding the destruction that was meant to follow from contradictions that Marx highlighted in his own massive account of capital in the nineteenth century – between means and forces of production – its success has continued to manufacture many different versions of yet another, related contradiction, one that is rendered visible in Scott's long view of society: that between value as defined in economic terms and values understood more generally as political, civic, religious, aesthetic and meritocratic.

Notes

1. Piketty, *Capital in the Twenty-First Century*, p. 2.
2. See for example Paul Krugman, 'Why We're in a New Gilded Age'; Stephen Marche, 'The Literature of the Second Gilded Age'; and Ted Underwood et al., 'Cents and Sensibility'.
3. Piketty, *Capital in the Twenty-First Century*, p. 2. In the Introduction to his follow-up volume, *Capital and Ideology*, Piketty again lists literary works among his primary sources, describing literature as 'often one of our best sources when it comes to understanding how representations of inequality change' (*Capital and Ideology*, p. 15). Austen and Balzac feature centrally in Piketty's latest account, but he also expands the range of authors he examines to include those writing about the non-western world.
4. Piketty, *Capital in the Twenty-First Century*, p. 106.
5. Ibid. p. 105.
6. Ibid. p. 1.
7. Ibid. pp. 408, 22.
8. Ibid. p. 22.
9. Ibid.
10. In an economics blog featured in *The Guardian*, Larry Elliott compares Piketty's *Capital in the Twenty-First Century* to Adam Smith's *Wealth of Nations*: see 'Thomas Piketty: The French Economist Bringing Capitalism to Book'; in a review for *The Washington Post*, Steven Pearlstein compares Piketty to other grand theorists of political economy, including Thomas Malthus, David Ricardo and Karl Marx: '"Capital in the Twenty-First Century" by Thomas Piketty'; and the cover pages of both the French and the US editions of Piketty's book, with 'Capital' written out in bright red letters, slyly suggest an update on Marx's magnum opus.
11. Dugald Stewart, *Lectures on Political Economy*, pp. 8, 10. See also Duncan Forbes, 'The Rationalism of Walter Scott', and Alexander Dick, 'Scott and Political Economy'.
12. Lukács, *The Historical Novel*, p. 58.
13. Piketty, *Capital and Ideology*, p. 172. 'Such discourse', Piketty continues, referring to meritocracy, 'would come into its own only later, with the rise of industrial and financial capitalism in the Belle Époch and especially in the hypercapitalist era 1990–2020'.

14. Walter Scott, *Chronicles of the Canongate*, p. 15.
15. Ibid. p. 27.
16. Ibid. p. 28.
17. Ibid.
18. Ibid. p. 29.
19. Devine, *The Scottish Nation*, p. 135.
20. Ibid. pp. 143–4; Scott, *Chronicles*, p. 26.
21. Scott, *Chronicles*, pp. 28, 27.
22. Ibid. pp. 17, 29.
23. Scott, *Saint Ronan's Well*, pp. 1, 135.
24. Ibid. p. 100.
25. Alexander, ed., *Introductions and Notes from the Magnum Opus*, p. 333.
26. Scott, *Saint Ronan's Well*, p. 6.
27. Ibid. p. 9.
28. Ibid. p. 21.
29. Price, *Reinventing Liberty*, p. 196.
30. Burgess, *British Fiction and the Production of Social Order*, p. 226; emphasis added.
31. Perkin, *The Rise of Professional Society*, p. 4.
32. Scott, *Saint Ronan's Well*, p. 9.
33. Perkin, *The Rise of Professional Society*, p. 117.
34. For Scott's own account of the rise of a growing professional class and its merit-based claims to wealth and power see *The Life of Napoleon Buonaparte* (1827), vol. I: chapters 1–2.
35. Scott, *Saint Ronan's Well*, p. 341.
36. Ibid. p. 342.
37. Ibid. p. 132.
38. Ibid. p. 124.
39. Ibid. p. 135.
40. Ibid.
41. Ibid.
42. Piketty, *Capital in the Twenty-First Century*, p. 239.
43. Scott, *Saint Ronan's Well*, p. 96.
44. Ibid. p. 371.
45. Ibid.
46. Ibid. pp. 371, 346.
47. Welsh, *The Hero of the Waverley Novels*, p. 80.
48. Dick also finds this tension explicitly laid out in Scott's account of the growth of print in *Tales of a Grandfather*. Scott, Dick writes, both 'underlines the importance of property and rank as the stabilising force of commerce' and suggests that 'the acquisition of wealth by those with the right combination of tenacity and know-how had led to the emergence of a distinct intellectual

class who could rival the power of the aristocracy'. Dick, 'Scott and Political Economy', p. 120.
49. Jameson, *Archaeologies of the Future*, p. 284.
50. Duncan, *Scott's Shadow*, pp. 103, 108.
51. Wordsworth, *The Major Works*, l: 10, l: 2.
52. Andrew Lincoln, *Walter Scott and Modernity*, p. 133.
53. Scott, *Rob Roy*, p. 186. See also Adam Smith, *The Theory of Moral Sentiments*, II.i.
54. Scott, *Rob Roy*, p. 315.
55. Duncan, *Scott's Shadow*, p. 108. Scott, *Rob Roy*, pp. 195, 205.
56. Scott, *Rob Roy*, p. 180.
57. Ibid. p. 182.
58. Ibid. pp. 183, 185.
59. Ibid. p. 311.
60. Ibid. p. 297.
61. Ibid. p. 315.
62. Ibid. p. 316.
63. Ibid. pp. 10–11.
64. Ibid. p. 185.
65. Ibid. pp. 317–18.
66. Ibid. pp. 317, 318.
67. Ibid. p. 342.
68. Ibid. p. 320.
69. Ibid. p. 318.
70. Ibid. p. 321.
71. Ibid. pp. 321, 11.
72. Piketty, *Capital in the Twenty-First Century*, p. 408.
73. Welsh himself, in his reading of *Rob Roy*, suggests that '[t]he riches gained in commerce merely assist the hero to secure his rightful lands'; *The Hero of the Waverley Novels*, pp. 124–5.
74. For more on the changing stances that Scott's fiction takes on the market and the contingency of value see Caroline McCracken-Flesher, *Possible Scotlands*, esp. pp. 127–38.
75. Jane Austen, *Persuasion*, p. 102.
76. Piketty, *Capital in the Twenty-First Century*, p. 417.
77. Matthew Stewart, 'The 9.9 Percent is the New American Aristocracy'; Daniel Markovits, *The Meritocracy Trap*.
78. Sen, 'Merit and Justice', pp. 8, 14.
79. Jedediah Purdy, *After Nature*.
80. Piketty, *Capital and Ideology*, p. 3.
81. Lukács, *The Historical Novel*, p. 49.

5

The General Undertaker: Scott's *Life of Napoleon Buonaparte* and the Prehistory of Neoliberalism

Celeste Langan

Question: Do I have a spending problem?
Answer: No, you have a revenue problem. You spent (n) amount of time typing this question. You therefore need to replenish your stock of time by an amount equal to or exceeding (n + 1). If you can't, well . . . as Simonides said, 'We are all debts owed to death.'

Posting on *Quora* website (2011)

No, if they will permit me, I will be their vassal for life and dig in the mine of my imagina[tion] to find diamonds (or what may sell for such) to make good my engagements, not to enrich myself. And this from no reluctance to allow myself to be calld the Insolvent . . .

Sir Walter Scott, *Journal* (24 January 1826)

It was extremely fortunate that he took up this scheme [of the *Journal*] exactly at the time when he settled seriously to the history of Bonaparte's personal career.

John Gibson Lockhart, *Life*

In his essay 'Death and the Author', Ian Duncan considers two intersecting narratives that together constitute an important moment in the concept of authorship. The first is the familiar 'progress' narrative of Walter Scott's literary career: the trajectory from writer of popular verse romances to 'Author of Waverley'. For Duncan, the narrative of Scott's career condenses or exemplifies an historical process by which the idea of 'Author' supplants that of the poet, establishing this 'Author' as 'the privileged bearer of human creative agency in industrial modernity' and, as such, 'the last fully human subject'.[1] But as Duncan points out, this narrative of the Author's 'birth' almost immediately intersects with another: that of the Author's 'death', this time represented by Scott's financial collapse in 1825–6. Insofar as financial ruin is 'the symbolic form of death in modern commercial society', Scott's self-anointment with the epithet 'the Insolvent' might be said to figure his subsequent career as a posthumous one.[2]

These two intersecting narratives of authorship and insolvency are no doubt operative in what Susan Manning has dubbed the 'critical question' framing the study of Scott's late literary production: the question of whether Scott's heavy investment in the market value of his work compromised his artistic integrity. 'Were Scott's last years – *pace* Lockhart – ennobled, perhaps even sanctified by the heroic determination to pay off all his debts single-handed', she asks, 'or . . . were they the inevitable outcome of hubristic grabbing after fame and fortune?'[3] Duncan, for his part, tends to read Scott's 'posthumous' career as a heroic endeavour ('the hard labor of recovery that brought on his actual death') and argues for 'the quality and interest of Scott's later fiction'.[4] In this chapter, I want to propose another way of reading the 'late' Scott, focusing in particular on the two *non*-fiction writing projects that Scott began to undertake at the moment of financial crisis: the private *Journal* (begun 20 November 1825) and the nine-volume *The Life of Napoleon Buonaparte*, published in 1827. Might we find in the 'posthumous' existence of 'the last fully human subject' narrated in these two projects a prehistory of the transformation of the 'Author' into 'indebted man',[5] and to that extent, a premonitory vision of our own condition as knowledge workers in the twenty-first century?

In *The Making of Indebted Man*, Maurizio Lazzarato describes 'indebted man' as an inevitable effect of the equivocal promise of neoliberalism: 'everyone a shareholder, everyone an owner, everyone an entrepreneur'.[6] A polity reimagined as a 'risk society' holds its members liable, in periods of financial crisis, for a 'debt' that has itself been transformed. Whereas 'sovereign debt' had been guaranteed by the state (backed, of course, by the state's monopoly on the power of taxation), what's been called 'the democratisation of debt' – the entry of an ever-greater proportion of a populace into relations of debt – constitutes Debt itself as sovereign. Recent experience of boom-bust volatility has alerted us to the structural dimensions of what Fiona Allon calls 'everyday leverage' – the sheer necessity, in periods of job precarity, wage stagnation and rising costs, for households to borrow against equity in order merely to survive.[7] Even those domains long thought to have been immunised against indebtedness by land grants, state support or private endowments – that is, public and private universities – now devote their budgets to debt servicing to an unprecedented extent. As the generalisation of risk society obscures the difference between the 'last human subject' and the 'willing slave of capital', it seems worthwhile to reconsider the late undertakings of the 'Author of Waverley' to assess the effects of indebtedness on the 'human and creative agency' of today's students and scholars.

As if in unconscious homage to Scott, educational policy theorists have described the twenty-first century 'university of excellence' as marking the end of one romance and the beginning of another: 'a new romance in which the enterprising academic is the central figure'.[8] Especially since the global financial crisis of 2008–9, when, as Rei Terada puts it, 'ever more limited opportunities for the extraction of profit' made universities 'worth mining', academics have been subjected to new norms of productivity, especially in the form of self-reporting.[9] Standards of excellence are redefined in quantitative terms, and past achievements are regarded as benchmarks to be exceeded. Tenure itself, as if nostalgically evoking feudal social relations, is rendered precarious if not obsolete, a kind of fixed capital ('bricks and mortar') that inhibits the flow of value-added information. Instead, scholars are encouraged to transform themselves into 'intrapreneurs', advancing the institution's interests through individual initiative and marketable innovation. In short, the twenty-first-century academic must learn the lesson Scott himself recites to mark his conversion from 'Author' into an indebted knowledge worker: 'When House and Land are gone and spent / Then Learning is most excellent'.[10]

It may seem perverse to propose Walter Scott as a figure of interest to critics of the neoliberal university. Scott embraced the speculative economy of the first era of financial capitalism wholeheartedly, seeking to profit not only from his writing but also from investment in Ballantyne's printing business and in other 'joint-stock' ventures (even as he leveraged his projected profits to buy land, as if nostalgic for pre-capitalist forms of wealth). But the financial crisis of 1825–6 transformed Scott's experience of writing: 'I can no longer have the delight of waking in the morning with bright ideas in my mind, haste to commit them to paper, and count them monthly as the means of planting such groves and purchasing such wastes', he writes in the long *Journal* entry of 18 December 1825.[11] Although Scott had always sought to make writing 'count' financially, in the immediate aftermath of his insolvency his writing consists almost solely of recounting: narrating the life of Napoleon, the age's most written-about subject, and keeping track in his journal of the sheer number of pages produced in each day's labour. In its increased emphasis on quantitative measures, the writing of the 'late' Scott prefigures the current conditions of academic labour, as Stephen Ball describes them: 'we are required to spend increasing amounts of our time in making ourselves accountable, reporting on what we do rather than doing it. There are new sets of skills to be acquired here – skills of presentation and of inflation, making the most of ourselves, making a spectacle of ourselves.'[12]

Etienne Balibar might well be writing about Scott's *Journal* when he describes the 'indebted subject': 'The life of the indebted subject thus appears as an endless race governed by the *calculation* of her debt's interests: how much has been repaid, how much remains to pay – meaning how much lifetime can be expected before redemption if this is to be achieved before death.'[13] Describing the psychic and practical effects of the general subjection to debts that are 'essentially *impossible to repay*', Balibar comments:

> In order to be able to bargain their deadlines and premiums, indebted subjects are those who must permanently account to the bank for their lifestyles, preferences, and expenditures, and in the end adapt their behaviour to what is supposed to be a rational pattern according to their resources and anticipated revenues.[14]

But critics of neoliberalism like Balibar and Lazarrato tend to refer to the 'democratisation' and 'sovereignty' of Debt only ironically, as perversions of political enfranchisement. What if we took that reference more literally, tracing in the experience of indebtedness Scott narrates in his *Journal* and the account he gives of the 'democratisation' of imperialism in *The Life of Napoleon Buonaparte* a composite genealogy of neoliberalism? One might thereby challenge Joseph Schumpeter's foundational opposition between the hero of capitalism, the 'rational' entrepreneur, and the 'objectless' imperialism he works to 'absorb into useful exploitation'.[15]

* * *

Even prior to the crash of 1825–6, Scott worried that he might have saturated the market for the Waverley brand (sales of *Redgauntlet* had disappointed) and/or exhausted his own imaginative resources (James Ballantyne, his informal editor as well as printer, had disparaged his latest manuscript, *The Betrothed*, as unworthy of publication). In these respects, Scott's own situation resembled the financial condition of the British economy circa 1825. The prior wartime expansion of the British economy, particularly a heavy debt-funded investment in capital goods (machinery for textile manufacture, for example) that intensified the rate of production, led to peacetime overproduction. With the end of the Napoleonic Wars, interest rates on government bonds fell and investors looked for higher rates of return in the market. Shares in South American bonds – particularly in mining companies – were particularly attractive; one economic historian suggests that investors were influenced by a 'generations-old belief in mythical indigenous treasures and unexploited minerals'.[16] Even in Great Britain, investments were drawn chiefly to 'extractive' as well as to logistical industries (railways and canals) aimed at the spatial expansion of markets. Indeed, Scott's chief publisher, Archibald Constable, sought such investments partly because high rates of return were needed to pay off large debts – including those incurred to pay advances to Scott – that were regularly renegotiated and rarely discharged.

Constable's global investments were related to his simultaneous plan to combat the exhausted market for books by radically expanding the number of domestic book purchasers with cheaper editions. Scott's *The Life of Napoleon Buonaparte* was conceived as part of Constable's *Miscellany*, a capital-intensive project to increase profits by larger-scale production and lowered costs. Constable planned to become 'The grand Napoleon of the reams of *print*', with the *Miscellany* constituting something like a new, proto-digital platform for which Scott would be a content provider.[17] Scott himself, according to Lockhart's 1838 biography, urged the appropriateness of taking 'that *other* Napoleon' as the subject of this content, suggesting that 'the vein of fiction was nearly worked out', and that 'history' might provide a new field of operations.[18] Scott seems to imagine 'history' – reams of French *Moniteurs* and already-written lives of Napoleon – as fixed capital (dead labour) he might enlist or requisition to underwrite his own commercial campaign. In short, Scott and Constable conceive a plan to profit on remainders of Napoleon.

The second project, the *Journal*, written in Scott's own hand (digital in a retronymic sense), was a corollary means of 'mining' Scott's mental resources. Aiming to increase surplus value from an intensification of labour, it constituted a version of what Marx describes as 'a closer filling-up of the pores of the working day'.[19] For Marx, the intensification of labour requires a shorter work-day, because of a 'self-evident law' that intensity or efficiency is 'in obverse ratio to the duration of its expenditure'.[20] Scott, however, seems at once to intensify and extend the working day, managing to increase the quantity of writing by filling his former leisure time with more writing. This technique depends on what Scott acknowledges as a kind of self-deception: 'I think this Journal will suit me well', he writes, one month into its composition, 'if I can coax myself into an idea that it is purely voluntary'.[21] Imagining writing as 'escaping from an imposed task' seems necessary at precisely the point when writing is identified as 'the imposition of a piece of duty-labour'.[22] That point – when writing becomes '*Peine fort et dure*' – occurs after Scott learns, in January 1826, that his creditor, the Bank of Scotland, considers his 'past present and future labours as compensated in full'.[23] Like the contemporary academic who works overtime to exceed institutional expectations (and to maintain the feeling of creative agency), Scott attempts to resolve the tension between what he *has* to write and what he *wishes* to write by doubling the amount of writing.

Most obviously, the *Journal* and *The Life of Napoleon Buonaparte* split the formerly integrated process of Scott's writing of fiction into two distinct operations: into a kind of 'free writing' on the one hand, and historical scholarship on the other. This splitting – also a doubling, since Scott regards the one as necessary to the other – is the primary form of knowledge work today. In addition to performing paid labour (for academics, a normative amount of teaching and research), academics apply endlessly for grants, fellowships and other funds that are essentially lines of credit; these applications require that knowledge workers engage in continuous self-assessment, accounting for the amount and value of already-performed labour. But more surprisingly, Scott's simultaneous prosecution of these apparently separate projects gradually seems to dissolve the difference between Scott's own 'posthumous' life and the afterlife of Napoleon. Those two lives chiasmatically intersect in what becomes Scott's double-entry process of writing. On the one hand, the *Journal*'s ongoing account of Scott's daily volume of writing (an account that requires even more writing) becomes the mirror of Napoleon's endless pursuit of glory. Narrating his attempt to write himself out of debt, the 'late' Scott represents his graphomania as a series of military campaigns: 'Here's a day's task for you: the Siege of Toulon. Call you that a task? d— me I'll write it as fast as Boney carried it on.'[24] On the other hand, in *The Life of Napoleon Buonaparte,* Scott represents the 'late' Napoleon – defeated and exiled – as possessed by a 'mania for scribbling' that rivals Scott's.[25] Dictating his memoirs on St Helena, Napoleon leverages the hands of his various amanuenses in a new form of mass conscription: a writing machine endlessly reproducing 'lives of Napoleon'. Far from having been defeated, the 'objectless' imperialism of the Napoleonic Wars moves to 'the realms of print', with Constable and Scott as its recruits. War and writing become parts of the same 'enterprise'.

At first, it might seem that war and commerce are distinct, even opposed. In *The Life of Napoleon Buonaparte*, Scott represents Napoleon's empire as built on unsustainable risk-taking, and strives to contrast France's fixation on military glory with Britain's commercial spirit. While acknowledging Napoleon's transformation of warfare by the entrepreneurial tactics of leveraging mass and speed, Scott measures the success of the French war machine critically against the number of bodies those successes cost. Yet Scott, in writing *The Life of Napoleon* chiefly as a commercial venture, ineluctably becomes part of the second phase of Napoleonic enterprise, part of the Napoleon life-writing machine. Moreover, he writes knowing the cost of his own financial risk-taking, and aware of the consequent pressures of acceleration and intensity on both the quality of his writing and the health of his body. Those costs are registered in the *Journal*, which functions at once as the form of self-accounting always required of the indebted subject, and as a kind of homeopathic remedy (writing to relieve the strain of writing to order). Far from being a safe haven for 'the last fully human subject', however, the *Journal* emerges as a transcript of conscription into the service of Debt. In its attention to the conditions of duress – call it conscription – under which *The Life of Napoleon* is written, the *Journal* discovers the deep continuity between war and commerce. Scott allows us to recognise in the entrepreneurial form of financial capitalism not the defeat but the *afterlife* of war.

Economic historians have already identified a causal relation between the end of the Napoleonic Wars and the 1825 collapse of credit – what I've alluded to above as a crisis of overproduction and falling rates of profit.[26] Scott's writing of 1825–7 allows us to trace a far more complex relation, one closer to Marx's description of the ramifying effects of a transformation in the mode of production. It is clear that the series of Napoleonic Wars – especially their escalated size and duration – constitute a transformation in the mode of production of war. For Clausewitz, that transformation depended on the transformation of society, what he calls 'the peoples' new *share* in these great affairs of state':

> Since Bonaparte, then, war, first among the French and subsequently among their enemies, again became the concern of the people as a whole, took on an entirely different character, or rather closely approached its true character, its absolute perfection. There seemed no end to the resources mobilized; all limits disappeared in the vigour and enthusiasm showed by governments and their subjects.[27]

And this 'democratisation' of war has a corollary effect of extending the sovereignty of Debt. The scaling-up of industries that service armies, from textiles to logistics, required or precipitated important economic changes in Great Britain: an exponential increase in the national debt, suspension of paper-to-gold conversion, and the imposition of an income tax.

This narrative, in which the 'democratisation' of war by revolutionary France leads to the sovereignty of Debt, turns out to structure Scott's *The Life of Napoleon Buonaparte*. Scott begins the *Life* not with Napoleon's birth or family, but with an account of economic conditions in Britain after the loss of the American colonies. In a (three-volume!) 'Preliminary View of the French Revolution', Scott makes Napoleon seem a remote but inevitable consequence of prior economic stagnation. 'The peace concluded at Versailles in 1783', Scott writes, 'was reasonably supposed to augur a long repose to Europe'. Conditions warranted an economic retrenchment: 'the decay of commerce during the long course of hostilities, with the want of credit and depression of the price of land, which are the usual consequences of a transition from war to peace, ere capital has regained its natural channel' meant that England should 'husband her exhausted resources and recruit her diminished wealth'.[28] Instead, the French Revolution, and the Napoleonic Wars that followed, required or allowed a debt-financed expansion. By describing the succession of civil governments in France prior to Napoleon as mere 'passing apparition[s]' leading to the 'Armed Head',[29] Scott narrates an historical pattern uncannily parallel to Giovanni Arrighi's in *The Long Twentieth Century*, except where Arrighi writes $M-T-M^1$ (Money-Territory-Money) as the materialist dialectic of international capital, Scott writes $W-C-W^1$ (War-Commerce-War).

Consider in this light the parallels between war and commerce drawn in two well-known stories of Scott's decision to write *The Life of Napoleon*. I have already alluded to the first, told by Scott's first biographer and son-in-law, John Gibson Lockhart. Scott nominates Archibald Constable as 'The grand Napoleon of the realms of *print*' because of the 'revolution in the art and traffic of bookselling' that Constable envisions in May 1825.[30] Significantly, the evidence for an untapped market of book-buyers comes from the tax rolls. The envisioned *Miscellany* 'had been suggested by, and w[as] in fact mainly grounded upon, a sufficiently prosaic authority – namely, the annual schedule of assessed taxes', Lockhart reports.[31] In a telling phrase, Constable describes the payers of a tax on hair powder as 'an *army*, compared to the purchasers of even the best and most popular of books'.[32] Although he presumably refers to excise-tax rolls, Constable's reference to an 'army' of taxpayers evokes as well the recently repealed income tax, levied from 1799 to 1816 to fund the war against Napoleon. Constable clearly imagines his print 'revolution' as a sort of privatisation of the state monopoly on taxation; the former taxpayer, a kind of discharged soldier, will become a subscriber to his *Miscellany*. Thus Lockhart's account of Constable's response to his anointment as 'The grand Napoleon of the realms of *print*':

> 'If you outlive me', says Constable . . . 'I bespeak that line for my tomb-stone; but, in the meantime, may I presume to ask you to be my right-hand man when I open my campaign of Marengo? I have now settled my outline of operations – a three-shilling or half-crown volume every month, which must and shall sell, not by thousands or tens of thousands, but by hundreds of thousands – ay, by millions! Twelve volumes in the year, a halfpenny of profit upon every copy of which will make me richer than the possession of all the copyrights of all the quartos that ever were, or will be, hot-pressed! Twelve volumes, so good that millions must wish to have them, and so cheap that every butcher's callant may have them, if he pleases to let me tax him sixpence a-week!'[33]

Constable's plan is emphatically an enterprise of scale, parallel to Napoleon's model of warfare. Napoleon's 'system', according to Scott, was to reduce warfare to a 'mathematical and arithmetical science', in which victory depends on 'who can assemble the greatest number of forces upon the same point at the same moment'.[34] In short, a leveraging of mass and speed.

Marshalling the resources made available to him by the mass conscription of soldiers, Napoleon achieves military leverage. Constable imagines exercising a similar leverage, 'turning' his fortunes with Scott's *Napoleon*. '[C]onsider[ing] the appearance of the second edition of the Life of Napoleon in his Miscellany as the great point upon which the fortunes of that undertaking were to turn',[35] Constable first amasses Napoleonic materials for Scott (no doubt on credit): 'Constable accordingly set about collecting a new library of printed materials, which continued from day to day pouring in upon him . . . The first wagon delivered itself of about a hundred folios of the Moniteur; and London, Paris, Amsterdam, and Brussels, were all laid under contribution to meet the bold demands of his magnificent purveyor.'[36] And Lockhart's description of Constable's procedure, in which various cities were 'laid under contribution', seems almost intentionally to recall Scott's account of Napoleon's own tactic, by which he converted the French military from a drain on revenues into a revenue generator:

> From the time that Napoleon passed the Alps, he inverted this state of things; and made the newly conquered countries not only maintain the army by means of contributions and confiscations, but even contribute to support the Government. Thus war, which had hitherto been a burden to the republic, became in his hands a source of public revenue.[37]

Of course, in the end – particularly in the Moscow campaign – Napoleon becomes over-leveraged. Catastrophic losses result in a 'credit squeeze' of a particularly morbid kind: soldiers' bodies cannot be replaced rapidly enough, and supply lines are attenuated by distance. But Constable's plan and Scott's *Life* use the defeat and death of Napoleon as a financial opportunity, 'inverting' loss into potential profit.

The second story of Scott's decision to write *The Life of Napoleon Buonaparte* appears in the Introduction to the 1825 edition of Scott's *Tales of the Crusaders*, an elaborate meta-fiction purporting to be the 'minutes' of a stock-holders' meeting (of the kind Scott knew well, as an investor in the Edinburgh Oil Gas Company), convened by the 'Eidolon' of the Author of Waverley, to persuade various narrators and characters from the earlier novels to seek an Act of Parliament formalising the 'Author of Waverley' as a corporate *'persona standi in judicio'*.[38] Two advantages of legal standing are advanced: it would allow the prosecution of 'encroachers' on the Waverley brand, and – more importantly – it would enable investment in a new 'little mechanism' designed to reduce 'the labour of composition of these novels . . . by the use of steam'.[39]

> Mr Dousterswivel has sent me some drawings, which go so far to show, that, by placing the words and phrases technically employed on these subjects, in a sort of frame-work, like that of the Sage of Laputa, and changing them by such a mechanical process as that by which weavers of damask alter their patterns, many new and happy combinations cannot fail to occur, while the author, tired of pumping his own brains, may have an agreeable relaxation in the use of his fingers.[40]

The proposed machine seems quite amazingly to prefigure the word-processing systems by which knowledge workers now mostly write (or, rather, type). We know that Charles Babbage was inspired by the jacquarding machine to use punched cards for his analytical engine; the punched cards allowed the machine to conduct different operations, just as, on a far more elaborate scale, the modern computer can operate as a typewriter, a telephone and a darkroom. When the Author of Waverley claims that the machine may allow 'an agreeable relaxation in the use of his fingers', though, his foresight seems to fail. For as we know all too well, the word-processing keyboard generally employs two hands.[41]

The Author of Waverley argues that the capital-intensive transformation of writing by the Dousterswivel machine is a necessary adaptation to a more general transformation of the mode of production. 'The age of Stock-companies', he opines, is a kind of dialectical inversion of the division of labour, making man once again 'his own weaver, tailor, butcher, shoemaker, and so forth'.[42] The difference is that speculative investment works as a kind of magical leverage, making each expenditure a source of profit:

> In fact, a man who has dipt largely into these speculations, may combine his own expenditure with the improvement of his own income, just like the ingenious hydraulic machine, which, by its very waste, raises its own supplies of water. Such a man buys his bread from his own Baking Company, his milk and cheese from his own Dairy Company, takes off a new coat for the benefit of his own Clothing Company, illuminates his house to advance his own Gas Establishment, and drinks an additional bottle of wine for the benefit of the General Wine Importation Company. Every act, which would otherwise be one of mere extravagance, is, to such a person, seasoned with the *odor lucri*, and reconciled to prudence. Even if the price of the article consumed be extravagant, and the quality indifferent, the person, who is in a manner his own customer, is only imposed upon for his own benefit. Nay, if the Joint-Stock Company of Undertakers shall unite with the Medical faculty, as proposed by the late facetious Dr. G—, under the firm of Death and the Doctor, the shareholder might contrive to secure to his heirs a handsome slice of his own death-bed and funeral expenses.[43]

We note that the joint-stock company seems to produce profit as automatically as the Dousterswivel machine produces narrative (or at least 'those parts of the narrative which are at present composed of common-places').[44] Working on the same principle of Joseph Bramah's hydrostatic press, the joint-stock company turns expenditure into investment; consumption fuels growth.[45] But the darker effect is to make the ultimate profit (for the joint-stock company of Undertakers) require the death of the subject.

In the context of the actual effects of financialisation on Scott's own work of writing, the dénouement of this fictional proposal to form a writers' joint-stock company is significant. Opposed first by Luddite 'murmurs' ('blown up', 'bread taken out of our mouths') from some members of the Board, the proposal ultimately fails because of a collapsed credit market: 'whereas last year you might have obtained an act incorporating a Stock Company for riddling ashes, you will not be able to procure one this year for gathering pearls'.[46] It is as a consequence of this credit collapse that the Author of Waverley decides to go it alone as an independent author: 'I will vindicate my own fame with my own right-hand', he declares, working into the *Tales of the Crusaders* a 'canny advertisement', as Evan Gottlieb puts it, for 'the LIFE OF NAPOLEON BUONAPARTE, by the AUTHOR OF WAVERLEY!'[47]

'Circumstances', of course, dictated otherwise ('Circumstances, however, unconnected with the undertaking, induced him to lay aside an *incognito*').[48] The 'Great Unknown' had become, to use Scott's own painful joke, the 'Too Well Known'.[49] For the Bank of Scotland to accept Scott's offer of a deed of trust, he had to reveal himself as the source of the Author of Waverley's extraordinary literary output. Although *The Life of Napoleon Buonaparte* was published in 1827 as the work of 'the Author of Waverley', in the 'Advertisement', Scott acknowledges the work as his own. Nor did he have clear title to the profits of the work. Constable, citing their verbal agreement about the *Miscellany*, claimed the *Napoleon* project as a commissioned asset, and Scott did not win the legal case until after the nine volumes were completed, in July 1827. Finally, the accrued profits went to pay off the creditors of what had essentially become a joint-stock company of debtors: Walter Scott, his printers, James Ballantyne and Robert Cadell, and his publisher, Constable.[50]

The Life of Napoleon Buonaparte did turn a profit on publication, but measured by conventional standards of 'aesthetic integrity', Scott's history is no doubt a failure. It seems bloated not just because of the materials Constable had requisitioned, but also from its 'just-in-time' mode of production. On 22 March 1827 Scott reports that Ballantyne had sent an 'urgent request in extending the two last volumes to about 600 each', and comments, 'I believe it will be no more than necessary after all. But [it] makes one feel like a dog in a wheel always moving and never advancing.'[51] In his rather scathing review, John Stuart Mill suggested that 'the celerity with which [Scott] projected and completed a work which, to execute it tolerably, would have required many years' reading' merely confirmed earlier evidence that Scott regarded 'any degree of pains employed on his productions, more than was necessary to their sale' as 'superfluous' – the judgement of a rational entrepreneur, one might say.[52]

What is most relevant about Mill's review, however, is his analysis of the *Life of Napoleon* as a bifurcated work. Mill regards the second 'half' of the work, devoted to Napoleon's career, to be the work of a 'tolerable poet' and 'much more than a tolerable novelist', but containing little to interest the historian.[53] For Mill, the enigma that requires an *historian* is not individual character (Napoleon), but the 'mighty power' unleashed by and as the French Revolution – the subject of the first part of Scott's history.[54] 'The moving forces in this vast convulsion, the springs by which so much complex machinery was now set in motion', Mill continues, 'were of a class for the laws of whose action the dictionary of historical commonplaces does not yet provide one established formula'. (Recall the Author of Waverley's admission that Dousterswivel's engine could only crank out ready-made phrases and plot elements.)

For Mill, a proper account of how that 'thing' which is called 'the people' comes into being requires not a novelist or poet but 'the man who is yet to come, the philosophical historian'.[55] Yet in some respects, Mill's description 'the *people*' as a product of the 'complex machinery' of the French Revolution seems more reminiscent of Scott's joint-stock company of leveraged subjects than an unprecedented self-organisation of democratic agency:

> That mighty power, of which, but for the French Revolution, mankind perhaps would never have known the surpassing strength – that force which converts a whole people into heroes, which binds an entire nation together as one man, was able, not merely to overpower all other forces, but to draw them into its own line, and convert them into auxiliaries to itself.[56]

Moreover, by representing the Revolution as a 'mighty power' which 'binds an entire nation together as *one man*', Mill seems precisely to evoke Napoleon, who harnessed power at once through charisma and conscription. Mill insists, however, that this mighty power exceeds the capacity of a single hand to control; it cannot be personified. More closely than it resembles Napoleon, it resembles the free market, at least as Joshua Clover describes the market in the liberal imagination: 'able to revalue every object with supple velocity according not to some ideological program but the aggregate will of the people – not just the invisible hand but the invisible spirit, as it were'.[57] Or – with Scott in mind – perhaps we should venture a new figure: the *visible* hand moved by an invisible agency. The *willing* slave of capital.

I refer, of course, to a famous anecdote about Scott's productivity from Lockhart's biography. Lockhart describes a modern version of Belshazzar's Feast, a scene in which the writing hand of Walter Scott casts a monitory spell on a young William Menzies, like Lockhart himself a would-be knowledge worker ('destined for the bar').

> I observed that a shade had come over the aspect of my friend, who happened to be placed immediately opposite to myself, and said something that intimated a fear of his being unwell. 'No', said he, 'I shall be well enough presently, if you will only let me sit where you are, and take my chair; for there is a confounded hand in sight of me here, which has often bothered me before, and now it won't let me fill my glass with a good will'. I rose to change places with him accordingly, and he pointed out to me this hand, which, like the writing on Belshazzar's wall, disturbed his hour of hilarity. 'Since we sat down', he said, 'I have been watching it – it fascinates my eye – it never stops – page after page is finished and thrown on that heap of MS. and still it goes on unwearied – and so it will be till candles are brought in, and God knows how long after that. It is the same every night – *I can't stand a sight of it when I am not at my books*.[58]

Lockhart attempts to assuage the young professional's anxiety by construing the 'hand' in the synecdochic sense of a labourer or wage-worker: 'Some stupid, dogged, engrossing clerk, probably', but is promptly contradicted – 'No, boys', said our host, 'I well know whose hand it is – 'tis Walter Scott's'.[59] But the difference between the hired 'hand' of a copyist and the authenticating 'hand' of the Author, that 'last fully human subject', is notably diminished by the crash of 1825. Indeed, on the day Scott came 'home through cold roads to as cold news' (16 January 1825), he holds out that hand to an old friend, declaring, 'give me a shake of your hand – mine is that of a beggar'.[60]

Which hand – the Author's or the beggar's – writes in this scene? Lockhart, by situating the scene in 1814, clearly wishes to identify it as the hand of the 'Author of Waverley'. Yet his first instinct is to see in the automatism, the almost perpetual motion of the hand, a figure of conscription. Certainly that's what his friend sees. Imagining himself in implicit competition with the disembodied hand, the young would-be knowledge worker feels he has been 'weighed and found wanting'. Of course, the pages of the MS are a mere 'heap', so the standard of measure must be entirely quantitative, not qualitative; to be 'at one's books', it appears, is to undertake the work of accounting.

The figure of the hand reappears later, when Lockhart distinguishes between the 'buoyant' work of fiction writing and the near-drudgery Scott undertakes in copying information for the *Life of Napoleon*.

> He had now to apply himself doggedly to the mastering of a huge accumulation of historical materials. He read, and noted, and indexed with the pertinacity of some pale compiler in the British Museum; but rose from such employment, not radiant and buoyant, as after he had been feasting himself among the teeming harvests of Fancy, but with an aching brow, and eyes on which the dimness of years had begun to plant some specks, before they were subjected again to that straining over small print and difficult manuscript which had, no doubt, been familiar to them in the early time, when (in Shortreed's phrase), 'he was making himself' . . . It now often made me often sorry to catch a glimpse of him, stooping and poring with his spectacles, amidst a pile of authorities – a little note-book ready in the left hand, that had always used to be at liberty for patting Maida.[61]

Again, surprisingly little emphasis is placed on the qualitative difference of the product; the distinction instead concerns the spirit with which the work of writing is undertaken – buoyant or dogged, spirited or servile. (Or on paying attention to what the left hand is doing: petting a dog or doggedly copying.)

Crucially for my purposes, this distinction of spirit corresponds to how Lockhart represents what I've called Scott's 1825–6 double-entry mode of writing (the simultaneous commencement of the *Journal* and the *Life of Napoleon*):

> It was extremely fortunate that he took up this scheme [of the daily journal] exactly at the time when he settled seriously to the history of Buonaparte's personal career. The sort of preparation which every chapter of that book now called for has already been alluded to; and . . . there were minutes enough, and hours, and perhaps days of weariness, depression, and languor, when (unless this silent confidant had been at hand) even he perhaps might have made no use of his writing desk.[62]

Lockhart suggests that Scott's *Journal* supplies the 'spirit' wanting in his somewhat overlaboured *The Life of Napoleon Buonaparte* – a judgement in which subsequent scholarship has largely concurred. But what if we consider the spirit exhibited in the *Journal* not as relief from conscription but its necessary counterpart?

In their account of neoliberal management strategies in *The New Spirit of Capitalism*, Luc Boltanski and Eve Chiapello remind us of why capitalism requires 'spirit'. Because the logic of infinite, 'insatiable' accumulation lacks intrinsic moral justification, 'capitalism must borrow the legitimating principles it lacks from orders of justification external to it'.[63] Only by 'borrowing' (a wonderfully apt figure) moral justification in this manner can capitalism motivate people to 'sacrifice' to the accumulation process. Even more pertinently, they point out that capitalism requires spirit because 'capitalism is not vested with the power of arms'. If this latter claim too quickly overlooks the imbrication of capitalism with state power, and the frequency with which war is an engine of capitalist development, it does throw a different light on Scott's disembodied hand. That hand represents 'the spirit of capitalism' insofar as it appears to act independently of 'the power of arms'.

Mill criticised Scott's *The Life of Napoleon Buonaparte* for its failure adequately to account for the 'complex machinery' set in motion by the Revolution, and for Scott's reliance on a 'dictionary of historical commonplaces'. But the history of its composition that the *Journal* records may partly counterbalance these charges – by representing Mill's 'man who is yet to come' as *indebted* man. Certainly Scott describes himself as submitting with delight to a streamlined model of 'just-in-time' production ('I love to have the press thumping, clattering and banging in my rear – it creates the necessity [which] almost always makes me work best').[64] His speed and productivity overawe (or disable) judgements of quality: 'I scarce know what is to succeed or not, but this is the consequence of writing too much and too often. I must get some breathing space. But how is that to be managed? There is the rub.'[65] No longer anonymous, Scott can offer his autograph directly to the printer, without employing a copyist. But Ballantyne complains that Scott's new laboursaving automatism costs *him* a good deal of labour: 'I have been reading over, critically what has been printed [of the *Napoleon*]; and I find the tautologies and inaccuracies very numerous indeed. Yet every one sheet costs me 5 hours labour, if it costs me five minutes.'[66] Ballantyne's experience may well remind contemporary knowledge workers of the entrepreneurial management strategy of 'Getting Things Done' (GTD) as Melissa Gregg describes it: 'The notion of freedom GTD celebrates is, perversely, the freedom to work. In practice it typically means liberation from a raft of unrewarding labour that others must still perform.'[67]

Reading *Life of Napoleon* can itself seem like unrewarding labour – especially when contrasted to the *Journal*'s more personal prose. But the apparently relaxed hand with which Scott writes may also be construed as the enlistment of *both* hands in the campaign of capital accumulation. Why does Scott wish to imagine his journal writing as 'free' rather than 'compelled', even though he will write *Life of Napoleon* in either case, to 'extricate' himself from debt? In *The Soul at Work*, Franco Berardi provides one possible answer, tracing an historical transformation in the concept of 'enterprise'. For Machiavelli, he writes, 'enterprise' was, like politics, a form of *action*, an emancipation from fate, and to that extent, opposed to labour. This opposition is sharpened and intensified by capitalism: 'Enterprise means invention and free will. Labour is repetition and executing action.'[68] But the conditions of *cognitive* labour, or knowledge work, confuse this distinction – especially when knowledge work itself becomes a target of capitalist exploitation. Berardi claims that digital technology for the first time makes possible the abstraction of cognitive labour; intellectuals 'are no longer a class independent from production, nor free individuals assuming the task of a purely ethical and freely cognitive choice, but a mass social subject, tending to become an integral part of the general process of production'.[69]

Asking 'Today, what does it mean to work?', Berardi answers: 'As a general tendency, work is performed according to the same physical patterns: we all sit in front of a screen and move our fingers across a keyboard. We type.'[70] Precisely when physical movements of cognitive workers become interchangeable, they begin to identify their mental labour as specific and personal; as *enterprise*. Because their ideation seems inimitable, knowledge workers do not regard their work as labour: 'on the contrary, they tend to consider their labour, *even if formally dependent*, to be an enterprise where they can spend the best part of their energy, independently from the economic and juridical condition in which it expresses itself'.[71] In answering the question, 'Why do such a large part of workers today consider work the most interesting part of their life, no longer opposing the lengthening of their working day and instead spontaneously choosing to increase it?',[72] Berardi helps us to understand the apparent paradox of Scott's doubled productivity. The more the work of 'compiling' the *Life of Napoleon* is experienced as labour, the more the *Journal* becomes a necessary adjunct, to keep the spirit of 'enterprise' alive.

Scott's *The Life of Napoleon Buonaparte* is best understood as a prehistory of this transformation of 'enterprise'. Careful to have represented Napoleon's reputed military 'genius' as owing as much to mass conscription as to personal qualities of energy and courage, Scott represents his pursuit of 'glory' as a perversion of enterprise, thus anticipating Schumpeter's critique of imperialism. 'Imperialism', Schumpeter writes in 1919, 'is the *objectless* disposition on the part of a state to unlimited forcible expansion'.[73] Schumpeter wants to distinguish 'objectless' military expansion from the 'concrete' motives of private enterprise in capitalism, yet admits that 'The modern businessman acquires work habits because of the need for making a living, but labors far beyond the limits where acquisition still has rational meaning in the hedonist sense.'[74] Indeed, Schumpeter links both war and industrial capitalism in an autopoetic tautology: '*Created by wars that required it, the machine now created the wars it required.*'[75]

Scott's portrait of Napoleon in defeat reinforces the parallel between 'objectless' imperialism and the trick of self-enterprise. In terms relevant to the birth-death of the Author as 'last human subject', Scott quotes Napoleon on Elba declaring, 'I am now a *deceased person*, occupied with nothing but my family, my retreat, my house, my cows, and my poultry.'[76] Yet in his 'afterlife' as a landowner resigned to 'devote himself exclusively to science and literature',[77] Napoleon merely applies his military tactic of leverage on a smaller scale:

> His propensities continued to be exactly of the same description at Elba, which had so long terrified and disquieted Europe. To change the external face of what was around him; to imagine extensive alterations without accurately considering the means by which they were to be accomplished . . . to apply to Elba the system of policy which he had exercised so long in Europe, was the only mode in which he seems to have found amusement and exercise for the impatient energies of [his] temper.[78]

Even though Napoleon resorts to his former methods of requisition, demanding that inhabitants of Elba pay their taxes early, and quartering his troops at their expense, these measures prove inadequate. Like Walter Scott ('I have been rash in anticipating funds to buy land. But then I made from £5000 to £10,000 a year, and land was my temptation'),[79] Napoleon experiences a collapse of credit: 'He had plunged into expenses with imprudent eagerness, and without weighing the amount of his resources against the cost of the proposed alterations', Scott reports.[80] And if Scott's Abbotsford is a smaller-scale Elba, Napoleon's entire career of over-leveraging is a mirror of Scott's own fertile imagination: 'Thus, we recognize in his government of this miniature state, the same wisdom, and the same errors, by which Buonaparte won and lost the empire of the world . . . Napoleon's impatience to execute whatsoever plans occurred to his fertile imagination, was the original cause of these pecuniary distresses.'[81]

But by far the most revelatory moment is Scott's representation of Napoleon's return from Elba to Paris in 1815. Trying to explain the enthusiasm for Napoleon's return on the part of a populace devastated by conscription, Scott writes,

> For a little time after Napoleon's return, crowds of artisans of the lowest order assembled under the windows of the Tuilleries, and demanded to see the Emperor, whom, on his appearance, they greeted with shouts, as *le Grand Entrepreneur*, or general employer of the class of artisans, in language where the coarse phraseology of their rank was adorned with such flowers of rhetoric as the times of terror had coined.[82]

Read quickly, this passage makes little sense. In what way can we understand the phrase '*le Grand Entrepreneur*' as at once the 'coarse phraseology' of artisans and a Terrorist rhetorical flourish? While the reference to Terrorist coinages might put us in mind of epithets for the guillotine like 'the National Razor', it's unclear how 'general employer' might operate as such an instance of morbid wit. For in truth, the 'coarseness' of the phrase depends upon Scott's own buried pun – one whose implications aren't evoked until the last pages of the ninth volume, when he writes in conclusion,

> The name given him by the working classes, of the General Undertaker, was by no means ill-bestowed; but in what an incalculably greater degree do such works succeed, when raised by the skill and industry *of those who propose to improve their capital by the adventure,* than when double the expense is employed at the arbitrary will of a despotic sovereign![83]

Scott is the only writer I know of who calls Napoleon 'the General Undertaker'. Many histories written before and after Scott's reproduce the cry – '*le grand entrepreneur est de retour; tout était mort, tout renait; nous étions oisifs, et aujourd'hui nous sommes tous occupés*'. But at least one English translation (1820) of a French source-text takes care to *avoid* Scott's pun, preserving the French *entrepreneur* because 'We have no single word in our language answering to this: it implies one who undertakes works of different kinds, including our architect and civil engineer.'[84] Scott himself first chooses 'general employer'; another, W. H. Ireland, translates the phrase as 'the great contractor'.[85] It seems clear that in choosing to translate *entrepreneur* as 'undertaker', Scott wishes to recall his earlier critique of Napoleon's risk-laden military strategy, to ironise 'le grand entrepreneur' as one who makes a business of burial: 'His system was ruinous in point of lives, for even the military hospitals were often dispensed with. But although Moreau termed Napoleon a conqueror at the rate of ten thousand men a day, yet the sacrifice for a length of time uniformly attained the object for which it was designed.'[86]

Yet instead of explicitly *capitalising* on the pun, as it were, by reminding readers that the measure of Napoleon's greatness is the number of corpses he helped to produce, Scott in his conclusion merely sounds the refrain of (neo)liberal doctrine. His conclusion claims that state-sponsored 'enterprise', even as aggrandising and rapacious as Napoleon's, cannot extract profit as efficiently as a market system which produces 'by an incalculably greater degree', and at half the cost, by the trick of self-enterprise ('the skill and industry of those who propose to improve their capital by the adventure').[87] Indeed, Scott's insistence on the superior productivity of the individual capitalist we call the *entrepreneur* recalls the legal argument he makes on his own behalf in contesting Constable's claim to the profits of his *Napoleon*. There he reminds the arbitrators that *Life of Napoleon* as yet exists only in his imagination: '[T]he author has the strongest possible hypothec upon that which, independent of his own voluntary exertions, can never have an existence', Scott writes, so that 'circumstances which call upon him to exercise such a hypothec for himself and others are very *imperious*'.[88] Echoing the resistance to 'duty' so often expressed in his *Journal*, Scott claims that 'free' labour is more efficient, more likely to pay off debt. 'The readiest mode of extricating these affairs', he writes to the arbitrator,

> rests on the author's own exertions, and the question is whether he is free to use these exertions for his own interest and that of his creditors, or whether he is to be chained to the oar for behoof of Messrs. Constable, through whose misfortunes it is that the labour is become at all a matter of compulsion.[89]

* * *

The *OED* does not consider Scott's citation and translation of the phrase *le grand entrepreneur* when it attributes to Carlyle, in 1852, the first usage of *entrepreneur* in its familiar economic sense – 'one who undertakes an enterprise . . . a person who takes the risk of profit or loss'. Nor does Schumpeter, who makes the *entrepreneur* the centre of his influential *The Theory of Economic Development*, allude to the epithet applied to Napoleon. Yet Schumpeter's classic account of the *entrepreneur* – 'one can only become an entrepreneur by previously becoming a debtor'[90] – is surely enriched by reading Scott's *Journal* and his *Life of Napoleon* together.

In 'Politics of the Debt', Balibar suggests that, as sovereign debt gradually supplants political-military sovereignty, people faced with the complexity and abstraction of a global financial market often imagine a 'Great Manipulator', even though financial markets operate outside of individual intention or control. That would be another way of translating *le grand entrepreneur*, perhaps. Scott, for his part, dreams something more complex: the deep identity of the *entrepreneur* and the undertaker. Or as Marx would later have it: 'What the bourgeoisie, therefore, produces, above all, is its own grave-diggers.'[91]

Scott's *Life of Napoleon* has often been read as a history told by the victors. But who or what proves to be victorious? The story it actually tells is merely a shift of theatre of operations; in the aftermath of military defeat, Napoleon on St Helena shifts to a writing-industrial complex as a mode of conquest. Always possessed by 'a mania for scribbling', according to Scott, he ingeniously manages to construct his own word-processing machine:

> [H]e was careful not to suffer his condition to be forgotten, and most anxious that the public mind should be kept carefully alive to it, by a succession of publications coming out one after another . . . Accordingly, the various works of Warden, O'Meara, Santini, the Letter of Montholon, and other publications upon St. Helena . . . although seemingly discharged by various hands, bear the strong peculiarity of . . . being arrows from the same quiver.[92]

'Arrows from the same quiver': an arresting figure, one which suggests that print capitalism of the sort we see represented here or in Constable's analogous *Miscellany* is a continuation of war – of objectless enterprise – by other means. And when we read Scott's *Journal* entries, can we avoid reading them as belonging to this 'succession of publications' as much as the *Life of Napoleon* does? This, for example, from 7 April 1827: 'I am a perfect Automaton. *Bonaparte* runs in my head from 7 in the morning till ten at night without intermission. I wrote six leaves to-day and corrected four proofs.'[93] Another day, Scott's effort to employ every moment of his time in writing extends to taking notes for the *Napoleon* while he's attending the Courts of Session; he misplaces them, and in the *Journal* imagines them 'shuffled in perhaps among my own papers or those of the Teind Clerks'.[94] 'What a curious document to be found in a process of valuation', Scott comments. Yet in a sense, Scott's *Journal* is similarly interleaved in *The Life of Napoleon Buonaparte*.

The same phrase with which Scott has the 'Author of Waverley' announce his hubristic decision to launch himself as an independent entrepreneur by writing *The Life of Napoleon Buonaparte* – 'I will vindicate my fame with my own right-hand' – also appears in the *Journal*. On 22 January 1826, Scott writes, 'My own right hand shall do it – Else I will be *done* in the slang language and *undone* in common parlance.'[95] One might say that the vindicating hand writes the *Life of Napoleon*, whereas the hand of the beggar writes the *Journal*. But what I have called the chiasmatic relation between the two projects disallows such a distinction. Instead, Scott seems to achieve something like the effect he describes as the '*double touch*':

> I believe the phenomena of dreaming are in a great measure occasiond by the *double touch* which takes place when one hand is crossd in sleep upon another. Each gives and receives the impression of touch to and from the other and this complicated sensation our sleeping fancy ascribes to the agency of another being when it is in fact our own limbs acting on each other.[96]

For in pursuing the two projects simultaneously, in finding that his 'right hand' no longer offers sufficient leverage, Scott experiences what Marx calls the economic paradox of capital: 'the economic paradox that the most powerful instrument for reducing labour-time suffers a dialectical inversion and becomes the most unfailing means of turning the whole lifetime of the worker and his family into labour-time at capital's disposal for its own valorization'.[97] The *Journal* entry continues, 'Well here goes – *incumbite remis*.'[98] Scott chains *himself* to the oar. (The next day's entry reads, 'Finished Vol. III of *Napoleon*.')

I began by alluding to a question raised by Susan Manning about whether the work of the 'late' Scott has 'aesthetic integrity' or whether that integrity was compromised by the condition of debt, and a consequent acceleration of productivity measured in quantitative terms (pages and hours). I have not argued that Scott's *The Life of Napoleon Buonaparte* is a work of deep aesthetic interest, although I hope to have suggested how Scott's representation of Napoleon as a failed *entrepreneur* becomes more compelling when read against his own deep involvement in finance capitalism and his parallel experience of failure as a posthumous existence. Instead, I have tried, by linking Scott's attempt to write himself out of debt with the condition of students and scholars in the neoliberal university, to raise a parallel question about *scholarly* integrity. In the humanities, where scholarship is rarely sponsored by or directly profitable to markets, the challenge to integrity is not so much falsification as it is overproduction. Scott's motto – *Nulle dies sine linea* – is certainly an admirable provocation to those of us for whom writing is a creative outlet or intellectual stimulant as well as part of our paid employment; it can remind us to *make time* for thought and expression. But we must be wary of making the number of lines the measure of value – both of the writing and of our lives.

Arguing 'There is no such thing as voluntary servitude. There is only passionate servitude', Frédéric Lordon helps us to recognise in the 'buoyant' spirit with which Scott keeps a work journal a metamorphosis in the 'spirit' of capitalism that now goes by the name of neoliberalism.[99] 'The justifications offered for contemporary transformations in employment practices – from longer work hours ("it allows stores to open on Sundays") to competition-enhancing deregulation ("it lowers prices") – always contrive to catch agents by "the joyful affects" of consumption, appealing only to the consumer in them', he writes. These justifications are designed to 'keep alive' not the human subject but desire. They ring a change on the refrain of liberalism, as Joshua Clover has suggested: not 'make live and let die', but 'make work and let buy'.[100]

Notes

1. Ian Duncan, 'Death and the Author', pp. 69, 68.
2. Ibid. p. 69.
3. Susan Manning, 'The Critical Question', p. 187.
4. Duncan, 'Death and the Author', p. 69 and 'Late Scott', p. 131.
5. Maurizio Lazzarato, *The Making of Indebted Man*.
6. Ibid. p. 9.
7. Fiona Allon, 'Everyday Leverage'.
8. Erica McWilliam et al., 'Developing Professional Identities', p. 69. Qtd in Stephen J. Ball, 'Performativity'.
9. Rei Terada, 'Two Hundred Years of University Reform'.
10. Walter Scott, *Journal*, 120.
11. Ibid. p. 49.

12. Ball, 'Performativity', p. 19.
13. Etienne Balibar, 'Politics of the Debt', 4.2.
14. Ibid. 4.1.
15. Joseph Schumpeter, *The Theory of Economic Development*, p. 36.
16. Ron Harris, 'Political Economy', p. 678.
17. The phrase was coined by Scott in response to Constable's ambition (Lockhart, *Life*, 6: 31, 28–32). In some respects, the project required the labour not of an 'Author' but of a copyist; Scott was provided with reams of French newspapers, histories of the war and other Lives of Napoleon, and constructed his history more or less as a commentary on those texts.
18. Lockhart, *Life*, 6: 31–2.
19. Karl Marx, *Capital*, p. 534.
20. Ibid. p. 535.
21. Scott, *Journal*, p. 28.
22. Ibid. p. 29.
23. Ibid. pp. 106–7.
24. Scott, *Journal*, p. 151.
25. Scott, *Napoleon* 9: 168.
26. See Larry Neal, 'The Financial Crisis of 1825', and also *The Rise of Financial Capitalism*, pp. 180–230. For more focused accounts of the effects on Scott and his coterie, see Alloway and Dick.
27. Carl von Clausewitz, *On War*, pp. 592–3; emphasis added.
28. Scott, *Napoleon* 1: 4, 5–6.
29. Ibid. 1: 18.
30. Lockhart, *Life*, 6: 28.
31. Ibid. 6: 29.
32. Ibid. 6: 29; emphasis added.
33. Ibid. 6: 31.
34. Scott, *Napoleon* 3: 91, 89.
35. Lockhart, *Life*, 6: 38.
36. Ibid. 6: 37.
37. Scott, *Napoleon* 9: 308–9.
38. Scott, *Tales of the Crusaders*, p. vi.
39. Ibid. p. viii.
40. Ibid. p. ix.
41. In *Capital*, Marx points out that technologies only gradually replace earlier efforts to increase the productivity of the body: 'The machine, therefore, is a mechanism that, after being set in motion, performs with its tools the same operations as the worker did with similar tools . . . The difference strikes one, even in those cases where man himself continues to be the prime mover. The number of implements that he himself can use simultaneously is limited by the number of his own natural instruments of production, i.e., his own bodily organs. In Germany they tried at first to make one spinner work two spinning

wheels, that is to work simultaneously with both hands and both feet. That proved to be too exhausting. Later, a treadle spinning wheel was invented, but adepts in spinning who could spin two threads at once were almost as scarce as two-headed men. The Jenny, on the other hand, even at the very beginning, spun with twelve to eighteen spindles' (p. 495).

42. Scott, *Tales of the Crusaders*, p. xvi.
43. Ibid. pp. xvii–xviii.
44. Ibid. p. viii.
45. Samuel Smiles, *Industrial Biography*, p. 236.
46. Scott, *Tales of the Crusaders*, p. xxi.
47. Ibid. p. xxv; Evan Gottlieb, *Walter Scott and Contemporary Theory*, p. 6; Scott, *Tales of the Crusaders*, p. xxvii.
48. Scott, *Napoleon* 1: ii.
49. Scott, *Journal*, p. 48.
50. Although Constable and Cadell opted for sequestration, where their assets were sold to pay part of their debt, Scott chose a deed of trust, promising to pay his debts in full, but gaining time to do so. Since he had signed accommodation bills for the others, he was effectively paying some of *their* debt as well. See the *Dictionary of National Biography* for a succinct accounting. See also John Gibson's *Reminiscences*; Gibson served as one of Scott's trustees, and recounts the bank meeting at which Scott disclosed his identity as 'Author of Waverley' in January 1826 (p. 15).
51. Scott, *Journal*, p. 329.
52. John Stuart Mill, Review of Scott's *Life of Napoleon*, pp. 252–3.
53. Ibid. p. 256.
54. Ibid. p. 255.
55. Ibid. p. 256.
56. Ibid. p. 255.
57. Joshua Clover, 'Busted'.
58. Lockhart, *Life*, 3: 128; emphasis added.
59. Ibid. pp. 128–9.
60. Scott, *Journal*, p. 71; Lockhart, *Life*, 6: 213.
61. Lockhart, *Life*, 6: 88–9.
62. Ibid. 6: 108–9.
63. Luc Boltanski and Eve Chiapello, *The New Spirit of Capitalism*, p. 487.
64. Scott, *Journal*, p. 105.
65. Ibid. p. 468.
66. Scott, *Letters* 9: 493.
67. Melissa Gregg, 'Getting Things Done', p. 195.
68. Franco Berardi, *The Soul at Work*, p. 77.
69. Ibid. p. 33.
70. Ibid. p. 74.
71. Ibid. p. 78; emphasis added.

72. Ibid. p. 80.
73. Schumpeter, *The Theory of Economic Development*, p. 6.
74. Ibid. p. 36.
75. Schumpeter, *Imperialism and Social Classes*, p. 25; original emphasis.
76. Scott, *Napoleon* 8: 275; emphasis added.
77. Ibid. 8: 264.
78. Ibid. 8: 264–5.
79. Scott, *Journal*, p. 47.
80. Scott, *Napoleon* 8: 280.
81. Ibid. 8: 282.
82. Ibid. 8: 425–6.
83. Ibid. 9: 321–2; emphasis added.
84. Pierre Fleury de Chaboulon, *Memoirs . . . of Napoleon*, p. 84n.
85. William Henry Ireland, *The Napoleon Anecdotes*, p. 83.
86. Scott, *Napoleon* 9: 310.
87. Ibid. 9: 321–2.
88. Gibson, *Reminiscences*, p. 31; emphasis added. Scott writes as a lawyer here: a 'hypothec' is a security a creditor holds in the property of a debtor.
89. Gibson, *Reminiscences*, p. 32.
90. Schumpeter, *The Theory of Economic Development*, p. 102.
91. Marx and Engels, *Manifesto*, p. 12.
92. Scott, *Napoleon* 9: 167.
93. Scott, *Journal*, p. 334.
94. Ibid. p. 124.
95. Ibid. p. 77.
96. Ibid. p. 180.
97. Marx, *Capital*, p. 532.
98. Scott, *Journal*, p. 180.
99. Frédéric Lordon, *Willing Slaves of Capital*, p. 17.
100. Joshua Clover, 'The Rise and Fall of Biopolitics'.

6

Scott and the Art of Surplusage: Excess in the Narrative Poems

Alison Lumsden

The Edinburgh Edition of Walter Scott's Poetry will be published in ten volumes. While it offers the first reliable edition of Scott's narrative poems and shorter verse it also renegotiates the significance of Scott's own extensive notes by bringing them to the attention of twenty-first century readers in ways that have been lost for generations. This understanding of the importance of the extensive notes that Scott provides for his long narrative poems arises out of the work done to establish a methodology for the Edinburgh Edition. Researching the creative evolution of Scott's poetry revealed two things, particularly when compared to that of Scott's fiction: firstly, that the lack of anonymity surrounding the publication of Scott's narrative poems leads to a far more 'socialised' version of publication (to adapt Jerome McGann's term) than that found with the novels and, secondly, that the publishing practices of posthumous editions of Scott's poetry (including Lockhart's 1833–4 edition) have obscured the relationship of his own notes to the narrative poems, thus rendering the full creative and critical potential of them invisible.[1] This chapter aims to recalibrate the role of these notes and suggest some avenues for further criticism.

Scott provided only very light annotation to the first editions of his novels: on the whole his notes to the fiction take the form of very brief glosses at the foot of the page. As a consequence, the Edinburgh Edition of the Waverley Novels, which generally takes these first editions as its base texts, does not contain the lengthy introductions and notes which, for much of the nineteenth and twentieth centuries, were a hallmark of Scott's fiction. These notes and introductions were, of course, added in the 1829–32 Magnum Opus edition of Scott's work, and as a consequence they appear in the Edinburgh Edition of the Waverly Novels in the supplementary volumes 25a and 25b with which the edition concludes.[2] The situation with the poetry is altogether different. Scott's notes were intrinsic to the first editions of the poems and clearly were part of their original creative conception. Moreover, the notes to the poems are copious, detailed and, one might add, altogether curious. To use the terms that Gérard Genette develops in his taxonomy of paratextual material, the notes to the novels are 'belated', while those for the poems are 'original'.[3]

The nature of these 'original' notes can be clearly illustrated with reference to what is arguably Scott's most well-known narrative poem, *The Lady of the Lake*.[4] In its first edition format the six cantos of the poem have the kind of light glosses at the foot of the page familiar to readers of the novels, but these are accompanied by over 129 pages of annotation, set in a smaller font than the 290 pages of the poem itself. This is no surprise to anyone who has studied Scott's poetry but modern readers may be forgiven if they are unaware of these notes. Moreover, textual investigation of the notes for the Edinburgh Edition reveals that if the poems themselves are 'socialised' documents, this is even more true of the notes that accompany them. This is evident even in the manuscripts of the poems; while the text of the poem is on the whole in Scott's holograph the notes are in a variety of hands and contain passages copied by Scott's wife, Charlotte, material sent by Scott's correspondents, and at times pages taken from printed books; they are, in many ways, from their very inception a collective endeavour. Moreover, while Scott demonstrates considerable hesitation about changing the main body of the text at his friends' prompting, he is far more willing to alter and expand the material in the notes as the poem is reprinted in early editions. As a consequence there are ten new notes in the second edition of *The Lady of the Lake* and several existing notes are significantly expanded.[5] Several errors in the notes are also corrected, such as in note 6 to canto 3 where it is pointed out that the Ben-Shie had been incorrectly equated with the Head of the Fairies, when in fact a female fairy should be implied. The note originally reads 'The Ben-Shie, or *Ben-Schichian*, implies the head, or Chief of the Fairies'[6] but is altered in the second edition to read 'The Ban-Shie implies the female Fairy', and a footnote is added to state: 'In the first edition this was erroneously explained as equivalent to Ben-Schichian, or the Head of the Fairies.'[7] Scott clearly cares about these notes and remains actively engaged in expanding and correcting them. It is also worth noting that the 'socialised' nature of their production is written into the second edition, the reading process that informs it becoming part of the text itself.

Examination of Scott's other narrative poems reveals a similar situation and in some instances the notes continue to expand and evolve beyond the point where the text of the poem itself becomes settled; for example, Gillian Hughes's investigation of *The Lay of the Last Minstrel* has suggested that while the text of the poem becomes relatively stable by the fifth edition (published November 1806) the notes continue to expand and evolve at least until the eighth edition (1808).[8] This poses an interesting textual dilemma; if, as we have agreed, the base text for the new edition should be that which represents the point where the poem reaches a 'finished' form, should this include the point at which the notes are 'complete'? What should we do if this is not the same point as that at which the text becomes stable, as with the *Lay*?

Vexing though these issues may be to textual editors they are perhaps less fascinating to readers of Scott or critics in general. However, the detailed scrutiny that developing a textual policy requires alerts us to aspects of a literary text that might otherwise go unnoticed, and this, in turn, opens up new avenues for critical debate. There have, of course, been several critical attempts to theorise Scott's habits of annotation in his poems and novels and perhaps, above all, in *The Minstrelsy of the Scottish Border*, his 1802 collection of traditional ballads. Indeed, a theorising of the wider practices which inform the activity of annotation is part of much commentary that surrounds recent work on Scottish Romanticism. For many, such impulses are indicative of the Enlightenment precursors of Romantic poetry, and they see the notes and commentaries that support *Minstrelsy* as springing from essentially antiquarian pursuits. Kenneth NcNeil, for example, argues that in *Minstrelsy* Scott's notes, like all antiquarian discourse, 'reinforced orality's static deadness' and reveal a 'keen desire on the part of its author to secure legitimacy in the conventional antiquarian discourse of his time'.[9] Katie Trumpener elaborates on the impulses that lie behind the collecting of ballad materials in the eighteenth and nineteenth centuries and makes explicit this connection:

> In eighteenth-century Ireland, Scotland, and Wales nationalist antiquaries edited, explicated, and promoted their respective bardic traditions; emphasizing the cultural rootedness of bardic poetry and its status as historical testimony, their work represents a groundbreaking attempt to describe literature as the product of specific cultural institutions and to understand literary form as a product of a particular national history.[10]

This practice, she argues, is closely linked to Enlightenment concerns with codifying and recording knowledge and, as a consequence, 'derives much of its investigative method, descriptive techniques, and discursive style from Enlightenment encyclopedias and treatises'.[11] As a consequence, she claims, notes serve a recuperative function in preserving interesting material but they are also simultaneously in danger of reducing Scottish culture to no more than a museum, or stagnant cultural artefact, a claim often levelled at Scott more generally.

Scott's notes to *Minstrelsy* thus have been read as a kind of paratextual act of containment by which the oral is surrounded and erased by the weight of antiquarian authority. Murray Pittock, for example, points out that 'Scott's border minstrelsy . . . thus very much fulfils the publishing practice of the Romantic collector satirized by Burns in 'Tam o' Shanter'.[12] While more recent re-evaluations have recognised that a binary opposition between print and oral cultures may be only partially adequate, at best Scott's notes are seen as a rather crude attempt to offer some kind of mediation between these two positions. Scott's notes, comment Celeste Langan and Maureen McLane, are a gesture to 'the embodied background mediations of poetry, the complex transactions that brought poetry "out of the mouths" of singers into printed books, alongside other source materials including manuscripts, broadsides and previously printed books', and as such reveal the transmedial complexities that underlie the writing down (and more significantly) the printing of oral ballads.[13]

Theories that position these notes as part of an act of antiquarian recuperation can be justified if we look at the nature of the notes to *Minstrelsy of the Scottish Border* and, in particular, if we consider Scott's own remarks in the Introduction to the first volume of the first edition. Scott writes:

> In the notes, and occasional dissertations, it has been my object to throw together, perhaps without sufficient attention to method, a variety of remarks regarding popular superstitions, and legendary history, which, if not now collected, must soon have been totally forgotten. By such efforts, feeble as they are, I may contribute somewhat to the history of my native country; the peculiar features of whose manners and characters are daily melting and dissolving into those of her sister ally.[14]

Scott's intentions seem clear: the ballads in the collections are illustrations of popular superstition, legendary history and the peculiar features of Scotland, and his impulse in collecting and annotating lies with salvaging, recuperation and preservation. The nature of the headnotes and endnotes in the first edition of *Minstrelsy* more or less fulfils this purpose. Many of the ballads are prefaced by an introductory headnote, and often these give information about the provenance of the ballad and attempt to explain contextual matters. They are concerned with what can be verified, what is supported by sources, and what can only be known through conjecture. The headnote to the opening ballad, 'The Sang of the Outlaw Murray', for example, begins by telling us what is 'certain', what is 'true' what 'may be supposed' and 'what is probable', before going on to tell the reader that 'the tradition handed down in this Song may have had more foundation, than it would at present be proper positively to assert'.[15] The writer is, however, more sceptical about some aspects of the ballad noting that 'it seems difficult to believe that the circumstances mentioned in the Ballad could occur under the reign of so vigorous a Monarch as James IV'.[16] What seems to be established here is a kind of Enlightenment hierarchy of authority concerning the material in the ballad: what can be ascertained will be codified and wherever possible backed up by source material, and what cannot be given authority will be described as custom or 'legendary history'. The ballad is also annotated with footnotes, which are generally glosses, and with endnotes, which record possible textual variants and give elucidating material on places and incidents in the poem.

The pattern set in 'The Outlaw Murray' is, generally speaking, one followed throughout *Minstrelsy*. As theories that would see these notes as antiquarian containments of an oral tradition would argue, some of the ballads do, indeed, seem overburdened and overwhelmed by their antiquarian paratexts: 'Lord Maxwell's Goodnight', for example, is a ballad of three pages long with a seven-page headnote and three and a half pages of endnotes.[17] Moreover, the purpose of these notes is primarily to elucidate and to support such elucidation by providing supporting and additional information. By these methods the notes thus apparently codify, in fairly familiar Enlightenment terms, what rests in authority, what can be supported by secondary witnesses and what rests in legend and cultural memory.

However, such approaches to Scott's habit of annotation seem rather harder to justify in relation to his own narrative poems. As is well known, Scott's first long narrative poem *The Lay of the Last Minstrel*, published in 1805, began life as one of the category of 'imitation ballads' contained in the third volume of *Minstrelsy*. Moreover, it was designed in part to provide some illustration of the history and customs of the Scottish border to the young Countess of Dalkeith, who came from England. In this sense it is perhaps hardly surprising that Scott should have annotated it as he did the traditional ballads in *Minstrelsy*. What is perhaps more surprising, however, is that he should have continued to annotate his own creative productions once they inhabit a space that is clearly fairly far removed from his collecting activities; why should Scott choose to annotate what are, after all, his own fictional creations where, we might imagine, he can recuperate as much of Scotland's past as he wishes? As Gillian Hughes argues, 'it is hard to believe that Scott would have carried over this material unconsciously or automatically from an editorial and antiquarian enterprise into the very different context of a narrative poem'.[18]

Yet Scott is not unique in the Romantic period in his habit of providing notes to his own poems. As Ann Rowland reminds us, annotation in Romantic poetry is a common practice followed by poets such as Byron and Southey as well as by Scott. Rowland notes that 'with its fascination for older times and exotic places, its habitual, self-reflexive structure of historical and cultural juxtapositions, and, significantly, its freedom to cross poetic and prose forms, the romance that emerged in the late years of the eighteenth century is a multifarious, composite form' and as a consequence the romances in verse that emerge in the Romantic period typically included extensive prose notes.[19] This is true but there is, arguably, something about the nature of Scott's notes to his own poetry that marks them out not only from those to *Minstrelsy* but also from the notes provided by his fellow Romantic poets.

In order to illustrate this it is worth considering a particular example. As noted earlier, Scott's notes to a poem like *The Lady of the Lake* are extensive, running to 129 densely packed pages. While many of these notes do follow the pattern developed in *Minstrelsy* of providing elucidating and clarifying contextual material, a significant number are of a very different nature. For example, as early as note 6 of the first canto Scott opens a note on the lines 'A grey haired sire, whose eye, intent, / Was on the visioned future bent' with the sentence 'If force of evidence could authorise us to believe facts inconsistent with the general laws of nature, enough might be produced in favour of the Second Sight.' A five-page note relating to second sight follows which, while it quotes extensively from Martin's *Description of the Western Isles* (much of which itself serves not to authorise but question such events), ultimately refers the reader back to literature (thus offering a self-reflexive circle) as the evidence for second sight.[20] This is a very different kind of hierarchy of knowledge to that found in the *Minstrelsy* notes. This pattern continues. Note 7 offers information on Highland bolt-holes in response to the lines 'There for retreat in dangerous hour, / Some chief had framed a rustic bower' and includes, rather bizarrely, information on the hiding places of Charles Edward Stuart after Culloden.[21] It is hard to see how such information is simply clarifying or elucidating a poem set in the sixteenth century.

By the second canto Scott is on an apparent roll. Note 3 is ostensibly about 'This harp which erst Saint Modan swayed' but states that in fact he has no information about 'Saint Modan' and whether or not he played the harp. As he is 'not prepared to shew that Saint Modan was a performer', he offers information about some other saints who played harps instead.[22] Note 10 offers information on magic swords, especially the magic sword Skoffnung, 'wielded by the celebrated Hrolf Kraka' (which does not feature in the poem),[23] while in response to the line 'That Monk of savage form and face' in canto 3 Scott provides us with a seven-page note on the state of religion in the Middle Ages that includes information about Friar Tuck and on Irish monks on the rather tangential basis that:

> As the Irish tribes, and those of the Scottish Highlands, are much more intimately allied, by language, manners, dress, and customs, than the antiquaries of either country have been willing to admit, I flatter myself I have here produced a strong warrant for the character sketched in the text.[24]

Some of the material in this note comes again from John Martin's *Description of the Western Islands*. This may seem like the kind of authorising impulse we might expect from our experience of *Minstrelsy* but this is qualified by the fact that Scott describes his authority as 'a strange mixture of learning, observation, and gross credulity'.[25] The first note to canto 4 provides extensive material on the subject of how to tell the future using dead cats. In the same canto the seven-page ballad 'Alice Brand' leads to a staggering seventeen pages of notes on superstition and fairy tale,[26] while one of the last notes to the poem, which explores the habits of James V, brings Scott to a discussion of Ariosto.[27]

It is hard to describe such an extensive act of free association (arguably akin to the kind of hypertext experience provided by a modern electronic edition) simply as elucidation or a codification of the material contained in the poem and arguably it is this that marks out the notes to the poems as serving a different function to those provided for either *Minstrelsy* or other Romantic poets such as Byron. This difference is, indeed, highlighted by the editorial problems which these notes provide for those producing modern scholarly editions. For example, the notes to *Minstrelsy* provide no methodological questions for their modern editors (a team led by Sigrid Rieuwerts at Mainz in collaboration with the School of Scottish Studies in Edinburgh) since they already serve a function of annotation and need little further elucidation themselves.[28] Similarly, the annotating function of Byron's notes is exemplified by the fact that in his seminal edition McGann simply incorporates the majority of Byron's commentary into his own endnotes, and even the longer notes on *Childe Harold*, which are presented at the end of the poem, are largely informative and transactional.[29] However, the notes to Scott's narrative poems provide significant problems for the team editing his work. On close examination it proves that they seldom fulfil any function of elucidation at all, and, perhaps worse, they are so bizarre that they require annotation themselves, resulting in potentially Borgesian labyrinths of annotation.

It is clear that the function of Scott's notes goes far beyond what we would normally recognise as the function of annotation. Such notes cannot simply be dismissed as an antiquarian or Enlightenment exercise in documentation, since what they document is no longer what is certain, verifiable and supported by witness, but a far more complex amalgamation of written authority, local folklore, literary heritage and what can only be described as parallel narrative. Rather than creating a taxonomy of knowledge, as the notes to *Minstrelsy* do, they bring many different forms of knowledge into play to create additional, or even alternative, forms of discourse to those offered by the text proper of the poem. Indeed, the nature of the notes raises the question of what actually constitutes the poem itself: Is the poem only that material written in verse or is the 'poem' both verse material and its prose accompaniment? Genette argues that 'the paratext is itself a text: if it is not yet *the* text it is already textual' and argues that paratexts also contribute to a 'convergence of effects'.[30] Following Philippe Lejeune, he suggests that paratexts may constitute a kind of 'fringe' or 'threshold' which in fact controls how we receive and perceive the text as a whole.[31] Alex Watson goes further and reminds us that Romantic annotation may constitute a 'zone of confrontational transactions' that can be obfuscated by editorial practices that 'make it difficult for general readers to appreciate a vital and exacting aspect of Romantic textuality'.[32] If we are alert to this we may recognise that Scott's notes in fact form an important part of the discourse we call his 'narrative poems'.

One explanation for this may be offered by suggesting that Scott is exploring the ways in which meaning can only be generated by an amalgamation of different forms of narrative and, arguably, by accommodating what might be recognised as an impulse for story. This tendency is described by Scott himself in his late work *Reliquiae Trotcosienses*. *Reliquiae* was a project proposed to Scott towards the end of his life by Cadell and

Lockhart to distract him from writing what they considered to be the 'bad' late novels. It was proposed that Scott would write a kind of catalogue of his antiquarian collections at Abbotsford. For many commentators Abbotsford has been seen as a kind of architectural continuation of the antiquarian impulses in the notes to Scott's poetry and fiction offering a Waverley Novels in stone. However, the text that Scott produced is a curious one, and one that suggests an altogether more complex relationship between historical artefact, antiquarian impulse and story than this would imply. Rather than providing a simple catalogue Scott revisits the persona of Jonathan Oldbuck, the eponymous hero of *The Antiquary* and, as in that novel, calls into question the whole antiquarian impulse on which the notes to his work are seen to rest.

This can be seen in the very structure of the text. The narrator of *Reliquiae* sets out for himself a careful plan as to how he is to proceed; he will first describe the house and then the objects that it contains and, somewhat unusually, Scott reports that he indeed wrote a plan for this text.[33] Yet, as the Author of Waverley has observed elsewhere, he is incapable of writing up to such schemes and inevitably he cannot stick to one here.[34] Describing the hall at Abbotsford, for example, he comments upon a peculiar suit of armour that includes a sword marked out with the days of the Catholic saints. He goes on:

> In a word, it is a calendar to direct the good knight's devotions. The other suit of armour, which is also complete in all its parts, was said when it came into my possession to have belonged to a knight who took arms upon Richmond's side at the Field of Bosworth and died I think of his wounds there. If one was disposed to give him a name, in all certainty the size of his armour might claim that he was John Cheney, the biggest man of both armies on that memorable day. I venture to think – for I feel myself gliding into the true musing style of an antiquarian disposed in sailors' phrase 'to spin a tough yarn' – I incline, I say, to think that the calendar placed in the hand of the little French knight in the right-hand niche, originally belonged to the gigantic warrior of Bosworth Field.[35]

What he has done here, he notes, is to '[infringe] on [his order]' by describing the items in the collection ahead of the house.[36] But this is, in fact, how narrative is generated in this text. Scott uses his antiquarian collections not to describe a kind of history of Scotland (that is to say, the objects in his collection are not witnesses to a coherent historical discourse) but as springboards for story, 'tough yarns' as he calls them. *Reliquiae*, and its overt departure from its author's self-proclaimed (and we suspect tongue-in-cheek) scheme, thus reminds the reader that antiquarian collections may not offer a coherent narrative of the past but, rather, provide the imaginative spaces within which stories about it may exist. As David Hewitt puts it, what emerges here is an oblique relationship between artefact and fact, and one which suggests that,

> For the Author of Waverley the past can never be finally located, but only approached via complex, multiplex and elusive acts of narration; via fictions which, just as they seem to offer us some fixed referent for the personal and national histories which they recount, repeatedly subvert their own conclusions, offering up a myriad of possibilities and opening spaces for further narratives.[37]

Scott's own late text, then, suggests an altogether more complex relationship between antiquarian object (both physical and textual) and commentary and potentially provides a way to consider his notes; read in this way, the impulse behind them is, similarly, not one of elucidation, containment or reclamation, but, arguably, a far more disruptive process generated by the impulse for story and storytelling that results in a form of excess that resists the closure of historical account into any one form of narrative.

Yet if this impulse to recast acts of narration in the form of alternative discourses is in itself disruptive there may be yet more complex subversions at play in Scott's inclusion (and seeming obsession with) annotation. Alex Watson argues that annotation can be read as an 'unruly zone'[38] that 'constitutes a textual prosthesis that exposes the text's incompleteness or imperfection'.[39] In other words, Watson sees annotation as a form of what we might also call excess, or surplusage. The term 'surplusage' or surplus has, of course, come to be associated with Jacques Derrida's concept of the supplement. Derrida argues that rather than offering a form of completion the concept of a supplement (which we could read here as Scott's notes) highlights a lack of completion in that which is deemed to be original (the narrative sections of the poem): 'The supplement is always the supplement of a supplement' he writes: 'One wishes to go back *from the supplement to the source*: one must recognise that there is always a supplement at the source.'[40] Interestingly, the term 'surplusage' has a history that pre-dates theory. It is fundamentally a legal term, and one that would encourage us to see it as relevant for the lawyer Scott. As the *Oxford English Dictionary* defines it, it is 'an excess or superabundance (*of* words); *spec.* in *Law*, a word, clause, or statement in an indictment or a plea which is not necessary to its adequacy'.[41] In other words it is that which is in excess of what is necessary and consequently does not support authority, but, in fact, undermines it by foregrounding its lack of completion.

Recent commentaries on Scott's poems and on Scottish Romanticism more generally support a reading of his poems in these terms. Recognising something of the bizarre hotch-potch that exists in Scott's notes, Celeste Langan and Maureen McLane have suggested that his poems are 'conspicuous orchestrations not only of historical material but also of historical *media* – especially oral and manuscript poetries, those preserved in that living archive that Scott, "the last minstrel," purports to remediate',[42] concluding that what emerges in Scott's poetry is not simply a hybrid mediation between oral and print cultures but something more complex. That something more complex was acknowledged even in contemporary responses to Scott which, typically, lamented his habit of genre mixing and complained that his poems could not be classified in any simple way. While complaints like this (Francis Jeffrey's famous attack on *Marmion* for example) are usually thought to apply to the *narrative* of the poem only, we cannot dismiss the idea that they also extend to the notes (although this in turn raises interesting questions about exactly how people read the poems).[43] Certainly Thomas Love Peacock's contemporary criticisms of Romantic poetry more generally as a patchwork of 'disjointed relics' that produce 'a modern-antique compound of frippery and barbarism'[44] seem to include features such as the notes we have been discussing here.

However, while it is intended as a condemnation of Romantic poetry, Peacock's idea of 'disjointed relics' also pre-empts the work of modern commentators who have suggested that the fragmentary nature of Scottish Romanticism may be read more positively and is, indeed, precisely what differentiates it from its English counterpart. The most pertinent example of this is Susan Manning's 2002 study *Fragments of Union*. Manning's study moves out from the evocative title of James Macpherson's *Fragments of Ancient Poetry* to suggest that the linguistic and narratological fragmentation that occurs in Scottish Romanticism is generated by and symptomatic of the fragmented state of the Scottish nation, and is at odds with dominant narratives of cohesion and unity. While Manning says very little about Scott's poetry, it is not difficult to see how her arguments can be applied to the diffuse and tangential nature of his annotation. Moreover, Manning draws a more overt connection when she discusses the poem that Oldbuck and Lovel plan to write in Scott's novel *The Antiquary*. She states:

> Lovel establishes the integrity of Scotland's past and future. In their projected collaborative historical epic of Scotland, Lovel will write the connected narrative and the Antiquary supply the fragmenting footnotes.[45]

Following this reading the poem itself is the unified and unifying object but it is the annotations (also, arguably, part of the poem) which, rather than containing or overburdening that content, pull it apart to disrupt its ostensibly unifying impulses. Matthew Wickman similarly recognises this impulse within Scottish writing in his study *The Ruins of Experience*. Wickman proposes that an apparent Enlightenment reliance on facts and artefacts belies more disruptive tendencies in Scottish writing suggesting that the spectre of the Highlands (that which cannot be contained by discourses of testimony and witness) thus comes to haunt Scottish writing, acting as the 'spectral underside to progress'.[46]

Read within these paradigms, the bizarre notes that accompany Scott's poetry may be recognised as a kind of haunting of their narratives that disrupts the apparent discourses of unity which they, arguably, inscribe. This can certainly be claimed for *The Lady of the Lake*. Elsewhere I have suggested that standard readings of *The Lady of the Lake* that see it as offering straightforward narratives of homogeneity, reconciliation and Scottish unity via the suppression of the Highland other may be inadequate.[47] Rather, Scott repeatedly foregrounds the constructed nature of his own poem and by drawing attention to its inherent artificiality deconstructs his own 'romance' narrative to suggest that the resolution at its end may be a false (and potentially destabilising) construct that cannot be relied upon as the basis of a discourse of national progress. However, if this is true of the verse narrative it is even more apparent if we read it alongside its notes. Read in terms of surplusage they emerge as an enactment of the impossibility of completion. Within this paradigm, Scott's care with notes such as that on the Ben-Shie and the extent of his notes on second sight, harp playing saints, magic swords and fortune-telling cats may be read not as offering a containment of Highland romance within antiquarian and Enlightenment epistemes of progress but rather as an 'unruly zone' that reasserts the presence of alternative paradigms. Similarly, while a note on the hiding places of Charles Edward Stuart may seem oddly anachronistic it is a reminder (such as we find throughout Scott's work) that whatever the apparent points of closure in the historical narrative, these moments will be reopened by further conflict and future historical ruptures. Rather than encasing his narrative in a form of stasis, these notes offer an 'uncanny resurgence of dead powers' that refuse to be settled into completeness.[48] The notes thus form a reminder that any narrative of national coherence is by definition partial and subject to the spectral presence of alternative possibilities that at any moment threaten to pull it apart.

A similarly disruptive quality has been recognised in other of Scott's poems. In spite of his sympathy for the disruptive potential within Romantic annotation, Alex Watson follows a fairly conventional line in interpreting Scott's poetry. He sees it as an attempt 'to envisage cultures as monological entities'[49] and reads the notes to the *Lay* as existing to 'legitimize the modern British nation'.[50] At the same time, he recognises that the notes may 'possess a latent capacity to subvert their own containment' thus following many critics in recognising a subversive element in Scott's work but in presuming that this is some kind of 'error' that goes against Scott's supposed progressive project.[51] Gillian Hughes offers a reading that suggests a more overtly subversive impulse in Scott's poem, arguing that under the guise of 'prolix antiquarianism' 'Scott's multiplying . . . tales' in the notes allow him a 'powerful argument against the disregard of the supernatural otherwise implied by his irony and carefully stated scepticism'.[52] Ainsley McIntosh offers an equally convincing case for the subversive capacity of the notes in *Marmion*, suggesting that the series of tales in canto 4 of the poem 'mimics the way in which storytelling itself proceeds, with one story begetting another. Scott joins in, inserting further ghost stories and tales of the supernatural into the notes, so that the sense of enclosure imposed by narrative form is undermined by the way in which narrative spills over into Scott's paratexts. Just as Constance's voice "bursts" free of the tomb', McIntosh suggests, 'the text appears to "burst" free from the prison-like containment imposed by structural form'.[53]

As has been recognised by several critics in recent years, Scott is potentially a far more disruptive writer than his critical heritage would allow, and part, at least, of this disruption lies in his enduring fascination with the ways in which different forms of discourse offer different negotiations of the historical record; the past, this suggests, cannot be located in artefacts, facts and written witness, but is shaped by the nature of the narratives by which it is mediated. Alex Watson argues that 'reading from the margins enables us to consider Romanticism from a fresh angle'.[54] It is clear that examining the notes to Scott's poetry with the kind of scrutiny required for textual editing and confronting the problems they pose for us as modern editors may alert us to the possibility that this disruptive impulse is evident even in his early work. Such attentiveness reveals that the notes do not contain the poems they pertain to annotate but rather, if we read them as a form of surplusage, their effect is to break up the apparent completion that the narrative of the poems may seem to endorse. By their very existence, the notes to Scott's poems call into question the authority of discourse itself and the possibility of its completion. They resist the act of containment that for two centuries they have been held to legitimise, thus offering the potential for critical responses that resonate for twenty-first-century readers.

Notes

1. McGann argues that Romantic poetry is not simply the product of an individual creative mind but that it reaches the reader via a socialised network involving compositors, publishers and the reading public. In her PhD thesis 'A Critical Edition of Walter Scott's *Marmion*', Ainsley McIntosh argues that in the case of *Marmion* this concept can be extended to a network of Scott's friends and readers who respond to his work both before and after publication, thus influencing its development. This process is particularly true in relation to his lengthy notes. Similar processes influenced Scott's other narrative poems and were an important factor in establishing the editorial policy for the edition. See Alison Lumsden, 'Towards the Edinburgh Edition of Walter Scott's Poetry'. The editorial policy is also articulated in volumes of the Edinburgh Edition of Walter Scott's Poetry.
2. J. H. Alexander et al., *Introductions and Notes From The Magnum Opus* (2012).
3. Genette, 'Introduction to the Paratext', p. 264.
4. Walter Scott, *The Lady of the Lake*.
5. Scott, *The Lady of the Lake*, second edition.
6. *The Lady of the Lake*, ed. 1, p. l.
7. *The Lady of the Lake*, ed. 2, p. 346.
8. Gillian Hughes undertook an investigation into the textual development of *The Lay of the Last Minstrel* as part of a pilot project for the Edinburgh Edition of Walter Scott's Poetry. See also, Hughes, 'Pickling Virgil?'
9. Kenneth McNeil, ' Ballads and Borders', p. 26.
10. Katie Trumpener, *Bardic Nationalism*, p. 4.
11. Ibid. p. 30.
12. Murray Pittock, *Scottish and Irish Romanticism*, p. 188.
13. Langan and McLane, 'The Medium of Romantic Poetry', p. 249.
14. Scott, *Minstrelsy* 1: cixcx.
15. Ibid. 1: 3.
16. Ibid. 1: 2.
17. Ibid. 1: 194–207.
18. Hughes, 'Pickling Virgil?', p. 52.
19. Ann Wierda Rowland, 'Romantic Poetry and the Romantic Novel', p. 128.

20. *The Lady of the Lake*, ed. 1, pp. vii–xii.
21. *The Lady of the Lake*, ed. 1, p. xiii.
22. *The Lady of the Lake*, ed. 1, p. xxi.
23. *The Lady of the Lake*, ed. 1, pp. xxviii–xxxi.
24. *The Lady of the Lake*, ed. 1, pp. xlvi–lii, p. l.
25. *The Lady of the Lake*, ed. 1, p. li.
26. *The Lady of the Lake*, ed. 1, pp. lxxii–lxxxviii.
27. *The Lady of the Lake*, ed. 1, pp. cxxiii–cxxix.
28. For more information about the *Minstrelsy* project see http://walterscott.eu/
29. For an interesting commentary on Byron's notes and their potential similarity to Scott's see Michael Gamer, 'Gothic Fiction and Romantic Writing in Britain', pp. 98–100.
30. Genette, 'Introduction to the Paratext', pp. 265 and 262.
31. Ibid. p. 261.
32. Alex Watson, *Romantic Marginality*, pp. 3 and 9.
33. Letter to Robert Cadell, 12 July 1831, NLS MS 1752, f. 387.
34. The best iteration of this is to be found in the famous introductory epistle to *The Fortunes of Nigel* where Scott writes about the 'daemon . . . on the feather of [his] pen' which prevents him following a laid down scheme (p. 10).
35. *Reliquiae*, pp. 33–4.
36. *Reliquiae*, p. 34.
37. David Hewitt, 'Introduction', *Reliquiae Trotcosienses*, p. xvi.
38. Watson, *Romantic Marginality*, p. 112.
39. Ibid. p. 5.
40. Jacques Derrida, *Of Grammatology*, p. 330; original emphasis.
41. *Oxford English Dictionary* online http://www.oed.com
42. Langan and McLane, 'The Medium of Romantic Poetry', p. 253.
43. Hughes suggests that Scott has two different audiences in mind, arguing that 'Scott's notes seem designed for a more specific constituency than the poems themselves, one of gentlemanly scholars'. See 'Pickling Virgil?', p. 54.
44. Thomas Love Peacock, 'The Four Ages of Poetry', p. 16.
45. Susan Manning, *Fragments of Union*, p. 103. Gillian Hughes also uses this example from *The Antiquary* in 'Pickling Virgil?', p. 52.
46. Mathew Wickman, *The Ruins of Experience*, pp. 7 and 13.
47. See Alison Lumsden and Ainsley McIntosh, 'The Narrative Poems'.
48. Ian Duncan, 'Walter Scott, James Hogg, and Scottish Gothic', p. 127.
49. Watson, *Romantic Marginality*, p. 12.
50. Ibid. p. 109.
51. Ibid.
52. Hughes, 'Pickling Virgil?', p. 59.
53. Ainsley McIntosh, '"Land Debateable"', p. 151.
54. Watson, *Romantic Marginality*, p. 4.

7

Performing History: Theatricality, Gender, the Early Historical Novel and Scott

Fiona Price

In Ellis Cornelia Knight's historical novel, *Marcus Flaminius* (1792), the Roman hero remarks on a 'theatrical performance' of 'PROMETHEUS of Eschylus' in first-century Naples:

> I do not believe that . . . [the] principle of liberty ever approached nearer to seditious turbulence . . . I was obliged to use every effort to moderate my sensations, and would have given millions never to have entered [the theatre].[1]

Marcus's lapse into eighteenth-century idiom ('millions') suggests Knight's horror at the power of performance. The spectacle of Jupiter's tyranny has the potential to agitate both Marcus, with all his hardy military vigour, and the pleasure-loving, superstitious and opulent Neopolitans. Knight has employed stadial history (which sees historical development in terms of stages) to produce a gendered narrative of decline. Both mid-stage masculine republicanism and feminised late-stage imperial luxury are disrupted by subversive theatricality. Although set in the first century CE, Knight's novel is an analysis of the causes of the French Revolution. Nor is the peril confined to 1790s France. In April 1815 at Drury Lane Theatre, Knight attends *Richard II*, a play not 'acted for a hundred years', in which 'many passages allusive to present times seemed to be spoken with peculiar emphasis, and *silence* was vociferated on these occasions'.[2] As Napoleon, like Bolingbroke, returns from exile, the anti-Corn Law 'riots' convulse London.[3] Staging the past stimulates political feeling.

Writing against a politics that positions public space as undifferentiated in terms of class and social structure, Rancière, in his 1978 essay 'Good Times, or Pleasure at the Barrière', draws attention to the way theatre, concerts and the working-class *café-chantants* in nineteenth-century Paris function as a site of struggle.[4] In the British context, this awareness of the political power of performance is enlarged by David Worrall's and Jane Moody's explorations of Romantic-period censorship and radicalism in both the licensed Theatre Royals and unlicensed playhouses. Influenced by Betsy Bolton's *Women, Nationalism and the Romantic Stage* (2001), which traces the 'performativity of theatre within political or gendered discourses', Worrall examines how amateur performance formed 'new types of sociability which sometimes clearly transcended demarcations of class'.[5] But how was the relationship between the performance of gender and political performance articulated and theorised in other genres, notably in the intensely political space of the historical novel? And what light does the work of Walter Scott and his precursors shed on our moment, a moment preoccupied by 'gender performativity', 'precarious lives' and empty political theatricality?[6] In *Notes Towards a Performative Theory of Assembly* (2015) Judith Butler argues that, 'what we are seeing when bodies assemble on the street . . . is the exercise – one might call it performative – of the right to appear', to become visible as citizens. Just as gender can be subversively performed to alter the 'norms', Butler suggests, 'bodily acts' of political assembly change who constitutes the people. Moreover, she notes, 'gender norms have everything to do with how and in what way we can appear in public space'.[7] For Romantic-period historical novelists, the performance of gender operates as a tool, changing who can be politically visible and to what end.

In the years after the French Revolution, public assemblages came under renewed scrutiny. Historical novelists like Ellis Cornelia Knight, Jane West and Jane Porter examined the mode, extent and advisability of public performance. Their interest in public performance arose in part because, as female subjects, they stood in an odd relation to both polis and nation.[8] They were simultaneously inside and outside, included through their constitutive familial role, and excluded as marginalised political subjects (a situation further complicated where the theatre was concerned by the uncertain social status of female performers). Historical fiction allowed women writers to examine this issue of their 'right to appear'. In particular, it enabled them to experiment with the dominant mode of historiography, stadial history. Associated with the Scottish Enlightenment, this form of history, in describing a move from (a potentially masculinised) 'rude' primitivism to feminised luxury, introduced the possibility of understanding, in Karen O'Brien's words, the 'gendered structures' of historical progress.[9] By challenging the way in which the performances of political life were gendered in past and present, women writers began to reshape the political future.

The resultant controversy continues to reverberate in Walter Scott's Waverley Novels. Scott's engagement with historical fiction, with gothic and the national tale has been established, as have his 'talents as a dramatist': besides his involvement with the Theatre Royal and the influential theatrical adaptations of his novels, his five published plays are, as Fiona Robertson remarks, 'varied, experimental and directly responsive to contemporary theories and practices of drama'.[10] Yet the relation between the treatment of the politics of performance in earlier historical fiction and in the Waverley Novels has received less attention. While Scott's first novels display the tensions arising from these earlier historical novels, they simultaneously attempt to minimise the importance of performance. Nonetheless, his later works, particularly *The Abbot* (1820) and *Kenilworth: A Romance* (1821), re-examine such anxieties. Although Scott's theatrical pageantry has been read, notably by Stephen Arata in relation to *Kenilworth*, as reflecting on the author's own practice, Scott's treatment of alternative types of political theatricality, his interest in the performance of gender, and his anxiety about the uneasy divide between audience and actors all speak to the political concerns of his predecessors.[11] On the one hand, Scott was, like Knight, painfully aware of the theatre's potential to produce a radicalising 'seditious turmoil'; on the other, he was cogniscent of the negative association (made by Mary Wollstonecraft, for instance) between the 'puppet show' religion of Catholicism and the ritualised theatrical displays of absolutist power.[12] Transforming such concerns about radical or Catholic performativity, Scott creates an interactive model of political performance, one that is gendered to support Protestant modernity. Scott's response to his precursors sheds some light on what Cairns Craig has described as the 'notorious' change in Scott's attitude to the theatrical between *Waverley* and King George IV's 1822 visit to Edinburgh.[13] Yet the theatrical compromise Scott eventually generates is precarious. Emily Allen has suggested that the nineteenth-century novel tends to 'define the novelistic against and through the theatrical'.[14] Found in the early historical novel, and reworked by Scott, patterns of political overdetermination in relation to performance (and the performative) shed light on this supposed 'expulsion of the theatrical'.[15]

While Sophia Lee's *The Recess* (1783–5) positions performance (notably the festivals at Kenilworth) as a function of monarchical oppression, during the French Revolution debate a more elaborately gendered account of theatricality emerges in historical writing. In his *Reflections on the Revolution in France* (1790) Edmund Burke had attacked Dr Price's sermons, suggesting 'the theatre is a better school of moral sentiments than churches'.[16]

Mary Wollstonecraft responded by critiquing the 'celebrated beauty' for his 'theatrical attitudes'.[17] In *An Historical and Moral View of the Origin and Progress of the French Revolution* (1794) she follows this manoeuvre by a critique of 'the grand theatre of political changes'.[18] For Wollstonecraft political performance extends beyond the court to public assemblies, notably the theatre. When Wollstonecraft mentions the mixed pleasures available in British theatres, where 'the boxes, pit, and galleries, relish different scenes', she alludes to the mixed constitution of Britain. In contrast, the French respond to 'a highly wrought sentiment of morality ... when one heart seems to agitate every hand'.[19] This unity is negative, dictated by the 'fear' of 'stray[ing] from courtly propriety of behaviour'.[20] The French stage forms an implicit analogue to the 'puppet-show religion' and the 'pageantry of courts' that characterise Catholic absolutism.[21] Striped of this pageantry, the revolution offers an alternative theatricality. Visiting Paris on 17 July 1789, the king for the first time properly sees the 'triumphant' crowd. 'Forcibly struck by the energy every where displayed', Louis responds by altering his own performance.[22] Nonetheless, for Wollstonecraft, a rational, 'manly' politics would ultimately reject the theatrical.[23] Jean-Jacques Rousseau makes a similar and even more clearly gendered point in his *Letter to M. D'Alembert* (1758). Public theatres, he argues, hurt the morals of the state by causing men and women to associate too much together, 'degrad[ing] us into women'. The matter, he adds, is of little consequence in a monarchy but 'in a republic, men are wanted'.[24]

Wollstonecraft's suspicion of performance and political spectacle was shared by more conservative British novelists, who, however, associated them not so much with the *ancien régime* as with the Revolution. In *Marcus Flaminius*, for example, after the Germanic tribes defeat the Romans at the Battle of Teutoburg Forest (CE 9), the 'rude' Cheruscans of Germania encounter the atheist Greek philosopher (and revolutionary) Philocles.[25] With a 'commanding' figure and 'easy and natural' elocution, this demagogue tells tales of 'the successful struggles of the Athenian people in the cause of freedom'.[26] Undertaken with the support of the corrupt priest, Norbert, these shows do not just describe a political process; rather, they are performative, that is, in Butler's words, they are a kind of 'utterance' that 'brings some phenomenon into being'.[27] Philocles's theatrics ensure that the 'barbarous' Cheruscans rebel, 'sink[ing] into effeminancy, without ever having risen to civilisation'.[28] In this gendered stadial narrative, superstition and radicalism stage a history that weakens contemporary society.

The feminising and potentially politically disruptive nature of radical performance is also emphasised by the anti-Jacobin novelist Jane West in her novel *The Refusal* (1810), a reply to Germaine de Staël's *Corinne, or Italy* (1807). In de Staël's novel, the first part of Corinne's 'improvisation at the Capitol' is a cultural history of Italy from its mythical origins to Ariosto.[29] Cheered by the crowds, Corinne gives a performance that retrospectively creates a nation and that summons a people into being. In contrast, Paulina, West's Italian seductress (whose performances also recall the attitudes struck by Emma Hamilton), shows a 'genius as flexible as her form': 'the delighted spectator sometimes gazed on the sober charms of Octavia'.[30] Despite the message of classical self-sacrifice, Paulina aims to seduce a leading politician, Lord Avondel. Ostensible content and embodied performance differ: radical theatricality is deceptive, enacting seduction. Although de Staël's text calls for revolt from Napoleonic imperialism, West indicates its purpose, too, is seductive: it will shift political focus from the ruler to the nation and its people.

Challenging such radical rewritings of history, West turns to historical fiction, first with *The Loyalists* (1812) (which Peter Garside suggests left traces on a number of Waverley Novels) and then with *Alicia de Lacy: An Historical Romance* (1814).[31] Placing West's political message concerning performance in both a stadial and a religious framework, the latter responds in part to Jane Porter's *The Scottish Chiefs* (1810). Like Porter's novel, *Alicia de Lacy* takes place in the reign of Edward II but, instead of carrying Porter's message of popular Scottish patriotism, it promotes the centrality of the English nobility in shaping the nation. Porter's William Wallace becomes a minstrel at King Edward II's court, his songs inspiring Robert the Bruce to join the struggle for Scottish independence. In contrast, West's hero, the Earl of Lancaster ('a bold supporter of the independance [sic] of the national church'), stands between two types of dangerous theatricality.[32] Countess Margaret of Lincoln, temper 'soured' by religious allegiance to Rome, watches 'mysteries' combining 'sublimest Christian doctrines with gross wit and coarse buffoonery'.[33] No less destabilising are the demands of the next generation. The Countess's patriotic daughter, Alicia, demands a 'Dwarf – Icelandic dog – cloth of gold cushion' – and a troop of performers.[34] 'Lord Lancaster', West writes, 'doubted the expediency of partially employing men who must, at other seasons, be itinerants'.[35] Nonetheless he temporarily succumbs to the demands of fashion and to the sexual pressure put on him by his wife. In West's novel Lancaster's masculine proto-Protestant virtue is caught between two feminising moments, between retrograde Catholic performance and the subversive spectacles of consumerism.

When Scott considers performance in his novels, he is thus entering into a complex field of associations. It is not only that the theatre is connected with femininity, Catholicism and the *ancien régime* on the one hand and with femininity, superstition and radicalism, on the other, but also that this opposition is further complicated by the demands of national identity. Further, as Michael Gamer recounts, Scott was aware on his own account of the reputational and political difficulties attached to dramatic writing.[36] After translating Goethe's *Götz von Berlichingen* (1773) in 1799, the following year Scott was disappointed by the failure of the attempt to stage *The House of Aspen*. His discontent with the size of the early nineteenth-century theatre, with the mixed audience attracted and the kinds of drama performed is signalled by his involvement, most notably between 1808 and 1810, with the Theatre Royal at Edinburgh.[37] Yet, Christopher Worth argues, having attempted to shape a 'rational' and national dramatic entertainment, Scott 'was faced with evidence of his inability to revolutionise audience practices'.[38] Thus in his early novels, as in *Alicia de Lacy*, Scott queries the argument in favour of the patriotic effectiveness of performance, promoted by Jane Porter in *The Scottish Chiefs*. Having Wallace play 'songs dedicated to glory set in the grave', Porter at once connected the performance of history with national identity and masculinised it.[39] In contrast, Scott does not allow Waverley to perform.

Instead, connecting performance with the feminine, Scott suggests that the more hortatory such dramatisations of history are, the more dangerous they become. *Waverley*'s heroines Rose Bradwardine and Flora Mac-Ivor rewrite the behaviour of Jane Porter's female characters, Helen and Joanna Mar, in the process suggesting the rhetorical power of historical performance needs to be correctly framed. In *The Scottish Chiefs* both the heroine and her antithesis indulge in a cross-dressing symbolic of their attitude to nation; Helen disguising herself as page boy, somewhat masculinised but humble and patriotic, Joanna becoming Knight of the Green Plume, inappropriately martial, selfish and treacherous. In *Waverley* neither woman cross-dresses but each performs the past: the military intervention of Porter's women is replaced by historical spectacle. While Flora admittedly lacks the selfish motives of Joanna Mar, her invocations of history are equally martial in intent, flamboyantly staged and ultimately destructive. In contrast, Rose's verses, which capture 'a peculiar superstition', are reframed by the Baron Bradwardine, her father, in historical terms. The lady who, in Rose's song, appeals to the 'Night-Hag' for news of her husband is ushered off by the Baron's bathetic story of a witch on trial.[40] The impact of the performance is contained, both by the civilised domestic setting and the law.

The performances of *Guy Mannering* (1815) are still more mundane than those of *Waverley*. Harry Bertram (the missing heir) stays at a 'd——d cake-house, the resort of walking gentlemen of all descriptions, poets, players, painters, musicians' but, the hero's musical serenades aside, little comes of the theatrical threat. Julia's father reads aloud but 'produces effect by feeling, taste, and inflection of voice, not by action or mummery', while the young women give entirely standard domestic musical performances.[41] In *The Antiquary* the connection between theatricality and politics is still more firmly negated. Oldbuck thinks that Lovel is one of the 'player folk', while 'friends of the public' suspect the hero to be a 'French spy'.[42] Yet Lovel, in fact the Protestant descendent of the Catholic Earl of Glenallan, has nothing to do with the stage or radical politics. Catholic superstition has not, after all, been replaced by empty theatricality (a recurrent anxiety in Scott's fiction) – the choice between corrupt performances faced by West's Lancaster has been avoided. Further, Lovel thwarts the 'mountebank', Dousterswivel, who performs using the 'jargon of mysticism' but is ultimately neither Jacobite nor Jacobin.[43] Particularly where it invokes the historical, theatrical trickery has little place in political modernity.

In *Theatric Revolution*, David Worrall remarks: 'By the late 1810s drama was the primary literary form mediating between the British people and national issues'.[44] Dramatisations of the Waverley Novels formed part of this mediation. Yet, despite Scott's discussions with Terry concerning his play *The Doom of Devorgoil* (not published till 1830), Scott continued to wish for a theatric revolution. In 1818 he expressed to Terry a need for 'a more simple & less meretricious taste in dramatic composition', in 1819 to Matthew Weld Hartstonge, a desire for smaller theatres and more select audiences.[45] At the same time, in his novels he struggled to shape a new kind of national performance, considering both the extent and dangers of popular participation. After the Peterloo Massacre (to which the pageantry of *Ivanhoe* [published 1819, dated 1820] partly responds), in December 1819, Scott wrote to Lord Montagu and Lord Melville with plans to create a militia of 'common people'.[46] His tactics to 'counter the approach of radical insurrection in Scotland' suggest to Miranda Burgess his interest in the 'performative'.[47] The same interest is present in *The Abbot* and *Kenilworth*. For Andrew Lincoln, indeed, the festivals of *Kenilworth* function as a 'form of communal action'.[48] There is, though, a more troubled thinking through of political performance in these novels than this narrative implies. In these later works Scott rejects the stark choice between political performance as Jacobin or Jacobite, between the feminised Catholic absolutist theatricality, on the one hand, and the feminised, subversive performances of modernity on the other. But while an alternative (anti-theatrical) masculine historical moment had been imagined by West in Protestant and by Wollstonecraft in radical terms, to Scott neither vision appears satisfactory.

Scott's need to reassess what a masculine historical moment might look like politically — and the theatrical direction of his thought — is suggested in the 1830 preface to *The Monastery* (the 1820 novel to which the *The Abbot* — also 1820 — is the sequel). Discussing the critical unpopularity of his characters, the White Lady and Piercie Shafton, Scott blames changing historical fashion. The comedy that displays the 'follies' and 'coxcombry' of a particularly civilised society rapidly palls (a problem Joanna Baillie had pointed to in her 'Introductory Discourse' to *Plays on the Passions* [1798]).[49] One civilised stage is as frivolous as the next. On the other hand, a savage existence has universal appeal: in 'civilised life' many men wish 'to exchange' 'the habits and comforts of improved society' for 'wild labours'.[50] Scott's comments (again like Baillie's) speak to a need to re-masculinise society by returning to previous habits. There was, moreover, a precedent for imagining such a return to previous, masculine habits in relation to Protestantism, as a stripping away of the supposedly corrupting practices that had come to mar the Church under Catholicism. For Thomas Fosbrooke, whose *British Monachism* (1802) was held in the library at Abbotsford, 'monachism ... was an institution founded upon the first principles of religious virtue', but had been 'wrongly understood and wrongly directed' by the Catholic Church, while the nonconformist Anna Letitia Barbauld suggests that the 'original purity' and 'auster[ity]' of a sect gives way to 'elegance and show' such as 'that accumulated mass of error, the Church of Rome'.[51] But a return to previous simplicity had its hazards. In *The Abbot* and *Kenilworth*, Scott explores how to perform a masculine Protestant politics while avoiding the disruptive potential of mass participation.

The duology of *The Monastery* and *The Abbot* seems to expand the concern visible in *The Antiquary* — that the superstition of the old political order will be replaced by even more empty performance.[52] Hence the supernatural White Lady of *The Monastery* (albeit she seems to have Protestant sympathies) is supplanted in *The Abbot* by play-acting and theatricality. Yet, in contrast to *The Antiquary*, in *The Abbot* such drama seems inevitable enough to require careful management. The first relevant instance occurs when Edward Glendinning's ordination is interrupted by the carnival of the 'Abbot of Unreason', one of the 'frolics of the rude vulgar', a note in the 1831 Magnum edition informs us, which had initially been allowed by the Catholic Church in an endeavour 'to compromise with the laity'.[53] Although Catholicism seems to blame, with an ambiguity typical of the novel's attitude to religion, the Abbot of Unreason and his followers are, as Burstein notes, Protestant.[54] Protestantism's connection with an earlier historical moment is imagined in negative, not in positive terms. Reading *The Abbot* alongside Scott's *Essay on the Drama* (1818), it becomes clear that the 'propensity to turn into ridicule that which is most serious', evident in such carnivalesque practices, has its 'origin' in the 'rude gambols' of ancient Greece.[55] To extrapolate, the performances of the Abbot of Unreason revive the 'barbarism' and the 'fantastic orgies' of the rites of Bacchus.[56]

Scott's fear of unruly audiences makes him suspicious of more participative modes of performance: Protestantism's interrogative mode (asking 'grave question[s]' concerning doctrine), its anti-prelacy, its urge to personal responsibility and hence to participation, all link its public performances with the 'orgies' of ancient Greece.[57] Instead of enacting a return to an austere form of masculinity, this barbaric crowd in which men are 'disguised as women, and women as men' experiments only superficially with gender to challenge naturalised hierarchy.[58] For Wollstonecraft, a 'taste' for the stasis presented on the French stage had encouraged a political life 'where old principles vamped up with new scenes and decorations, are continually represented', but Scott produces a more anarchic picture of the drama's political manipulation over time.[59] Traditional practices license a kind of atavism in the Protestant performers. When his narrator describes the 'shouts of a multitude, now as in laughter, now as in anger', the repeated preposition suggests the indecipherability of the people's utterances and the impossibility of responding to their arbitrary desires.[60] Confronting the king, Wollstonecraft's crowd had generated a new type of political performance; the confrontation between the Abbot of Unreason and his officially ordained counterpart offers no such possibility.

In the *Essay on Drama* theatrical 'perfection' only arises with a greater separation between audience and actors and with a Chorus which tells the audience how to react.[61] However, in *The Abbot* more structured forms of drama prove equally problematic. Outside Loch Leven Castle, Mary Queen of Scots's prison, the protagonist Roland views a 'play, or dramatic representation' 'of recent origin in Scotland'.[62] Avoiding the 'magnificent decorations and pomp of dresses and of scenery' that Scott associates with Athens and the modern theatre, this performance eschews the feminising influence of luxury.[63] With the spectators 'raised' on an 'artificial bank', sat, like the audience at a masque, with Doctor Lundin, the 'dignified Chamberlain', 'in the centre', the scene also offers the illusion of a naturalised social order.[64] As the *Essay* has it, a 'disorderly mob' becomes an 'attentive audience'.[65] Yet this arrangement, although both properly masculine and Protestant, remains politically unstable due to the satirical impulse of Presbyterian authority. Andrew Lynch notes that Scott, responding anonymously in the *Quarterly Review* to the Reverend Thomas McCrie's criticisms of *Old Mortality* (1816), excused his own wit by citing the vicious humour associated with John Knox's *History of the Reformation in Scotland* (1559–66).[66] Here, however, the punitive (and misogynistic) humour of Dr Lundin's mock test of chastity appears dangerous. When the satire, involving a vinegar which makes incontinent damsels sneeze, is directed against a 'damsel' who is set 'a sneezing violently', the 'insulted maiden' gives the jester a hearty 'buffet'. Unrest threatens, not least because Dr Lundin, offended, orders 'two of his halberdiers to bring the culprit before him'.[67] Injured pride stimulates the doctor, a failing practitioner, who has himself provided the sternutatory 'vinegar of the sun'.[68] Unlike, for example, West's *The Loyalists*, which associates healing political medicine with Church and state, *The Abbot* demonstrates that the dramas of Protestant authority can act as an irritant.

Neither the 'barbarism' of radical Protestant participation nor the more authoritarian approach favoured by West is politically desirable: such aggressively masculine performances are destructive. For performance to be healthy for the state, the way the play-actors and their audiences are invited to stage gender must be carefully managed, not least because traditional gender hierarchy is at once an instantiation of and a metaphor for the operation of power. With the episode of the sneezing maiden, Scott indicates some rethinking of the performance of gender is necessary. The 'damsel' who sneezes so violently is actually the heroine's brother, the Catholic Henry Seyton, but Roland, the hero, mistakes the 'maiden' for Catherine herself. This error is not Roland's first. At St Michael's in Edinburgh, Roland encounters Henry in male clothing but is 'mazed' to see what he thinks is 'the form and face of Catherine Seyton; in man's attire'.[69] The ease with which the Catholic Henry is read as female might seem to fit into a common stadial narrative: in this kind of reading, when Henry dies, a feminised Catholicism will be replaced by a masculine alternative. But in Scott's more complex narrative Seyton's lability facilitates political struggle. His 'attitude of firm defiance' to the 'halbediers' swiftly changes into a 'modest and maiden-like' 'fashion': a shift in genders allows strategic choice. When the 'damsel' rediscovers her 'natural grace of manner', the re-establishment of courtesy diffuses hostility.[70] Scott implies that even if the new order is tempted to condemn Catholicism, it needs some version of the courtly 'drapery' with which Edmund Burke's *Reflections on the Revolution in France* had clothed the power of the *ancien régime*.[71] Otherwise, opposition will result.

Yet this courtliness must be more than mere display. Scott uses Henry to suggest that a more sophisticated performance of gender is needed, one which will integrate the masculine and the feminine and generate a fresh understanding of the way power functions. Repeatedly confronted by Catherine's brother, what Roland fails to identify is masculinity – and Seyton himself responds inadequately to such challenges, proving maleness only through violence. The epigraph to the chapter in which Roland encounters Seyton at St Michael's contrasts a 'mirror' (Henry) with the 'living substance' (Catherine).[72] This implied superficiality recalls Wollstonecraft's description of Catholic absolutism as a 'puppet-show' but it also suggests the need for a reintegration of the masculine and the feminine. Here the Scottish Regent offers Roland both warning and opportunity. Having gained authority only through the imprisonment of his sister, the Earl of Moray has the 'marks' of his sociality wiped from his face like 'bubbles' disappearing in 'the darkness of a still profound lake'.[73] Despite Moray's depth and purpose, his separation from his sister produces a disjunct between man and performance, suggesting Scott's unease about the role of secrecy in masculinist Protestant rule.

Nonetheless, Scott uses the occasion to hint at the possibility of an alternative mode of performance. Admitted behind the scenes of the Regent's display, Roland is, Scott's narrator remarks, 'controuled by the moral superiority, arising from . . . elevated talents and renown' rather 'than by pretensions founded only on rank or external show'.[74] The difficulty is to gain 'renown' through internal qualities properly displayed – through, that is, the right performance (one that genuinely reflects interiority), for the right audience (one that is properly discerning). As C. M. Jackson-Houlston remarks, Roland must shed his 'immature masculinity'.[75] This shift involves a more discerning approach to the spectator's demands. Instead of being provoked to immediate violence by insults to his ancestry, as he is at the beginning of the novel by Adam Woodcock, the English falconer, at the end, even when criticised for cowardice by both Seyton and Halbert Glendinning, Roland stays out of battle to protect his Queen. Thus he gains the praise of another onlooker, Catherine, at once feminine yet masculine enough to be mistaken for a man. Roland's masculine caution meets Catherine's feminine boldness in a re-gendered performance of power relations.

Jackson-Houlston argues that 'Gender, for Scott, complicates the question of legitimate rule, inherent in his early interest in Jacobitism'.[76]

However, the matter goes beyond the behaviours of the ruler to a broader re-imagining of the gendered moral qualities necessary to perform the modern state. While *The Abbot* suggests the need to rethink the performance of masculinity, *Kenilworth* presents such performance as both inevitably combative and pervasive. Sailing in a barge down the Thames, Sussex and Leicester debate, at Elizabeth's request, the rival merits of bear-baiting and the Shakespearian theatre. But this debate about the theatre is a meta-quarrel about performance in political life. The pair have already quarrelled at Westminster for court favour, a struggle that also has a ritualised dimension, as Scott makes clear by prefacing the clash with an epigraph from *Richard II*. As such, Sussex and Leicester offer two rival understandings of political performance. Queen Elizabeth, who anachronistically praises Shakespeare's Chronicles, must learn how to stage power more successfully than either Shakespeare's King Richard or her own courtiers.

Asked to choose between the theatre and Orson Pinner's bear-baiting pit, the 'martialist' Sussex praises Orson as 'a stout soldier' and defends Shakespeare on similar grounds, commenting on the dramatist's knowledge of manly sport (he is a 'stout man at a quarter staff') and virility (in supposedly kissing the keeper's daughter).[77] The merits of performance are connected with actual violence; for Sussex, as for Seyton, masculinity involves destructive bravado. Elizabeth, however, rejects his account of Shakespeare's behaviour as exaggerated and her later remarks suggest that even the supposedly more authentic violence of the bear-pit is fundamentally theatrical. When Sussex praises the 'royal game of bear-baiting' instead of the actors' 'mere mockery of a stout fight', the Queen responds to his blow-by-blow description with laughter: 'had we never seen a bear-baiting, as we have beheld many, and hope, with heaven's allowance, to see many more, your words were sufficient to put the whole Bear-garden before our eyes'.[78] Both Elizabeth's remarks and, ironically, Sussex's own recitation highlight the combat's repetitive staging. The meaning Sussex takes from such performance, of violence as end in itself, is a political construction: the show instantiates and encourages martial behaviour.

If Sussex tries to reject theatricality in favour of a violence that is somehow unmediated, Leicester embraces theatrical spectacle as a distraction from brute force: 'witty knaves' like Shakespeare are useful because 'rants and jests keep the minds of the commons from busying themselves with state affairs'.[79] Although Elizabeth argues that she does not want to withdraw 'the mind of [her] subjects' 'from the consideration of [her] own conduct', elsewhere Leicester seems to identify his tactic as properly Protestant.[80] Showing Amy the 'splendour' of his court costume, he scoffs at those who think more of 'the jewels, and feathers, and silk' than 'the man whom they adorn'.[81] Read in terms of the 1790s debate, these words distance Leicester from the empty theatricality of Catholic absolutism and imply his fundamental masculinity. Yet Leicester falsely 'courts the severe and strict sect of puritans', adopting a stance which even the villainous Lambourne rejects as hypocritical.[82] Ultimately, the morality of the inward man is less important to Leicester than the costume that leads to power. When Protestantism uses theatre as distraction, without belief in its public performances, it invites a distorted return of previous political practices. Worse still, detached from genuine religion, Leicester comes to believe in astrological predictions of his own greatness. In the absence of divine right, Scott fears, any scheming politician may harness religion while superstitiously serving the cult of his own self.

Where *The Abbot* displays the flaws of both popular and more hierarchical drama, *Kenilworth* suggests that the first has a role in counterbalancing the second: the Commons and aristocratic authority are in necessary tension. Sibyl Laneham, who 'hath played the devil ere now, in a Mystery', is 'taken in labour' while travelling in a troop of actors, giving Amy a chance to escape from Leicester's followers.[83] Whereas in *Alicia de Lacy* West had condemned Catholic mummery and the itinerant actors of modernity, in *Kenilworth* both combine to help Leicester's wife. Similarly, Amy's guide, Wayland, has both taken '[him]self to the stage' and aided the superstitious illusions of the 'quacksalver' to whom Leicester is in thrall.[84] To avoid misrule, the disruptive forces which Scott and his conservative precursors had suspected must be allowed to compete. Moreover, the pageants at Kenilworth indicate that this violent competition must be visibly performed. The men of Coventry who 'represent the strife between the English and the Danes' in 'rude rhymes' and 'hard blows'; the Lady of the Lake, with her list of Kenilworth's successive owners; even the fireworks, 'burning darts' which make the spectators 'vengeably afraid' – all perform the clash of powers within the state. Even the audience tremble on the urge of rebellion: only the 'profuse distribution of refreshments' keeps 'the populace in perfect love and loyalty towards the Queen'.[85] The potential for brutal disorder is persistently displayed.

This display is not the 'transcend[ence]' of historical violence that Anthony Jarrells associates with Scott.[86] Rather, for the author of *Waverley* this drama, with all its clunky combativeness, is not just a performance but performative. Alongside historical violence, it enacts contemporary conflict, creating a new understanding of politics not as a balance of powers but as a struggle of factions. Further, it suggests that, in such struggle, the only hope is to combine qualities usually considered masculine or feminine. Standing before the gates of Kenilworth, the porter announces that he governs by violence ('my club gives law'). Yet when he sees the Queen his language becomes more chivalrous ('What dainty darling's this—what peerless peer?').[87] He is markedly more gallant than the porter described in the contemporary 'Langham Letter', who is merely impressed with 'a personage so evidently expressing an heroicall Soveraintee'.[88] *Kenilworth*'s porter indicates both masculine strength and feminised courtliness are necessary. Scott refines the point using the Queen herself. Elizabeth combines feminine 'propriety' with masculine 'strength of mind'.[89] Yet she can also represent more exaggerated gender qualities: she 'stamp[s] on the floor with the action . . . of Henry himself' or displays tearful femininity.[90] Although Elizabeth desires to conceal these extremes, Scott's text will not let her. Instead, *Kenilworth* endorses the Queen's earlier preference for transparency. The Protestant subject, understanding the Queen's 'true motives', will also understand the need for self-control, the need to moderate gendered qualities into something useful.[91]

Like the *Kenilworth* festivals, King George IV's visit to Edinburgh appeared to perform harmony while enacting the potential for violence, both physical and satirical. In this staging of the necessary violence of political modernity, Scott transforms the previous debate. While radicals rejected Catholic absolutist theatricality, more conservative writers denounced radical politics as equally staged. Imagining an alternative (antitheatrical) masculine political moment, Wollstonecraft had emphasised rational mass participation in the public sphere; West replied by envisaging a structured Protestantism of Church and King. Initially following his predecessors in rejecting feminised theatricality, Scott later looked afresh at the masculine political moment they had imagined. Insisting upon the inescapability of the politically performative, Scott critiqued both radical mass public theatricality and the more conservative vision of hierarchy proposed by West. In *The Abbot* he suggests each is potentially too aggressive, proposing a more moderate performance of masculinity inflected by feminine qualities. In *Kenilworth*, however, he accepts the need to stage the brutality of historical conflict. In these scenes, both masculine violence and feminine courtliness are on display – and both are, he suggests, moderated and improved by the very act of performance.

Scott's new drama is fundamentally knowing: actors and audience merge in self-conscious participation. In this performance, what is at stake is not, after all, the 'right to appear'. On the contrary, all must participate in this alarming process. Such participation is necessary because, for Scott, Protestant modernity is marked by a waning belief in the sovereign function. In such a society, the ceremony and theatricality of absolutism is terrifyingly open to re-appropriation. While Knight and West feared the radical demagogue who would exploit an historically informed rhetoric of freedom, Scott, even more pessimistically, imagines the theatricality of the old order seized and transformed by aspiring members of the ruling class. The resulting performance, underpinned by no belief except egotism, is reminiscent of the display Judith Butler associates with US President Donald Trump. 'Taking up the screen', he 'postur[es] as the center of the world, and gain[s] power through that posturing'.[92] In such a 'post-truth' moment, performing past conflict offers a mode of resistance.

Nonetheless, this vision of political performance is hardly reassuring, making the ostensible anti-theatricality Allen remarks in the Victorian novel more explicable. Instead of moving towards the tidy resolution of conflict, *Kenilworth* suggests it must be perpetually staged and restaged. Such theatrical violence reminds a no-longer-innocent Protestant public that the demagogue's interests are not their own, no matter what contrary claims are made. In this process of political (re)embodiment gender is central. Scott's reconstructed history of the operation of gender sheds light on the connection Butler makes between 'gender performativity' and 'precarious lives'. It is not just that there is a continuum of oppression between those who perform gender non-normatively and the precariat. Rather, Scott's work reveals how the performance of gender structures political life, shaping our imaginary of how power should – and does – operate. As such, shifts in the performance of the masculine and feminine do not only affect individual lives but have implications for our understanding of class and social hierarchies more generally. To change the performance of gender, to challenge its binaries, is to rewrite the operation of power at a fundamental level.

Notes

1. Knight, *Marcus Flaminius*, 2: 27–8.
2. Knight, *Autobiography*, 2: 42–3.
3. Ibid. 2: 41.
4. Jacques Rancière, 'Good Times', pp. 175–232; David Worrall, *The Politics of Romantic Theatricality*; Jane Moody, *Illegitimate Theatre in London*.
5. Worrall, *Politics*, pp. 9, 2; Betsy Bolton, *Women, Nationalism and the Romantic Stage*.

6. Judith Butler, *Notes Towards a Performative Theory of Assembly*, pp. 25–6.
7. Ibid. pp. 24–5, 29, 34.
8. Fiona Price, 'National Identities and Regional Affiliations', p. 186.
9. Karen O'Brien, *Women and Enlightenment in Eighteenth-Century Britain*, p. 2.
10. Fiona Robertson, 'Castle Spectres', p. 444. For theatrical adaptations of Scott's work, see Barbara Bell, 'The Performance of Victorian Medievalism'. For Scott's precursors see Fiona Price, *Reinventing Liberty*, pp. 170–206; Ina Ferris, *The Achievement of Literary Authority*; Fiona Robertson, *Legitimate Histories*.
11. Stephen Arata, 'Scott's Pageants', p. 102.
12. Mary Wollstonecraft, *The Works of Mary Wollstonecraft*, 6: 18.
13. Cairns Craig, 'Scott's Staging of the Nation', p. 14.
14. Emily Allen, *Theater Figures*, p. 8.
15. Terry F. Robinson, '"Life is a Tragicomedy!"', p. 144.
16. Edmund Burke, *Reflections on the Revolution in France*, p. 176.
17. Wollstonecraft, *Works*, 5: 8.
18. Ibid. 6: 6.
19. Ibid. 6: 19.
20. Ibid. 6: 25.
21. Ibid. 6: 18, 30.
22. Ibid. 6: 120–1.
23. Ibid. 6: 108.
24. Jean-Jacques Rousseau, *Letter to M. D'Alembert*, pp. 134, 135.
25. Knight, *Marcus Flaminius*, 1: 5.
26. Ibid. 1: 35, 1: 70.
27. Butler, *Notes*, p. 28.
28. Knight, *Marcus Flaminius*, 1: 46.
29. Germaine de Staël, *Corinne, or Italy*, pp. 28–30.
30. Jane West, *The Refusal*, 2: 318.
31. See Peter Garside, 'Walter Scott and the "Common" Novel'.
32. Jane West, *Alicia de Lacy*, 1: 96–7.
33. Ibid. 1: 96, 1: 217.
34. West, *Alicia de Lacy*, 2: 50.
35. Ibid. 2: 48.
36. Michael Gamer, 'Authors in Effect', p. 852.
37. Christopher Worth, '"A Very Nice Theatre at Edinr."', pp. 88–92.
38. Ibid. p. 92.
39. Jane Porter, *The Scottish Chiefs*, p. 501.
40. Walter Scott, *Waverley*, pp. 64–5.
41. Scott, *Guy Mannering*, pp. 90, 157.
42. Scott, *The Antiquary*, p. 35.
43. Ibid. pp. 101–2.
44. Worrall, *Theatric Revolution*, p. 274.

45. Walter Scott to Daniel Terry, 22 February 1818, *Letters* 5: 89; Scott to Matthew Weld Hartstonge, 11 November 1819, *Letters* 6: 13.
46. Scott, *Letters* 6: 71.
47. Miranda J. Burgess, 'Scott, History, and the Augustan Public Sphere', pp. 123, 124.
48. Andrew Lincoln, *Walter Scott and Modernity*, p. 83.
49. Scott, *The Monastery* (Waverley Novels New Edition, 1830) 18: xxiv.
50. Ibid. 18: xxiii.
51. See Fosbrooke, 'Art. V. *British Monachism*', p. 40; Anna Letitia Barbauld, 'Thoughts on the Devotional Taste', 2: 248, 250, 253.
52. For the relationship between *The Monastery* and *The Abbot*, see Christopher Johnson's 'Essay on the Text' in Walter Scott, *The Abbot*, esp. pp. 379–85.
53. Scott, *The Abbot* (Waverley Novels New Edition, 1831) 20: 206–8.
54. Miriam Elizabeth Burstein, *Victorian Reformation*, p. 46. For ambiguity, see Michael E. Schiefelbein, *The Lure of Babylon*, pp. 15–55, 16, 44–5.
55. Scott, *Essays on Chivalry*, p. 246. (First published as a supplement to the *Encyclopedia Britannica*, 1818.)
56. Scott, *Essays*, pp. 222, 221.
57. Scott, *Abbot* (Waverley Novels New Edition, 1831) 20: 207.
58. Scott, *Abbot*, p. 105.
59. Wollstonecraft, *Works*, 6: 25.
60. Scott, *Abbot*, p. 102.
61. Scott, *Essays*, p. 220.
62. Scott, *Abbot*, p. 249.
63. Ibid. p. 250
64. Ibid. pp. 250, 249, 250.
65. Scott, *Essays*, p. 223.
66. Andrew Lynch, '"Simply to Amuse the Reader"', p. 172.
67. Scott, *Abbot*, p. 252.
68. Ibid. p. 253.
69. Ibid. p. 165.
70. Ibid. p. 252.
71. Burke, *Reflections*, p. 171.
72. Scott, *Abbot*, p. 159.
73. Ibid. p. 152.
74. Ibid. p. 153.
75. C. M. Jackson-Houlston, *Gendering Walter Scott*, p. 114.
76. Ibid. p. 107.
77. Scott, *Kenilworth*, pp. 132, 173–4.
78. Ibid. pp. 174–5.
79. Ibid. p. 175.
80. Ibid.
81. Ibid. p. 57.

82. Ibid. p. 83.
83. Ibid. pp. 170, 245.
84. Ibid. p. 103.
85. Ibid. pp. 362, 291, 285.
86. Anthony Jarrells, *Britain's Bloodless Revolutions*, p. 172.
87. Scott, *Kenilworth*, p. 288.
88. Ibid.; *Letter Describing a Part of the Entertainment unto Queen Elizabeth at Killingworth Castle* (1575), John Nichols, *The Progresses, and Public Processions, of Queen Elizabeth*, p. 6. The letter's authorship is disputed. See David Scott, 'William Patten'.
89. Scott, *Kenilworth*, p. 365.
90. Ibid. p. 272.
91. Ibid. p. 175.
92. Judith Butler, 'Reflections on Trump'.

8

Where We Never Were: Women at Walter Scott's Abbotsford

Caroline McCracken-Flesher

In early nineteenth-century Britain, literary genius acquired a habitation and a name: 'Abbotsford'. Whereas Shakespeare was long gone from Stratford before David Garrick reconceived his birthplace as an artistic and tourist mecca,[1] and Horace Walpole fled from Strawberry Hill under press of visitors,[2] Walter Scott was 'at home' and reachable in the Scottish Borders. Scott had produced poems and novels aplenty that dramatised return: the Bruce beats homeward in *The Lord of the Isles* (1815); Edward Waverley finds a Scottish home away from his English estate in *Waverley* (1814). Now, having directed his characters' and readers' steps north, Scott had built his own retreat. That home signalled access. As W. S. Crockett affirmed in 1905: 'But for Abbotsford [Scott] would not have been *our* Scott – our man among men – our Immortal'; and he reflected: 'A glance at the Abbotsford life will bring us nearer Scott as a man.'[3]

If Scott wrote of home, and built a home, he was also hospitable. 'Our house is the least that ever harboured decent folks since the traditionary couple who lived in the Vinegar bottle', he wrote to Sarah Smith the actress in 1814. Still, he assured her of Abbotsford under construction, 'if you come . . . we will find a corner for you'.[4] Washington Irving dropped by with a letter of introduction from Thomas Campbell the poet, sat with Scott among the building works, stayed for four nights and earned from the author the accolade of 'one of the best & pleasantest acquaintances I have made this many a day'.[5] And Scott's literary appeal, together with his importance as a public figure, invited all sorts to squeeze themselves into his rising home. Edward Everett, himself cited by H. J. C. Grierson to explain the author's 1818 reference to 'receiving visitors chiefly travellers',[6] having achieved a welcome through a friend soon wrote to introduce another friend. Everett hoped to spare that friend the embarrassment of two less fortunate 'pilgrims' he had encountered who had 'wandered over

[Scott's] estate for two days, in the design of falling in with you'.[7] Even less welcome, during the electioneering season of 1819 the two dull sons of Sir James Hall, a dull father, 'establishd themselves for the night', forcing on their host 'devouring feelings' and a stomach ache.[8] Many sought and some actually gained accommodation under Scott's roof – to the degree that the author's hospitality and its abuses became a theme in the explanation of his later financial challenges.[9]

Asserting themselves as insiders to Abbotsford, such visitors show us something about authors' houses, modernity, access and ourselves that we might carry into our era of intensified celebrity culture. They came, as Lawrence Grossberg asserts of today's fans, for different reasons.[10] But whatever an individual's 'mattering map' of personal concern, in their need 'to organize moments of stable identity, sites at which we can, at least temporarily, find ourselves "at home"', such visitors could appropriate all the physical and intellectual space available – so much so that Scott built himself a private staircase to separate his work from his hospitality.[11] They inhabit a Derridean paradox. Derrida posits that the notion of hospitality requires foreignness in both guest (as other than host) and host (as other than guest).[12] Moreover the intrusions of modernity – in this case, tourism – put the home under pressure as both penetrable and inviolable if true hospitality is to ensue.[13] With mattering maps situating Abbotsford as 'home' and Scott as host, the imperative is towards homecoming as well as hospitality. To achieve that double welcome – in Derrida's terms, to achieve proximity to Scott without rendering him 'hostage' or themselves as 'hostile' – not a few guests negotiated their presence relative to others.[14] They placed themselves at home by effectively expelling those normally situated at the hearth. Perversely, the family's females were rendered foreign.

Of course, a substantial proportion of Scott's visitors were women. Miss Smith, Joanna Baillie and Susan Ferrier came as invited. Charlotte Brontë and Harriet Beecher Stowe figure among authors touring Abbotsford after Scott's death. Many more appear anonymously in the guest books that mark the house's transition to a museum, often showing up as 'wife', or 'and party'. Still, most visitors in search of either the living or the late Scott proved curiously blind to the house's other inhabitants, specifically its women. Young Walter left to become a Hussar; Charles went off to study; but Scott's wife Charlotte and daughters Sophia and Anne were integral to his domestic establishment, were present through waves of visitors, and were succeeded by a female line that maintained the site as open to paying tourists. Yet even the writer Horace Smith, who had just met

Anne in Edinburgh, visiting Abbotsford felt only that every stone 'prated [Scott's] whereabout'.[15] As Abbotsford, increasingly replete with relics and cultural significance, became the national home and an international home away from home, and in the moments before Sarah Stickney Ellis and Coventry Patmore would deify the woman within the house,[16] its women proved the token that allowed access, but were expended in the process. Derrida notes that without the right of hospitality, a new arrival is 'a parasite ... liable to expulsion or arrest', but that 'in order to constitute the space of a habitable house and a home ... you have to give up a passage to the outside world'.[17] Scott's women found themselves on the outer end of that passage.

This chapter, then, considers the dynamic between Abbotsford, its guests and its inhabitants. It ponders the constitutive function of visits to this author's house, and particularly of author visits to such houses. Given Abbotsford's role as a place of memory, it pursues how the memories constructed by Abbotsford's visitors resist other presence – especially when that presence is family and female.

Notoriously, the fantasy assemblage of 'Sir Walter Scott and His Literary Friends at Abbotsford', painted by Thomas Faed in 1849, features none but men.[18] People who never met together surround Sir Walter. Even Byron is evidenced by the urn he gifted to his fellow author. But there is no sign of a Joanna Baillie, a Maria Edgeworth or a Susan Ferrier – the first two both intimates and colleagues of Scott,[19] the third an author he, at least, counted as a friend. And by 1849, the little that was known of Scott's female relatives was fading into the past. Although J. G. Lockhart, Scott's biographer, was also his son-in-law, scant reference to these women appears in his seven-volume *Memoirs of the Life of Sir Walter Scott, Bart*. Rather, Lockhart expended effort protecting the women from appearing in print. When James Hogg sought to publish his own memoir, with a reference to Charlotte's cloudy origins, Lockhart worked to keep it out of print in Britain.[20] Proto-Victorian notions of propriety, decorum and respect can explain this omission, still it is worth noting that stories of the family, when they are told, focus on Scott. An 1820 cavalcade to hunt hares is interrupted when '*the Lady Anne* broke from the line, screaming with laughter, and exclaimed, "Papa, papa, I knew you could never think of going without your pet"'.[21] Scott is being followed by 'a little black pig frisking about like a pony', and Lockhart can then turn to discuss Scott's unusual attraction for all dogs, pigs, chickens and donkeys. The 'wicked' humour of Anne, who had christened the donkeys 'Hannah More and Lady Morgan' is a thing of the moment; like all beasts of the field, all biographers (necessarily) turn to Scott. But something is lost nonetheless.

This loss encourages Alison Booth to consider Abbotsford the touchstone for 'homosocially male' authors' houses.[22]

Booth has a point. But that homosocial community is constructed from elsewhere than Abbotsford, and differently than we might expect. Certainly, Scott was the host in his home, and the guests were predominantly male. On the cavalcade to hunt hares, Lady Scott and Sophia, who would marry Lockhart, unpacked the picnic basket,[23] but it is Scott, Lockhart, William Allan, Humphrey Davy, Dr Wollaston, Henry Mackenzie, Mackenzie's black attendant, William Laidlaw and Tom Purdie who make the narrative that is the hunt and the story of its aftermath.[24] Davy wonders that it is by hunting he comes to visit 'the scenery of the Lay of the Last Minstrel', and quotes with abandon; gathered round the evening fire and swapping stories with Scott, he prompts Laidlaw to declare this a 'very superior occasion!' and wonder 'if Shakespeare and Bacon ever met to screw ilk other up?'[25] In the *Lay*, the story hangs upon the lady, and her inheritance of magic from her father;[26] here, guests vie to share Scott's physical and intellectual space with little reference to the gender politics of the origin story they cite or acknowledgement of the women who facilitate their festivity.

Interestingly, too, they understand their access to Scott and his home on an individual scale. All wondered, Lockhart tells us, about the extent of Scott's hospitality:

> The humblest person who stayed merely for a short visit, must have departed with the impression, that what he witnessed was an occasional variety; that Scott's courtesy prompted him to break in upon his habits when he had a stranger to amuse; but that it was physically impossible, that the man who was writing the Waverley romances at the rate of nearly twelve volumes in the year, could continue, week after week, and month after month, to devote all but a hardly perceptible fraction of his mornings to out of doors' occupations, and the whole of his evenings to the entertainment of a constantly varying circle of guests.[27]

That is, each guest thought they must be the unique object of Scott's attention.

They were often equally sure that the house's women, even when evident, were functionally absent. James Hogg typifies the pattern. Much is made of his first meeting with Mrs Scott, in 1803. In this story, Hogg figures in the Scotts' Edinburgh home.[28] Stretching himself out on a sofa in emulation of Charlotte Scott and, in Lockhart's telling, bearing 'legible marks of a recent sheep-smearing', Hogg effectively displaces the lady of the house. When his proposed memoir later points to Charlotte's possible opium addiction through her last illness and questions her birth he may, as Fiona Robertson suggests, claim a 'shared tangentiality to polite Edinburgh life'.[29] However, if Hogg was a farmer who became a friend, and Charlotte French and female, she was nonetheless Scott's wife. Given the discourse of the day, Lockhart was right to register the denigratory and distancing potential of Hogg's comments for his mother-in-law's role in the family.

Significantly, Hogg was not alone in distancing Charlotte Scott. She was persistently ostracised by outsiders to the family. An Edinburgh lawyer characterised her as a 'little, made-up sort of personage . . . luxuriant, dark, and I should say not natural curls, shading a yellow face, blushing under a real or artificial bloom of crimson, a very little figure' set beside the 'manly plainness of her illustrious husband'.[30] To Helen Graham, who appreciated her hospitality, she was nonetheless 'a funny looking little bodie and very fond of showy dress, and completely foreign both in manner and appearance'.[31] Scott's daughters, too, came in for their share of abuse. Anne, Helen Graham continued, was 'very satirical': 'I fancy as Sir Walter's daughter, she thinks she ought to be clever, which she is not, I am sure.'[32] Men and women alike distance Scott's wife and daughters from the great man, and by such authoritative determinations, situate themselves in their place.

As guests, acquaintances and even biographers seek to stand by the author, their inclusion, it seems, begets a gendered exclusion. Perhaps it is ever thus: David Garrick did not go to Stratford in search of Ann Hathaway; there was no spouse to seek at Strawberry Hill; one might legitimately think of Bronson Alcott even when drawn to Orchard House by his daughter, Louisa May Alcott, and not of Louisa's three sisters except as the predecessors of *Little Women*. Still, this phenomenon of exclusion, specifically the exclusion of women, is rendered highly visible in the hothouse of homeliness that was Abbotsford. What biographers, acquaintances, visitors and even scholars seek in asserting their proximity to a writer stands both provided and compromised by the myth of hospitality that was Walter Scott's home at Abbotsford – and uniquely traceable.

What visitors sought, of course, is not hard to find. Herman Melville made his trip to Abbotsford.[33] In London en route, Melville's biographer declares, he met 'Scott's cold-fish son-in-law John Gibson Lockhart and knew Scott had worked himself to death to save Abbotsford for his heirs'.[34] This is 'a perturbing story for a tourist whose Scottish father had squandered a fortune but had not heroically recovered it [like Scott] before dying'. Melville, here, is triply related to Scott: as Scot, as writer, and as son – at a slight cost to Lockhart. Melville's own role is thereby informed. Irving extends the case. He left an Abbotsford under construction to build his Sunnyside. Similarly James Fenimore Cooper, who never got to Abbotsford but who corresponded with Scott, built a house characterised as 'Abbotsford' for America's author.[35] Mark Twain, signing as Samuel Clemens, visited in 1873 and, whatever his later critiques of Scott, built a similarly expensive and expressive author's house in Hartford – where he would write the novels that cemented his fame.[36] As Paul Westover has made clear, Scott at Abbotsford became the formative node in a network of houses that valued their owners as authors.[37] These authors became insiders to their own spaces by aligning themselves with Scott in his. Short-circuiting their Derridean foreignness by standing as more sympathetic than Lockhart (in Melville's case) or more astute even than Scott (in Clemens's case), they could be at home at Abbotsford and validated elsewhere.

Hawthorne became suspicious of Abbotsford's narrative glamour. On his first visit in 1856, 'Its aspect disappointed me . . . It is but a villa after all.'[38] Perhaps he was soured by the guide suggesting that if he sat in Sir Walter's chair, he might 'catch some inspiration' not through primary relation but as a secondary effect.[39] Still, he felt the want of a guidebook since 'every pant of the engine carried us over some spot of ground which Scott has made fertile with poetry'.[40] But in 1857 he concluded: 'I do abhor this mode of making pilgrimages to the shrines of departed great men . . . it seldom or never produces (in me, at least) the right feeling'.[41]

Felix Mendelssohn, a drop-in guest during Scott's lifetime, figured out the problem. The issue is the affect. He declares:

> Most astonished friends! O most amazed readers! Under us the great man is snoring, his dogs are asleep and his armoured knights awake . . . and we look down very much on Europe.[42]

But then fascination turns to farce:

> P.S. – This is all Klingeman's invention. We found Sir Walter in the act of leaving Abbotsford, stared at him like fools, drove eighty miles and lost a day for the sake of at best one half-hour of superficial conversation. Melrose compensated us but little: we were out of humour with great men, with ourselves, with the world, with everything. It was a bad day.[43]

Visitors – especially authors – and authors' houses subsist in a network of meaning. Abbotsford constitutes the *lieu de mémoir* for a collective authentication project that is nonetheless experienced individually. It is a space with no room for actual residents, or, at least, no room for those who might contest a visitor's proximity to greatness. Hawthorne, in 1853, demonstrated this dynamic when as consul at Liverpool he met two sons of Robert Burns. There could be no contest for place – having served in India the poet's sons now lived in Cheltenham, and the meeting took place far from Alloway and from Burns's humble abodes. Yet Hawthorne nonetheless enacted the contest for proximity: he found in the colonel and the major 'no resemblance . . . to any portrait of their father'.[44] Pleasant company though they proved to be, Hawthorne effectively constructed and ejected Burns's family as foreign. Equally, at Abbotsford there was no room for the women who might complicate the narrative of access to greatness for visitors as unique individuals.

Hawthorne astutely observed: 'a house is forever after spoiled and ruined as a home, by having been the abode of a great man. His spirit haunts it, as it were, with a malevolent effect, and takes hearth and hall away from the nominal possessors.'[45] Yet if there is a tussle for home, as Abbotsford shows it is not between fathers and children. Mendelssohn's spoof reads more completely:

> Under us the great man is snoring, his dogs are asleep and his armoured knights awake: it is twelve o'clock, and the sweetest ghostly hour which I have ever spent, for Miss Scott makes the most delicious marmalade . . . Never was a letter begun with greater relish.[46]

Mendelssohn, that is, imagines suffering indigestion through Miss Scott's very hospitality. If visitors seek to elide the Scott women, it is because with their regular lives and family relationships, and in the nicest and homeliest of ways, they disrupt the visitors' affecting Abbotsford experience. It is for that reason they must be ejected.

Scott may have welcomed all and sundry to his home, but his women friends, from their own domestic role, also saw a problem. Some advised him to bring in the welcome mat. Maria Edgeworth, that much sought guest, did not want anyone else to show up, denigrating 'that odious Caledonian bore [Mr. Hall] and his wife . . . Heaven forbid they shd come to Abbotsford while we are there.'[47] Joanna Baillie, with less attention to her own comfort and more of an eye to what it took to maintain open house, and certainly with more understanding of what Scott's visitors sought, warned to avoid 'idle Travellers' who might 'make an Inn of your house . . . that they may boast in their stupid Tours afterwards of the great attentions they received from their <u>Friend</u> Mr Scott'.[48] And Mrs Scott, registering the reconstruction of the family as outside help, was rumoured to have called their mode of hospitality 'A hotel widout de pay.'[49]

Susan Ferrier, a long-time family friend but with the agenda of a competing author, shows what was at stake for author and family alike. Revisiting Scott without her father, Scott's colleague, and late in Scott's life, she saw him entangled in his own narratives of place, thralled to their continuing performance. He is the same kind and available host as ever, offering 'the same inexhaustible flow of legendary lore, romantic incident, apt quotation, curious or diverting story', but the evening songs seem 'little else than a mockery of human life . . . the glee seemed forced and unnatural'.[50] Friend Sophia at her harp, illness notwithstanding, but unable fully to join in the foot-stamping singing, is turning into a thing among things. Ferrier alone presumes an insider position and gaze, and that gaze translates family into furniture at best.

This is the issue at Abbotsford. Women, perversely displaced in their home *as* home by the ethos of entertaining, risk becoming functions. Yet, functioning as female, as the hidden, essential members of a household, they inevitably disrupt the self-serving narratives of proximity to place and to the person of Walter Scott sought by visitors to Abbotsford. They must consequently figure as foreign – or as mere furniture.

William Wells Brown, visiting in 1851 to a house distressingly 'undergoing repairs and alterations', gives a striking example of how this phenomenon continued, even when the author who had made Abbotsford a noted home was no more.[51] 'In passing through the library', he remembers, 'we saw a grand-daughter of the Poet':

> She was from London, and was only on a visit of a few days. She looked pale and dejected, and seemed as if she longed to leave this secluded spot and return to the metropolis. She looked for all the world like a hothouse plant.[52]

He determines:

> I don't think the Scotch could do better than to purchase Abbotsford, while it has some imprint of the great magician, and secure its preservation; for I am sure that, a hundred years hence, no place will be more frequently visited in Scotland than the home of the late Sir Walter Scott.

In Wells's eyes, the house belongs to the nation as the author's home. Anyone should be able to visit. But it cannot in spirit belong to the young woman who actually owns it, and who he infers as anxious to leave.[53] Brown, who had escaped slavery in Ohio in 1834, perhaps was driven by his own anxieties. The Fugitive Slave Act of 1850 meant he now had no American home to which to go. And with Abbotsford already overdetermined as 'home' by Scott's stories and now by a generation of public visitation, Brown uproots Charlotte Hope Scott as a 'hothouse plant', a foreign and misplaced growth that is pining for the city. He clears space for those who appreciate it more – who '[visit] Abbotsford because of the genius of the man that once presided over it'.[54] The house, that is, should allow the visitors who are Scott's real intimates (perversely) unique access. The woman, however, with her descent from Abbotsford and the author, cannot appreciate the relation between author and visitor. Indeed, she disrupts it, and must be reconceived as a thing and ejected.

Harriet Beecher Stowe, a literary lion herself, in 1853 looked around her with a significant difference. *Uncle Tom's Cabin* had been published in 1852, but in 1869 Stowe would publish a housekeeping manual.[55] Thus, Stowe saw all the women who made Abbotsford work. Speeding into Scotland on the train, at first Stowe seems unselfconsciously committed to Scott's national romance:

> The sun went down, and night drew on; still we were in Scotland. Scotch ballads, Scotch tunes, and Scotch literature were in the ascendant. We sang 'Auld Lang Syne,' 'Scots wha ha',' and 'Bonnie Doon,' and then, changing the key, sang Dundee, Elgin, and Martyrs.
> 'Take care,' said Mr. S.; 'don't get too much excited.'
> 'Ah,' said I, 'this is a thing that comes only once in a lifetime; do let us have the comfort of it. We shall never come into Scotland for the *first time* again.'
> 'Ah,' said another, 'how I wish Walter Scott was alive!'[56]

And the party progresses through a landscape that it maps through the works of Scott.

Singing themselves into a Scotland where they have never been, Stowe and her companions seem to enact all the intrusive cultural coding that twentieth-century critics such as Tom Nairn have considered a national blight founded in Scott's discourses of homecoming.[57] But Stowe was on a consciousness and fundraising abolitionist tour. She was recognised as the author of *Uncle Tom's Cabin* at every stop, and bound for work. Looking around her, she sees working people and ponders national and human relations. She sees the women. At Abbotsford, her first thought is of the guide who facilitates her tour: 'came a trim, little old woman in a black gown, with pattens on; she put up her umbrella, and we all put up ours'.[58] Of the house, she ponders how it 'violates one's ideas of housewifery utility', while recognising that there are other questions to ponder around such an unusual home.[59] She enjoys a chat about Scott busts with the old lady and is amused, not threatened, by her 'regard for the old laird scarcely less than idolatry'.[60] Moreover she remembers 'Scot's only surviving daughter' – properly, his granddaughter.[61] She even takes a certain wry pleasure in hearing the old lady repeat the same speeches to the next tour – and thus eject successive groups from their 'unique' proximity to Walter Scott at home.[62] For Stowe, Abbotsford wasn't about her.

The gendered problem of Scott's Abbotsford, then, is in ourselves. Whether as needy visitors or as biographers focused on the great man, 'ideas are what we project', as Leo Stein has it and, by contrast, '[things] are what we encounter'.[63] In projecting our idea of ourselves across and through the fictions of Abbotsford, in making ourselves at home, its women cannot simply be at home. They are what we encounter as we seek our singular and constructive communion with a spirit in its place. Consequently they strike us and strike against us, in Bill Brown's terms, like things.[64] But if there is a negative – they must be made foreign, or fade into the woodwork – there is also a positive.

Biographers have praised Scott's touch with common men like Tom Purdie (the erstwhile poacher, turned Scott's shepherd and then forester) or Dalgleish the butler. These functionaries visibly supported the myth of Walter Scott as 'the healthiest of men', and visitors' participation in Scotland's literary mystique as the land of the heather and the deer.[65] At the same time, biographers have ignored the daily operations of Scott's household to the degree that their readers might wonder who, at Abbotsford, did the dusting.[66] But Scott himself frequently participated in domestic discussions, and reports them in his letters. In February 1818, for instance, he discusses the need for a housemaid 'to look to scrupulous cleanliness within doors, and employ her leisure in spinning, or plain-work . . . she would be expected to cook a little in a plain way, and play maid of all work . . . she would assist the housemaid and superintend the laundry'.[67] Abbotsford's women domestics were essential, and thoroughly integrated in a cross-class community that in fact allowed the illusion of direct access to Walter Scott.[68]

If, cued by Derrida, we shift our focus from the narrative of great men at Abbotsford, and from outsider anxieties, we see a complex picture. We see women in their own space, and, at the least, as mutually foreign with those who aim to supplant them. Son-in-law Lockhart eventually came to rest at Scott's feet, as close as Charlotte Scott, in the family's Dryburgh Abbey grave plot. And not surprisingly, given the competition for positioning around even the remains of Walter Scott, in the moments after the author's death Lockhart quarrelled with William Laidlaw, a failed farmer and latterly Scott's steward, when Laidlaw wanted to publish his reminiscences of the author in potential competition with Lockhart's *Life*.[69] Thus Lockhart's stories of the great and the good circulated from 1837, while Laidlaw's 'Abbotsford Notanda' did not appear until thirty-two years later. These banished stories translate what has been expelled as foreign back into the familiar, and reveal the strangeness of what we take for granted. Here we find Scott's care for his workers and even instructions to the maids: 'I think of my books amongst this snow-storm; also of the birds, and not a little of the poor. For the benefit of the former I hope Peggy throws out the crumbs.'[70] We glean hints of how Scott's family supported the circulation of visitors. Whereas the traditional narrative focuses on Scott's remarkable availability to his guests, Laidlaw shows that the burden fell on the household. When Lady Byron visits, 'Miss Anne Scott and Lady Byron rode to Newark'.[71] And we hear of the behind-the-scenes adjustments to Scott's financial losses of 1826: in a letter to Laidlaw that Lockhart does not quote, Scott mentions that 'I must keep Peter and the horses for Lady Scott's sake, though I make sacrifices in my own [case]'.[72]

A peek into letters between women and across classes proves even more enlightening.[73] Published sixty-eight years after Lockhart's authoritative volumes, letters between the governess Miss Millar and her charges Sophia and Anne hint at a quite different social network without which Lockhart's would have collapsed. Mrs Scott asks Miss Millar to tell the cook about the next week's guests, but also to let her know that Charlotte has done a lot of the shopping already.[74] Charlotte jokes about encouraging the male inside help to clean the plate stands. When Miss Millar leaves, the whole family stays in touch, enquiring about her new pupils, asking her to visit time and again, and supporting her when she is job hunting once more.[75]

Networks also overlap. Sophia and Anne tell of their escapades, and it is thus that we see them on excursions along with everyone else – on the one hand, restricted from visiting Rob Roy's cave because of the lack of accommodation other than an ale house, but on the other, striding out across the Largs battlefield where the Scots met the Danes.[76] When Sophia rejoices in the gift of a boat for Caulshields Loch, we recognise that 'home' is not, in fact, divorced from the outside.[77] The girls place themselves differently than we might expect at Abbotsford, as well: Sophia gleefully, and not without irony, tells that with Abbotsford advancing in construction, 'We spend most of our time in airing ourselves upon the top, and I think it will be wonderful if it is finished without any of us breaking our necks.'[78] When she wearily steps in to thank Miss Millar for a gift of fish, acknowledging that she has 'witnessed the destruction of three different epistles of Anne's by the hand of the fair authoress', family dynamics and inner character show richly layered variability, making a nonsense of the 'foreign' and the 'familiar'.[79] Girls who are cyphers even for Lockhart, and impediments to Scott's admirers, spring into rich, connected life.

Importantly, this complex, supportive network trends towards the critical. Scott, in fact, taught his children how. The author who celebrated strong female characters such as Jeanie Deans, Di Vernon and Rebecca took time for his daughters.[80] Thus Miss Millar's letters include one from 1810 that lays out an interactive history lesson for Sophia. She is tasked to list kings, assess their reign as peaceful or warlike, note their governmental strategies, assess their goodness, and determine for each 'Whether the condition of his subjects was amended or became worse under his reign.'[81] So when Sophia later reports that 'our poor house has been honoured by a visit of his Royal Highness Prince Leopold', she takes a view at once literary, political, domestic and acerbic. The visit is, comically, 'as great an event . . . as Lady Margaret's dejeune at Tiltetudelum' (either a misspelling or a double joke upon Tillietudlem in *Old Mortality*).[82] With all Scotts present at the prince's visit of form to Selkirk, he promptly invited himself to tea for 'it would be impossible for him to leave Scotland without seeing Mr. Scott in his own house'.[83] Scott recounts Charlotte's 'scream' of 'What have we to offer him?' and her despairing cry at his suggestion of 'Wine and Cake': 'Cake!!! Where am I to get cake.' He rejoices in the humour – and the success – of her 'domiciliary search for cold meat through the whole city of Selkirk which produced *one shoulder of cold lamb*'.[84] 'Figure', Sophia declares, 'the dismay of the female part of our family'.[85] And yet, the prince was fed, was pleased and departed. In an event that ironised both host and guest, honour was upheld, but not, by the women, uncriticised.

Not surprisingly, whatever the foibles of his many satellites, the author who spent time with his daughters and cultivated their intellects appreciated and celebrated all the womenfolk of Abbotsford. When he found that Charlotte and the girls had been tricked into hospitality to two wandering young men without the appropriate introductory letters, he and Charlotte turned into an efficient and humorous team to eject the intruders. 'Mrs Scott', Lockhart remembers:

> was a sharp observer; and she, before a minute had elapsed, interrupted the ecstatic compliments of the strangers, by reminding them that her husband would be glad to have the letters of the friends who had been so good as to write by them . . . there were no letters to be produced; – and Scott, signifying that his hour for dinner approached, added, that as he supposed they meant to walk to Melrose, he could not trespass further on their time.[86]

On their departure, Scott jokes about his house turning into an inn. In telling terms, he ponders a signpost, and positions himself not at home but as mine host: 'no traveller of respectability could ever be at a loss for such an introduction as would ensure his best hospitality'.[87] And against the undue hospitality sought by the invading horde, he throws up the barrier of homely intimacy shared with his wife. He laughs: 'Hang the Yahoos, Charlotte – but we should have bid them stay dinner.'

While biographers have been keen to denigrate, distance and disconnect Charlotte from their hero, even terming her a 'blackamoor' – a Victorian slur against her origins as well as her looks – and as Scott's second choice for a wife, Scott consistently shows his respect, value and love for her.[88] Alison Lumsden has found traces of Charlotte's hand in Scott's manuscripts,[89] and his letters are full of their shared stories, marked by an appreciation of a marital communion founded in strangeness. Whether entertaining princes through creative housekeeping, wading through floodwaters after a sightseeing expedition to the Falls of Clyde, showing as 'the best *lady-whip* in Edinburgh', standing against Britain's casual cruelty to animals, or resisting writing in English, Charlotte was a source of Scott's domestic pride.[90] When she is gone, and he sits at work, 'The solitude seemd so absolute – my poor Charlotte would have been in the [room] half a score of times to see if the fire burnd and to ask a hundred kind questions.'[91] He remembers her efficient and excellent housekeeping, her human sympathy and their shared discussions of an evening – the daily communication and support of their life together that enabled his public roles and constituted his private joys.[92]

Nor does Scott forget his daughters, nor find them obtrusive. In 1809, we find Scott soliciting music to support 'my little girl' and her interest in song.[93] Subsequently, Irving noted that a seventeen-year-old Sophia sang at her father's request: 'She never waited to be asked twice, but complied frankly and cheerfully.'[94] With Sophia gone, Anne takes on the role, at some cost to herself. 'Anne is practicing Scots Songs', Scott writes. This 'I take as a kind compliment to my own taste as hers leads her chiefly to foreign music. I think the good girl sees that I want and must miss her sister's peculiar talent in singing the airs of our native country ... and so if she puts a constraint on herself for my sake, I can only say in requital God Bless Her.'[95] So if Susan Ferrier did not appreciate the singing that characterised Scott's hospitality, within the family it represented respect and generosity. As family these 'foreigners', whether from France or as female, were at home at Abbotsford. Indeed, by their intimacy yet difference they constituted a level of protection between Scott and those who sought to find him uniquely accessible at home.

Their generosity, however mocked, allowed the hospitality and facilitated the proximity that visitors sought to Scott. Irving was enchanted by the manner in which Scott's young family supported his visitors and he recognised that they had the potential to weave those visitors into a more intimate relation with the author. With 'no one present, but the family', young Charles is enlisted to show him over Melrose Abbey, while Sophia reveals the intimacy that 'papa shed a few tears when poor Camp [the dog] died'.[96] When Charlotte is on her death bed, Anne acknowledges to Miss Millar that 'we have had so many people here, that I have never had a moment's time to myself, particularly as Mamma has not been very well, and had to keep her own room a good deal, so all the trouble of entertaining visitors has fallen on me'.[97] She concludes with an excuse for her haste: 'I have written this in a great hurry, as I must go to play the agreeable to Lady Ravensworth.'[98] Anne, that is, participated in a family strategy that managed what Derrida warns against as the parasitism of visitation;[99] rather than belonging inside or outside, Scott's family negotiate the space between on the author's behalf.

Yet if Scott recognised the human generosity of his womenfolk's contribution to the family industry, allowing all and sundry the illusion of access to the great man, he also appreciated them for their difference and the very disruption they constituted within that access – the foreignness they figured that critiqued the notion of home as shrine to authorship. In *The Antiquary*, Jonathan Oldbuck is outraged by the intrusion of women with dusters (both niece and maid), into his sanctum: 'I assure you', he tells his guest, 'that the last inroad of these pretended friends to cleanliness was almost ... fatal to my collection'.[100] However 'Amid this medley [of books and antiquarian trumpery], it was no easy matter to find one's way to a chair, without stumbling over a prostrate folio ... or ... overturning some piece of Roman or ancient British pottery.' Women intrude, but they facilitate; in facilitating, they obtrude. But Oldbuck's study, a place of delusion as much as of enlightenment, could use a bit of practical disruption. Similarly, when Captain Clutterbuck encounters the 'Eidolon, or Representation, of the Author of Waverley', it retells the story of the cookmaid who used antiquarian folios to clean pots and light fires. The cook's depredations, however, have actually increased the value of those 'greasy and blackened fragments . . . which were not totally destroyed'.[101] So it is with the women of Abbotsford.

While descriptions of Scott at Abbotsford are more likely to celebrate his dogs than his daughters, it is the women of the house who have contributed most to visitors' experience in the past, and who also help to understand it most. Dogs do not disturb what Lawrence Grossberg calls the 'mattering maps' that help us position ourselves in the world; they are more likely to situate us, as he says, 'temporarily . . . at home'.[102] Women – and women have facilitated access to Abbotsford since Scott's day in an almost unbroken line of female descent – point to the author's other relations.[103] Whether in the person of that fascinating Frenchwoman, Charlotte Charpentier, her annoyingly musical or satiric daughters, or that haunting granddaughter with her London money, the women of the house unbind the links of sentimental sympathy between author and visitor. They disrupt the visiting identity as it attempts formation through a selective act of cultural memory at Abbotsford.

Hawthorne worried that the spirit of a great man and the tread of his followers take 'hearth and hall away from the nominal possessors' of an author's house.[104] Perhaps he need not have worried so much. Watching visitors' resistance to the female presences at Abbotsford gives us those women's unique gift: the gift of questioning our own positioning, our own assumptions, our own identities in formation. If Scott notoriously did not like a 'literary picnic', refusing the editorial intrusions of his male coterie in his later life, the author who joked about a 'joint-stock company' for novel production actually embraced such a relation with his wife and daughters.[105] Abbotsford may be, as some have suggested, a 'fiction'.[106] In that case, Scott's wife and daughters are surely its co-authors. And if 'ideas are what we project' but 'things are what we encounter',[107] in our encounter with these women who we would rather elide or eject, they author us, as visitors, too. Towards visitors' selective and exclusionary acts of cultural memory they stand, inevitably, as contradiction and critique. If we are pilgrims, they show that we are also problems to ourselves. Ever seeking a meeting with ourselves through association with a person and a place, we are ever tripping over the narrower relations of our hero in all the intimacy of home. We 'foreigners' can never be quite at home; Abbotsford is too strange a place for that. The anonymous 'wife' or 'party' numbered in the guest books might appreciate the irony.

Notes

1. Julia Thomas, *Shakespeare's Shrine*, pp. 15–17.
2. Walpole wrote: 'I keep an inn: the sign; "the Gothic Castle" . . . my whole time is passed in giving tickets for seeing it and hiding myself while it is seen' (Marion Harney, *Place-making for the Imagination*, pp. 18–19).
3. W. S. Crockett, *Abbotsford*, pp. 44, 51.
4. Letter to Miss Smith, 13 February 1814, *Letters* 3: 411.
5. Letter to John Richardson, 22 September 1817, *Letters* 4: 532.
6. *Letters* 5: 187, n.
7. David Douglas, *Familiar Letters of Sir Walter Scott*, 2: 24–5, n. The Massachusetts Everett (twenty-four at the time of his visit) was a Unitarian minister and Professor of Greek at Harvard. He became Ambassador to Britain, President of Harvard, Governor of Massachusetts, Secretary of State and Senator. He was introduced by William Gifford, editor at the *Quarterly*.
8. *Letters* 5: 377.
9. Thomas Carlyle, Review, pp. 327–30; Horace Smith, 'A Graybeard's Gossip about his Literary Acquaintances', p. 298.
10. Lawrence Grossberg, 'Is there a Fan in the House?', p. 55.
11. Ibid. pp. 57, 60.
12. Jacques Derrida, *Of Hospitality*, p. 35.
13. Ibid. pp. 51–2.
14. Ibid. p. 55.
15. Horace Smith, 'A Graybeard's Gossip', p. 294. Smith remembers an 1827 tour of Abbotsford.
16. Sarah Stickney Ellis, *The Women of England*; Coventry Patmore, *The Angel in the House*.
17. Derrida, *Of Hospitality*, p. 61.
18. Left to right, *seated*: Thomas Thomson, James Ballantyne, Archibald Constable, Thomas Campbell, Tom Moore, Sir Adam Fergusson, Francis Jeffrey, William Wordsworth, John Gibson Lockhart, George Crabbe, Henry Mackenzie, Walter Scott, James Hogg; *standing*: Humphrey Davy, David Wilkie, William Allan, John Wilson and the urn Byron gifted to Scott.
19. Robert Mayer, *Walter Scott and Fame*, pp. 75–89.
20. See Douglas S. Mack, ed., *James Hogg*, pp. xii–xvi.
21. Lockhart, *Life*, 5: 8–11.
22. Alison Booth, *Homes and Haunts*, p. 170.

23. Lockhart, *Life*, 5: 10.
24. Ibid. 5: 7–11.
25. Ibid. 5: 12.
26. Walter Scott, *The Lay of the Last Minstrel*, canto 1: 1, 11.
27. Lockhart, *Life*, 5: 1–2. Lockhart is not quite correct, though, that every guest would have known of Scott's authorship of the Waverley Novels.
28. Valentina Bold questions the story's authenticity, calling it 'defamatory': Valentina Bold, *James Hogg*, p. 73; Douglas Mack questions Lockhart's reporting of a distant event (Mack, ed., *James Hogg*, p. xvii). Hogg, however, wrote a letter of apology dated 24 December 1803 (Lockhart, *Life*, 1: 408–11).
29. Fiona Robertson, *Lives of the Great Romantics II*, 3: 47.
30. Quoted in W. E. K. Anderson, ed., *The Journal of Sir Walter Scott*, p. xxxix and fn 1.
31. Ibid.
32. Ibid. p. xli and fn 3.
33. The guest book signature is for 5 November 1856.
34. Hershel Parker, *Herman Melville*, p. 297.
35. Paul Westover, 'The Transatlantic Home Network', pp. 156–8. Notably, Cooper, as consul at Lyon, helped to trace Charlotte Charpentier's family tree in defence of her legitimacy. *Letters* 11: 8–9; and NLS MS 1846, f. 37–8, MS 3905 24–5.
36. Abbotsford Visitor Book, 1873–5, entry for 8 August 1873. Mark Twain, *Life on the Mississippi*, chapter 46.
37. Paul Westover, 'The Transatlantic Home Network', chapter 7.
38. Nathaniel Hawthorne, *Passages from the English Note-Books*, 2: 46.
39. Ibid. 2: 48.
40. Ibid. 2: 52.
41. Ibid. 2: 295.
42. David Jenkins and Mark Visocchi, *Mendelssohn in Scotland*, p. 57.
43. Ibid. pp. 58–9.
44. Hawthorne, *Passages from the English Note-Books*, 1: 44.
45. Ibid. 2: 295.
46. Jenkins and Visocchi, *Mendelssohn in Scotland*, p. 57.
47. See R. F. Butler, 'Maria Edgeworth and Sir Walter Scott: Unpublished Letters, 1823', p, 35. Maria Edgeworth letter, dd. 24 June 1823.
48. Joanna Baillie, *Collected Letters*, 1: 282–3.
49. Given in W. S. Crockett, *Abbotsford*, p. 67.
50. Robertson, *Lives of the Great Romantics II*, p. 351; Susan Ferrier, *Memoir and Correspondence of Susan Ferrier, 1782–1854*, p. 240.
51. William Wells Brown, *Three Years in Europe*, p. 189.
52. Ibid. pp. 191–2.
53. Charlotte Scott, daughter of Sophia and Lockhart, was born in 1828. She married James Hope in 1847 and would have been twenty-three at the time of Wells's visit.

54. William Wells Brown, *Three Years in Europe*, p. 190.
55. Catharine E. Beecher and Harriet Beecher Stowe, *The American Woman's Home*.
56. Harriet Beecher Stowe, *Sunny Memories of Foreign Lands*, 1: 49.
57. See for instance Tom Nairn, 'The Three Dreams of Scottish Nationalism'.
58. Stowe, *Sunny Memories of Foreign Lands*, 1: 131.
59. Ibid. 1: 133.
60. Ibid. 1: 134.
61. Ibid. 1: 135.
62. Ibid.
63. Quoted by Bill Brown, 'Thing Theory', p. 3.
64. Ibid. pp. 3–4.
65. Carlyle, Review, p. 305.
66. Crockett lists off William Laidlaw, Tom Purdie, John Usher and Peter Mathieson the coachman with no hesitation, noting (significantly) that they provide 'the most perfect pen-portraits in Lockhart' (Crockett, *Abbotsford*, p. 65).
67. Scott, *Letters* 5: 72.
68. Scott, *Journal*, p. 133.
69. See Major Scott's (Scott's son Walter) letter to Robert Cadell (Scott's publisher) 29 July 1833, NLS MS 21003, f. 164–5.
70. William Laidlaw, 'Abbotsford Notanda', p. 589. The magazine's introduction to Laidlaw's materials (edited by R. C. – Robert Chambers – focuses on his recognition by Scott, and others' recognition of Scott in the form of agricultural products relevant to Laidlaw's work as steward: 'The Duke of Buccleuch sent bushels of acorns; the Earl of Fife presented seed of Norway pines; Lord Montagu forwarded a box of acorns and a packet of lime seed' [p. 587]).
71. Ibid. p. 592.
72. Ibid. p. 681. In Lockhart, this letter appears only by reference in a quotation from Scott's *Journal*: 'Wrote to Laidlaw, directing him to make all preparations for reduction.' Some editions that follow the 'Abbotsford Notanda' quote briefly from its appearance there. *Memoirs of the Life of Sir Walter Scott*. 5 vols (Boston: Houghton Mifflin, 1901); 4: 451 and fn 1.
73. For example: John Wilkins, *Letters Hitherto Unpublished*.
74. Ibid. p. 39.
75. Ibid. pp. 40, 47, 51, 82, 101.
76. Ibid. pp. 41–2.
77. Ibid.
78. Ibid. p. 42.
79. Ibid. p. 57.
80. See Scott's *The Heart of Mid-Lothian* (1818), *Rob Roy* (published 1817, dated 1818) and *Ivanhoe* (published 1819, dated 1820).
81. Wilkins, *Letters Hitherto Unpublished*, pp. 37–8.
82. Ibid. p. 60.

83. Ibid. pp. 62–3.
84. Scott, *Letters* 5: 505.
85. Wilkins, *Letters Hitherto Unpublished*, p. 62.
86. Lockhart, *Life*, 4: 200–1.
87. Ibid.
88. William Howitt, *Homes and Haunts of the Most Eminent British Poets* (4th edn), at first characterises her as Scott's 'charming young wife', but describing his encounter with her portrait actually at Abbotsford, erupts: 'Oh! Such a round-faced little blackamoor of a woman! One instantly asks – where was Sir Walter's taste? Where was the judgment which guided him in describing Di Vernon' (pp. 454, 477).
89. See Alison Lumsden, in this volume.
90. Scott, *Letters* 1: 382; 9: 43; 1: 189; 2: 90.
91. Scott, *Journal*, p. 172.
92. Ibid. pp. 186, 178, 305.
93. Scott, *Letters* 2: 227.
94. Robertson, *Lives of the Great Romantics II*, p. 146.
95. Scott, *Journal*, pp. 35–6.
96. Robertson, *Lives of the Great Romantics II*, pp. 127–8, 137.
97. Wilkins, *Letters Hitherto Unpublished*, pp. 108–9.
98. Ibid. p. 114.
99. Derrida, *Of Hospitality*, p. 61.
100. Scott, *The Antiquary*, p. 21.
101. Scott, *The Fortunes of Nigel*, pp. 11–12.
102. Grossberg, 'Is there a Fan in the House?', p. 60.
103. Scott's immediate heir, Walter, remained in the army. After him the line is female, with the exception of Mary Monica Maxwell-Scott's son, Walter, who was succeeded by Dame Jean (1923–2004) and Lady Patricia (1921–1998), the last Scott descendants to occupy the house.
104. Hawthorne, *Passages from the English Note-Books*, 2: 295.
105. Walter Scott, 'Introduction' (1831), *Chronicles of the Canongate* (Waverley Novels New Edition, 1832), p. xxxi; 'Introduction', *The Betrothed* (1825), pp. 3–11.
106. Nicola Watson, *The Literary Tourist*, pp. 94–101, esp. 101.
107. Leo Stein, qtd in Brown, 'Thing Theory', p. 3.

9

Reading Walter Scott in the Anthropocene

Susan Oliver

To say that Walter Scott speaks meaningfully to a twenty-first-century anthropogenic world defined by accelerating climate change, species loss, plastic pollution and human migration is a bold claim. Scott published between 1799–1831, mainly about Scotland, although with some attention to a wider Britain, Europe, North America and Asia.[1] Nuclear technology was more than a century in the future. Plastic as a synthetic polymer substance was not invented until 1907, seventy-five years after Scott's death, although James Watt's improvements that made the steam engine industrially viable and kick-started the carbon economy of modern times occurred during his childhood. I will show in this chapter how Scott's relevance to the environmental crises of the twenty-first century can be understood through an ecocritical approach to ways in which his poems, fiction and non-fiction addressed species loss resulting from two of the most known and connected events in Scottish history: that is, the agro-economic drive for 'improvement' in land management practices, and the clearances that decimated human populations across large areas of rural Scotland. Scott critiqued farming practices and programmes such as deforestation that have been active contributors to the Anthropocene.

The shepherds, drovers, small farmers, Highland clansmen, fisher-folk, itinerant beggars and gypsies who are some of the most interesting and popular characters in the Waverley Novels and Scott's short stories struggle to survive in a nation that was either heading towards or going through 'improvement' and clearance. Alongside those characters and the animals and plants with which many of them are directly associated, a vibrant network of other flora and fauna that teems in Scott's writing also fought for survival. Together these human and non-human witnesses, often victims, of violence against the land and those who live on it raise multiple questions of environmental and ecological justice, land ethics and bio-politics. Scott provides us with an important if constrained narrative of extirpation and extinction that resulted from forms of clearance that took place in and beyond the Highlands and the long eighteenth and early nineteenth centuries. His altered habitats include rivers with fewer fish, mountains that stand silent apart from the wind, meadows without wildflowers and river valleys without trees, all of which question the conventional separation of human and non-human interests. Set against these depleted environments, sheep do well as the predominant species, helped along by the human provision of food and interventive control of predators. Even particular groups of people, notably the rural poor, lose their habitats to sheep.

Scott repeatedly draws attention to the land as a vast site of cultural memory precisely because of its ecological vibrancy. To that extent, he identifies the ethical concept of a 'biotic community' comprising interdependent parts, more than a century before that term was introduced into popular use by Aldo Leopold in *A Sand County Almanac and Sketches Here and There*.[2] More recently, revisiting Lawrence Buell's well-established questioning of 'what sort of literature remains possible if we relinquish the myth of human apartness?', the journal *English Studies* devoted a special number to ecocriticism's revision of narrative theory.[3] One of the forward-looking implications to be taken from these recent studies is that ecocritical approaches to Scott need to take account of how memory studies extend beyond the human.

The effects of the losses and extinctions that Scott documents, together with coincidental declines in bird and animal populations that we know about from scientific studies, result from changes in land use that continue to define a Scotland that exists in the popular cultural imaginary in our own time. Damaged environments, the absence caused by population and species loss, and re-made, consumer-oriented, aesthetically pleasing landscapes all reflect as well as continue to create cultural meaning. It hardly needs to be said here that the wildness of the Borders, Highlands and islands is almost never what it might seem. Thomas Devine has recently suggested the term 'derelict landscape' as a more appropriate descriptor than 'wilderness' for these cleared places.[4] William Cronon's analysis of aesthetic constructions of wildness and wilderness provides a transnational, temporal and aesthetic framework that necessitates a reappraisal of Scott's use of 'wild' settings.[5]

Why Ecocriticism?

Ecocriticism has never been a singular form of enquiry. Instead, it comprises a network of strategies for interpretation in which dialogues and responses, sometimes antagonistic, mimic those that occur in organic communities. Ecocriticism, then, comprises a kind of ecology of theories. While some approaches are more compatible than others, even disagreement contributes to an energy that impels thinking forward. Scott provides a model for ecocritical enquiry not least because of the extent to which he draws attention to the interdependence of people, other living things and place. Until recently, criticism focused mostly on the human themes in his writing. Scott's innovation and onward influence in putting representative, ordinary people into the foreground of historical fiction has been acknowledged since Georg Lukác's groundbreaking publication in 1937 of *The Historical Novel*. Beyond human concerns, however, the attention that Scott drew to the predicaments facing a wider world of vital but endangered ecologies needs more recognition, since it establishes him as a precursor of, as well as someone whose writing is more latterly illuminated by, ecological theories.

How, then, can contemporary ecocriticism connect with, rather than work against, the substantial body of valuable enquiry into Scott's works that already exists? Lukács remains pivotal, because of his onward influence on critical approaches. His Marxist humanist repositioning of Scott generated a rigorous reappraisal of attention, mainly focused on the Waverley Novels, to subsistence economies that exist at or beyond the edge of communities. This focus on marginality and exclusion took Scott studies towards the ecocritical field of environmental justice before that term was in popular use. Questions asked include how, why and with what consequences the poorest people and most vulnerable biotic communities find themselves living on the most damaged, unstable land.[6]

Devine's *The Scottish Clearances* examines the 'sheep frontier' (a term which more than hints at mythmaking and analogises the pioneer transformation of the American West) as a key catalyst for the dispossession and movement of people from the rural Borders and Lowlands as well as the more written-about Highlands. Seen in this wider geographical and temporal framework, clearance takes many forms including coercion and historically spans 1600–1900. The first two of those centuries are the years in which most of Scott's fiction is set, although some of his works take their narratives forward into the early 1800s. Devine argues that the Sutherland clearances, for their systematic destruction and relocation of Highland villages along with their attempts to find alternative work for a redundant labour force, amounted to an exceptional act of social engineering.[7] Fredrik Albritton Jonsson's interdisciplinary scientific and literary exploration shows how those and the similarly impactful Argyll clearances were also prime examples of ecological engineering that drove non-human species to the point of extinction. Jonsson cites a memorandum to the Countess of Sutherland that urged her to 'extirpate' foxes and eagles, claiming these species had already been 'driven from other counties'.[8] The basis for Hugh Rose's recommendation was that 'A great part of Sutherland is well calculated for feeding moderate stocks of sheep', providing predators could be eliminated.

If we look at the overwhelming shift from cattle to sheep in Scottish livestock farming during the eighteenth and nineteenth centuries (the southwestern Lowlands, where cattle farming has remained dominant, are an exception), along with the extirpation of designated 'nuisance' species such as raptors and larger predatory mammals, changes in grass varieties, flora and tree species, the conclusion must be that improvement and clearance amounted to a strategic restructuring of the nation's ecologies. Scott's *The Heart of Mid-Lothian* (1818) includes a substantial account of the Duke of Argyll's estate, his native and non-native livestock breeds and the combination of cultivated and wild food that is available for local people. At one level, the Duke of Argyll, as well as Jeannie Deans, who persuades him to keep farming native domestic cattle (the old Ayrshire breed), and the residents of Knocktarlitie contribute to a model of sustainable farming and foraging. To that extent, Scott's fictional narrative prefigures codes of practice for responsible farming, employment and recognising local culture that are generally welcomed in the twenty-first century. Moreover, food security is a key focus of environmental justice, as is the provision of 'decent work' that is now a Sustainable Development Goal of the United Nations.[9] At another level, the enlightened depiction of farming and employment in *The Heart of Mid-Lothian* constitutes a warning when read in the wider context of the novel's period of publication through to the present day. Its apparent benevolence ignores the silent catastrophe suffered by species whose existence obstructs land management policies designed to maximise food production and other animal products along with providing rural leisure pursuits. In this instance, markedly contrasting with others that I shall discuss, Scott does not comment on strategies that would result in an example of ecophobic species reduction.[10]

Migration to North America, particularly in the nineteenth century, has been well written about as a key consequence of clearance. What was effectively an exchange of people for trees amounted to a major transatlantic trade, in which emigrant Scots provided the labour in a North American lumber industry that exported vast quantities of timber to Britain.[11] Meanwhile in Scotland, the relocation of communities to existing and new coastal villages where the inhabitants were expected to contribute to a growing fishing industry (particularly the herring trade) led to other economic and environmental problems. The clearances and the ideology of improvement that led to them, then, raise major questions where environmental and ecological justice is concerned. They also require a critical reappraisal of the aesthetic integrity pertaining to a post-clearance landscape, which had been created to maximise profit from modern farming and from leisure and tourism industries.

Returning to Scott criticism, the sociological nature of much work until recently was shaped by theories that emerged in the last decades of a twentieth century during which social mobility, protest movements, political oppression, the displacement of people for reasons of war and economic change, and the need to confront poverty were major local and global concerns. In different circumstances, these issues all pertained to the nation undergoing improvement and clearance that we find in Scott's published work. Significantly for my enquiry here, another theory cluster was coming into the foreground during the 1990s that likewise connects with Scotland. I refer to the interdisciplinary, scientifically grounded theory of a new Anthropocene epoch, according to which the years of Scott's lifetime, 1771–1832, and the middle to late years of the twentieth century are particularly 'hot' or decisive moments because of world-changing technological developments. As I shall go on to show, a much older Scotland that dates back to the early Neolithic period features in the argument for an earlier start to that new epoch. Scott's writing could not have anticipated the nuclear arms race, global climate change, or that synthetic substances including the already mentioned plastic would be found on every part of the planet and inside a frighteningly large number of life forms by the time this chapter is published.

In our twenty-first century, faced with species loss that might soon include human beings, the next step in interpreting Scott has to be the interrogation of how centralised and edge economies impacted the non-human life forms in his writing, to the point where that life becomes notably damaged or exterminated. After all, history and its manifestation in the form of literature discloses precedent as a warning, requiring us to think about how we did not see today's problems coming.

Rob Nixon's well-recognised theories of slow violence and the environmentalism of the global poor show how capitalism has commoditised time and place, accelerating first-world lifestyle rhythms to a dizzying pace that makes it difficult or impossible for economically successful individuals and social groups to recognise acts of violence that are not spectacular or that are remote enough to be out of sight.[12] People who think and speak using a vocabulary of fast gain pass by the slower-paced poorest workers and never-will-haves (Nixon's phrase) without seeing their predicament and without understanding the global impact of the damaged environments in which poverty is grounded. Slow violence on the one hand and spectacular moments of historical viciousness on the other both have a prominent place in many, indeed most of Scott's best-known works, so are made visible. The ballad 'Lord Soulis' in the *Minstrelsy of the Scottish Border* (1802) records how, centuries after an incident of torture, plants do not grow in lead-poisoned soil despite the blood and bone meal that would normally boost growth;[13] in *Old Mortality* (1816) the luxuriance of trees, grass and wildflowers continues to make visible a burial site of bodies, following a massacre of fugitive Covenanters during the 'Killing time'.[14] In the early Reformation novel *The Monastery* (1820), the distinction between people and trees is remarkable when a monk is unsure whether he sees the spectre of a dead woman or the decaying relic of a birch tree as he makes his way home during a misty night along a river valley where murders have historically taken place and where birches were, by Scott's lifetime, notably rare. The point here is not just the monk's comedic credulity, but the fact that the tree is a ghost in any case – a decaying remnant of the region's lost woodland. Scott situates this incident shortly after his interpolated disquisition on historic township farming practices, reminding his readers that the improved farmland around Melrose is also haunted by visible earthwork remains from old fields.[15] Ecogothic, with its focus on environmental haunting and ecohorror, provides a useful theoretical framework for exploring these poems and novels.[16] Storytelling in a Gothic mode is a powerful medium by which Scott raises questions about real-life ecological problems that resonate into our own Anthropocene age. *Waverley*'s devastating account of a post-Culloden Scotland cleared of clan society and trees, and converted to sheep pasture, is an obvious example that I will deal with shortly. Indeed, in 1814 this first of his novels explicitly establishes a principle that is fundamental to everything that he wrote: that those who really know a place can see environmental damage in the form of absence, even when the evidence has been systematically erased:

> Not only had the felled trees been removed, but, their stumps being grubbed up, and the earth round them leveled and sown with grass, it was evident that the marks of devastation, unless to an eye intimately acquainted with the spot, were already totally obliterated.[17]

Nothing haunts a landscape more profoundly than the absence created by human departure coupled with species loss. Scott's point here is that obliteration is deliberate, so that only those 'acquainted with' what existed previously can be fully aware of such a haunting. *Waverley* ends with a view of a newly created garden and redesigned estate in Perthshire, on the border between the Lowlands and Highlands. The vista is of grass. Tully-Veolan's lawn and parkland clearly analogises an improved Scotland in which old mixed farming had given way to extensive monocultural pasturage for sheep. Edward Waverley and Rose Bradwardine's wedding doubles as a funeral for an older Highland way of life and all the people and species that went with it, at least as much as does the excessively violent execution of clan chieftain Fergus Mac-Ivor and his lieutenant Evan Dhu Maccombich. The black cattle that Fergus Mac-Ivor's cateran clansmen stole at the beginning of the story are gone, along with the clan itself. Sheep in large numbers are all that is needed to complete the picture.[18]

Interdisciplinary Theories

Although the clearances that took place in the Highlands during the late eighteenth and nineteenth centuries are probably the most commonly recognised demographically transformative event in modern Scottish history, that does not mean they are the best understood in terms of their impact on ecologies. That the managed removal of people who were regarded as surplus to the needs of commercial land use involved concomitant violence against non-human species cannot be disregarded. Understanding the nature of that violence is helped by theories, including environmental victimology, that explore the interaction of people, animals and plants. Eco-criminologist Rob White explains the tensions as well as the interrelatedness that are revealed when theory addresses damage that is both social in its human context and ecological because extending to habitats and non-human species. The categories for enquiry that White identifies are environmental justice (human and social), ecological justice (habitats and environments) and species justice (concerned with particular animals and plants).[19] Taking Scott as a writer who demonstrates each of those related areas, I will now show some of the ways in which his tales of specific acts of ecological violence, including instances of ecocide, are instructive for twenty-first-century readers when read within an analytical framework that looks beyond Scotland to include 'glocal' and archipelagic theory as well as Anthropocene studies. The inter- and transdisciplinary compass of ecocriticism is paramount here, since these enquiries draw on investigations in green sociology, environmental criminology, biogeographical history and environmental paleontology as well as literary environmental criticism.

Glocal theory as defined by sociologist Roland Robertson and eco-critic Ursula Heise, requires local and global conditions to be interpreted in terms of mutual impact. That impact, in turn, emphasises local resistance to national or centrally administered forms of power. Glocal studies shows how deep ecological, local knowledge enhances rather than occludes awareness of global problems.[20] It follows that local environmental consciousness is often seen as in need of suppression by central political power because of its disruptive tendencies. Species with the propensity for 'bad behaviour', including occupying space that could otherwise be used profitably, are labelled predators, vermin, pests, weeds or just non-contributors. The regulation of rural Scotland during improvement and the clearances, through the control of species that included people with no work, was coterminous with the rapid period of expansion of the British Empire and therefore was glocal in its context. Many Scots left their nation as soldiers or to seek fortunes as part of Britain's colonial and imperial expansion. Serjeant More MacAlpin in the frame narrative of *A Legend of the Wars of Montrose* (1819), a figure to whom I shall return towards the end of this chapter, and Guy Mannering in the novel of that name (1815) return 'home' to a dramatically changed nation, each providing an account of transformation that is ecological as well as sociological.

Environmentalism that runs alongside and in critical counterpoint to the wealth-generating objectives of colonial and imperial politics can also be approached through archipelagic theory. Such a method fundamentally reconfigures how land and its ecologies are imagined, replacing conceptualised national and centrally organised international landmasses with vibrant assemblages and networked communities. Scotland is surrounded by sea on all except one of its borders (that with England) and includes more than 790 offshore islands. Therefore, it is archipelagic in a conventional sense. But Brian Roberts and Michelle Stephens have shown how thinking archipelagically does not need to involve actual islands and is more expansively a way to understanding how human relations with material geographies connect to encircle the planet.[21] George B. Handley argues that these alternative human and biogeographies are premised upon a 'phenomenological encounter with natural forms'.[22] Both approaches give a twenty-first-century dimension to the botanical metaphor of the rhizome that was introduced into theoretical enquiry by Gilles Deleuze and Félix Guattari. The rhizome according to Deleuze and Guattari describes how counter-hierarchical relationships or assemblages operate laterally and multiply, in data as well as in critical and material studies.[23]

During clearance, long-standing archipelagic assemblages were lost when the sheep frontier displaced older ways of life. However, with the relocation of thousands of Highlanders to coastal towns, attention became refocused on fishing communities. Scotland has long been a fishing nation, controversially involved in fishing wars and international trade conflicts over quotas and access to its waters.[24] Fishing communities are notably treated by Scott in *The Antiquary* (1816), *The Bride of Lammermoor* (1819), *The Pirate* (1822) and *Redgauntlet* (1824). Archipelagic theory highlights the fragility of those communities but also their capacity for vitality. If we ignore sequence of publication in the interest of geographical network mapping and historical continuity, *The Bride of Lammermoor* configures Wolf's Hope on the Lothian coast as a village where the inhabitants, who have relocated from a dependent, peasant existence on the estate formerly managed by Edgar Ravenswood's family and latterly by Sir William Ashton, are optimistic about their future. They supplement their fishing income with smuggling and keep domestic animals including chickens.[25] The period is the early eighteenth century and the cleared area is the Borders, which Scott wrote about repeatedly as a region in which the biodiversity that included people had been decimated. Looking forward in time and northwards along Scotland's coast, the small fishing community in which the Meiklebackit family lives in *The Antiquary* struggles for survival. The economics of a fishing market in which customers determine the price of the produce being sold makes it necessary for the fishermen increasingly to risk their lives in bad weather or further from shore along a dangerous stretch of coast. *The Antiquary* is set in 1794, which is just before Scott's own writing career began. Although the action appears to be located along the Aberdeenshire or Morayshire coast, David Hewitt has shown that Scott had in mind the representation of a wider expanse of the northern and eastern coasts of Scotland.[26] Hewitt proposes that Scott probably began writing *The Antiquary* in 1815, which is concurrent with the middle of the 1806–21 period in which the Countess of Sutherland and her husband removed thousands of people from their land to tiny crofts on what Devine describes as an 'inhospitable eastern coast [and] habour-less maritime environment'. There, the less-than-subsistence capacity of the land provided was designed to 'force crofters to take up fishing', swelling the number of people fishing inshore in order to make a living.[27] This was not the herring fishing industry for which Scotland would become renowned. Jonsson has shown how fishing was imagined to be an opportunity to offset redundancy from the land.²⁸ The trade-off magnifies rather than diminishes the need for environmental justice.

The Pirate maps the network still further northwards to Shetland, where Scott describes fishing that is venturing further out into the deep sea towards Norway and Iceland. *Redgauntlet* and *Guy Mannering* confront the modernisation of the southwest of Scotland's coast.²⁹ *Redgauntlet* is well known for its comparison of a salmon hunt on horseback, using spears, with modern, more efficient methods of fishing including stake nets that were substantially reducing fish stocks in the nation's rivers. Decaying stake beds and old salmon stations are still visible in many of Scotland's estuaries, establishing visible memorials to a technology that was only ended in the twenty-first century by legislation to protect wild salmon stocks. The remains of the nets also provide a material reminder that 200 years ago Scott used fiction and his role as a founder of the River Tweed Commissioners to warn against the effects of overfishing.³⁰

Scott and the Anthropocene

Anthropocene studies need to be critiqued if they are to be helpful in reappraising Scott for a present-day audience. The use of a singular term risks a level of simplification that might render his work, along with improvement and clearance, insignificant by comparison with global issues – which it is not. Of the several point-of-origin theories for the Anthropocene, two are especially pertinent to my enquiry: the early (Neolithic) and later (carbon industry) origin theories. Marine biologist Eugene Stoermer and atmospheric scientist Paul Crutzen, who first drew attention to the term, have argued for the Anthropocene's emergence during the same historical period in which the clearances began to accelerate and when Scott was a child. They identify Scotland as the fulcrum and catalyst in global change because of James Watt's development of steam-engine technology.³¹ A main argument of Anthropocene studies is the culpability of a rampant, carbon-fuelled Capitalocene, to use Donna Haraway's related term, which began by empowering nineteenth-century manufacturing while relegating older, rural agro-economics.³² Another Anthropocene-related term, 'Plantationocene', shifts the focus back onto agro-capitalism and the environmental damage caused by the systematic use of industrial farming methods. As Haraway, Anna Tsing and a group of scholars from the University of Aarhus have said, Plantationocene farming alienates land by disciplining it to become different.³³ Vibrantly diverse, multi-species biotic communities are strategically replaced with new, scaled-down systems of production in which there is no place for anything that does not contribute to profit. The agronomics of improvement-driven sheep farming and commercial forestry in Scotland, like those of the British Empire, were Plantationocenic. It is their financial success that impels the changes recorded in novels including *Rob Roy* (1818), which centres on the decline of droving, and *The Heart of Mid-Lothian*, with its account of modern farming in Argyll.

The depopulation that is the clearances' most recognised feature affected many more places than the Highlands north of the geological fault line, which stretched from coastal to coastal environment, and from fishing community to fishing community (the Isle of Arran west of Glasgow to Stonehaven, south of Aberdeen). Moreover, the removal of species from the land involved more than just people, extending beyond the large mammals and birds whose absence has been relatively easy to notice, and some of which have returned or have been reintroduced. The wildflowers of Scotland that analogise war casualties in ballads including Scott's anthologised, extended, two-part 'Flowers of the Forest' in *Minstrelsy of the Scottish Border* – the forest itself indeed – as well as the nation's grasslands declined markedly in biodiversity in the nineteenth century, as a narrower range of introduced non-native species aimed at improved economic return gained ground. The wholesale use of lime fertiliser on sheep pasture, for example – advocated in just about every farming advice publication from the 1790s onwards – changed the pH balance of the soil, while the programmatic draining of peat bogs and other wetlands altered water levels and contributed to a rise in atmospheric greenhouse gasses long before the latter were recognised as a problem.[34] At a historical level, then, the clearances were a managed 'improvement' that dramatically impacted the well-being and survival prospects of non-human as well as human life.

Food production and its economics has long been an initiator of ecological change. Scottish Enlightenment stadial theories of human history, the term notably used by John Millar in 1771, concluded that critical shortages of food relative to population were the catalyst for the great cultural shifts from hunter-gatherer society to settled farming, then onward into feudalism and clan cultures, and latterly into modern civil society.[35] Seen in a global context, land management, food production and food security have linked local and wider environmental changes for at least 8,000 years. William Ruddiman's early Anthropocene hypothesis argues that the local and global impacts of human land management first synthesised around 5,000 years after the end of the last great glaciation; that is, around 6000 BC. Settled farming across continents at that point in history led to large-scale forest clearance by burning, with land quickly reassigned to arable crop cultivation and pasturage for domesticated animal husbandry.[36] Livestock farming flourished from Neolithic times onwards, with the increase in domestic animals that we know today to be a contributor to climate change even then matched by corresponding strategies to extirpate predators. Donna Haraway vividly captures in her *Companion Species Manifesto* how wolves became dogs, and how many of those dogs became – and still are – 'technology' in an agro-tech farming industry. Returning to the Neolithic clearances of trees, paleo-botanists and forest historians have identified how and over what period the burning of woodland took place in Scotland, with significant reductions in mixed tree cover that comprised mostly birch, alder, hazel, hawthorn and rowan, with some conifers including Scots Pine dominating further to the north.[37] Jim Conroy, Andrew Kitchener and Jack Gibson's study of the extinction of the Scottish beaver argues that by 50 BC Scotland had already lost much of its tree cover through forest clearance, with the remaining woodland reorganised around river courses.[38] It is worth noting that the early Anthropocene argument for global change depends on analyses of carbon sink layers that provide evidence of how the CO2 and methane contents of the atmosphere between 6000–3000 BC significantly increased, producing levels of global warming that prevented a new major glaciation.[39]

Walter Scott could not have known about climate science of this kind, nor that the large-scale, systematic draining of peat bogs (for which he showed considerable fascination, and from which he notes the bones of beavers were exhumed[40]) would release into the atmosphere huge quantities of carbon dioxide that had been stored underground for millennia. But he did know something about the remnant of ancient woodlands, their precarious existence and their connection with fauna and flora facing extinction in his own time. References to lost forests and the value of replanting native species feature so frequently in his writing, and usually relating to times so long before the clearances, that I am not going to identify examples here. However, I do want to note a particular, remote and ancient kind of woodland that during his own life – coincidental with improvement and the accelerating clearances – became perilously scarce due to drainage. I will come back shortly to bog-pine woodland in *A Legend of the Wars of Montrose*.

I turn now, though, to aesthetics and the wild places for which Scotland has become so renowned in a popular cultural imaginary – places that are as much a creation of the economics of improvement and clearance as they are of the more usually cited progenitors, Walter Scott's poems and novels. The power of fiction cannot be underrated, but neither should the prerogative of making money. Put into a historical context, Scotland's nineteenth-century picturesque and sublime landscapes of wildness (think Landseer's *Monarch of the Glen*, 1851) were a fiction in their own right – a story created out of environmental censorship and fake authenticity.[41] Those landscapes had not been devoid of human settlement and community activity for millennia, until the clearances. Scott, in *A Legend of the Wars of Montrose*, refers to communities that had lived for 'years that have gone by' in Glencoe, establishing that region as an exemplary indicator not of wilderness but of traumatically and violently cleared land.[42] Moreover, absence speaks in the case of the Romantic sublime through a created landscape of loss and vacancy. The ending of Scott's 1810 poem *The Lady of the Lake*, which is set in the middle of the sixteenth century but was written during the clearances, famously leaves the reader with the wind echoing through an otherwise silent and empty landscape where the people, goshawks, ravens, goats and so many other species mentioned throughout this cacophonous tale have disappeared to leave only mountains, lochs and heather:

> And now the mountain breezes scarcely bring
> A wandering witch-note of the distant spell –
> And now, 'tis silent all! – Enchantress, fare thee well.
> (VI: xxix)

Read as a comment on cultural and ecological aesthetics, the vibrant diversity of this landscape has been lost but so also has its affective capacity to generate enchantment and magic. The poem begins with a deer hunt, which would have appealed to field sportsmen in Scott's own time and to the Victorian gentry who succeeded them in the hospitality industry that surrounded grouse shooting and deer stalking. The removal of local communities and the persecution to extinction of predators that feed on game birds played a major part in the practice of clearance. Where Scotland's wild birds are concerned, the Capercaillie became extinct in 1785, due to deforestation and the loss of its native pine forest habitat. It was reintroduced into northern forests in 1837 as a game bird, during the rise of sporting estates that took place alongside the clearance of human populations.[43] Gamekeepers contributed substantially to the extinction during the nineteenth century of the goshawk, osprey, white-tailed sea eagle and red kite. These birds, all of which feature in nineteenth-century literature including Scott's poems and fiction, have each been reintroduced (Osprey 1954; Goshawk mid-1960s; Sea Eagle 1975; Red Kite 1991).[44] A non-predatory species, the bittern, became extinct in 1830 in

Scotland due to the drainage of wetlands and destruction of the reed beds in which it breeds.[45] These birds all lived on in nineteenth-century literature at the same time that they died in the landscape.

Literature, then, has confronted extinction and the threat to undomesticated species. The enchantment that Scott wrote about analogises the creative 'wonder' that he associates with his nation's history of ecological diversity. Yet the popularity of his and other Scottish romances during the early nineteenth century became part of the problem, by contributing to a heritage tourism industry and country-estate field sports culture that wanted mountains, heather, grouse, hares and deer but not poor, rural Scottish families, their goats and their dogs.

Scotland's wider agro-economy turned farming into an industry in which resources were measured and refined in order to maximise financial return. Chris Bambery has recently drawn attention to what was recorded by Sir John Sinclair in the reports from every parish in the nation in his first, twenty-one-volume *The Statistical Account of Scotland* between 1791–1799 and in the fifteen-volume *New Statistical Account* published between 1834–5.[46] Bambery's point, supported by evidence from the *Statistical Accounts*, is that Cheviot and Blackface sheep introduced from the North of England and the Scottish Borders northwards across the Scottish mainland (substantially in the early years of the nineteenth century) were not only larger and therefore more profitable, but required more pasturage per animal.[47] Those breeds also needed to be brought down from summer high-ground grazing during winter, and so required alternative land to be available. Cheviot and Blackface not only replaced older, smaller, less profitable breeds in the Highlands. The demand for grazing to maximise their meat and wool yields, along with a catastrophic reduction in the human population that had kept more diverse domestic animals, led to the loss of black cattle and mixed meadows, as well as to the removal of areas of old mixed species woodland. The treatises on sheep farming mentioned earlier consistently advised on planting trees in new formations that would provide protection for sheep rather than encouraging woodland biodiversity.[48] At a more popular level, especially given the extensive circulation of his fiction, the contemporary frame narrative of Scott's third series *Tales of My Landlord* novel, *A Legend of the Wars of Montrose*, lays bare this narrative at its outset, in a homecoming tale told by fictional former Highland soldier and customer of the Wallace Inn, Serjeant More MacAlpin. In receipt of an army pension after losing the use of an arm in the Napoleonic Peninsular Wars, MacAlpin had 'retired with the purpose of enjoying this income in the wild Highland glen, in which, when a boy, he had herded black cattle and goats'. He found not only the change in livestock but also a place altered by migration and depopulation. The violence involved in the changes is visceral:

> The fires had been quenched upon thirty hearths – of the cottage of his forefathers he could but distinguish a few rude stones – the language was almost extinguished – the ancient race from which he boasted his descent had found a refuge beyond the Atlantic. One southland farmer, three grey-plaided shepherds, and six dogs, now tenanted the whole glen, which in his youth had maintained, in content, if not in competence, upwards of two hundred inhabitants.[49]

What is not recorded here is the impact on an entire biotic community, beyond domesticated animals and the emigration that MacAlpin mentions.

Most of Scott's writing about the wider Scottish environment and the need to preserve native flora and fauna was informed by his local knowledge of changes in the land around where he lived. If we turn from his prose fiction to life writing, a journal entry in 1826 records his despair at lost wildflower and mixed grass meadows at the Tweedside Ashiestiel farm, near Selkirk. Scott lived as a tenant at Ashiestiel between 1804–11, before purchasing Abbotsford. While acknowledging that improvements in agriculture were inevitable if Scotland was to survive in a modern world, his anxiety relates to the loss of plant biodiversity already incurred because of improvement and for reasons of fashion and profit. He laments that his cousin and one-time landlord, James Russell, had developed part of the Ashiestiel estate into two artificially engineered environments: 'a *thriving* plantation . . . and a park *laid down in grass*'.[50] Scott uses adjectives associated with waste in a critique of this local contribution to a Plantationocene environment, describing as 'lean' and 'wanting' the two-species rye grass and clover meadow that had replaced 'the rich graminivorous variety which nature gives it[s] carpet'. His observation is visionary in the light of the current Scottish Rural Development Programme begun in 2014, which categorises arable land and pasture according to a list of 'sensitive plants' found in concentration only in unimproved Lowland grassland. The sensitive plants include twelve native grass species.[51]

The clearance of animal species has to be accounted for alongside that of people if we are to bring environmental ethics into the picture. I will close with an ecogothic encounter with an apex predator and keystone species. Wolves in Scotland – like the beaver – were extinct by Scott's lifetime and before the clearances began, but they haunt the ongoing changes. A final question is: What can reading Scott tell us about the consequences of assuming that we are intellectually in control of boundaries between the human and non-human?

Scott was a hunter. He neither critiques the idea that killing wolves was brave nor indicts lupocide as an instance of violence against the environment. Rather, an environmental, eco and species justice critique emerges from outside the bounds of authorial intentionality. No one can know where or when the last wolf in Scotland died. Competing narratives of their extinction populate the gaps in knowledge with a lively folklore. In woodland near Furness – a small iron-smelting town by the late eighteenth century, hence its name – a large, rough stone marks the place where the last wolf in Argyll is rumoured to have been shot. There is no date. Furness is on the banks of Loch Fyne, which we will see shortly has significance. Thomas Pennant claimed that wolves were 'wholly extirpated' by 1680.[52] Another source dates the extinction more recently to 1743, with a shooting in woodland at Findhorn near Inverness.[53] A dark irony aligns that death of the last wolf almost contemporaneously with the 1745–6 Jacobite rebellion that ended with the nearby Battle of Culloden and led into the clearances. Ecocritically, environmental and species justice boundaries here begin to converge, as they do in my final example from Scott's historical fiction.

During the period that Scotland's wolf population declined towards extinction, in the already mentioned main story of *A Legend of the Wars of Montrose*, the Children of the Mist, led by Ranald McEagh, live in bog-pine woodland on the Perthshire border with Argyll. Scott notes the woodland to be a rare relic of ancient forest found only in the 'the morasses', or wetlands. Almost entirely lost during the drainage programmes of agricultural improvement and with its remnants now protected, bog-pine woodland not only constitutes a remarkably efficient carbon sink (the trees are rooted in peat), but also supports an extremely rich biodiverse ecology.[54]

Scott explains McEagh to mean 'son of the mist', but J. H. Alexander corrects that etymology to 'son of a wolf'.[55] Ecogothic and environmental justice show how boundaries between the human and non-human, and between living things and inanimate elements such as water, air and stone, become tenuous in this novel when property and survival is at stake. Threatened with execution, Son of the Mist Ranald MacEagh protests that he 'is a man', not a wolf:

'Do you call yourself a man', said the interrogator 'who have done the deeds of a wolf?'

'I do,' answered the outlaw; 'I am a man like my forefathers – While wrapt in the mantle of peace, we were lambs – it was rent from us, and ye now call us wolves. Give us the huts ye have burned, our children whom ye have murdered, our widows whom ye have starved.'[56]

The zoomorphic analogy with wolves, which like outlaws could be legally hunted and shot, refers to circumstances in which the Children of the Mist had crossed a threshold from their condition of perceived wildness and savage living onto the estate of the king's forester. They have committed murder. But they had earlier been driven from land on which their families had lived. The violent actions in this novel uncannily foreshadow the managed cruelty of the clearances, in which whole villages were burned to force their inhabitants to leave the land. McEagh internalises his status to later claim that he is both a wolf and a raven, likening himself also to a tree whose branches have been lopped from its trunk (he awaits his roots being torn from the soil) and comparing his people with eagles and foxes who dwell 'in the thicket of the wilderness'.[57] Risking a spoiler, he dies but his son and clansmen disappear into Argyll above Loch Fyne (see above for an extant connection with the extinction of wolves). Rumour has it that they are occasionally seen.[58] The Romantically sublime Scotland with which this novel ends is one where the thrill of glimpsing rare species has an aesthetic value premised upon things living onwardly on the edge of extinction.

Conclusion

In this chapter I have argued that ecocriticism provides us with a way to reinterpret Scott's writing for a twenty-first century immersed in crises of extinction, species loss and environmental justice relating to people living on the land. Improvement and clearance, situated in a wider temporal and spatial context, have provided the foci for exploring a literature of extirpation and extinction, as well as of a substantial reduction in Scotland's biodiversity. My aim has been to show how an assemblage of theories rather than a singular approach can refocus attention on matters of environmental, ecological and species justice that are a direct legacy of the clearances. Deleuze and Guattari, for example, here meet Heise and Nixon. The circumstances that Scott describes and records are not merely historical but resonate onwardly and meaningfully into our own time. In a world where economic interests and environmental concerns are increasingly conflicted, and where the migration of people displaced by poverty is a concern of global proportions as well as local concern, we can do worse than look at Walter Scott's fiction and the sympathies it identifies between marginalised people, animals and plants. Scott emerges as an authorial precursor of twenty-first-century environmentalism, and not just someone whose writing has been made visible or different by ecocritical theory.

Notes

1. *Guy Mannering* (1815), *Saint Ronan's Well* (1824) and 'A Surgeon's Daughter' in *Chronicles of the Canongate* (1827) all include or refer to episodes that take place in India. *The Talisman* (1825) is set mainly in a Palestine that comprises modern-day Gaza Strip, West Bank and Jordan, so its fertile and desert landscapes are still the habitat of ecologies impacted by religious, cultural and political conflict.
2. Aldo Leopold, *A Sand County Almanac*, pp. 204, 210–11 and Lawrence Buell, *The Future of Environmental Criticism*, pp. 101–2. For types and periods of clearance that include but look beyond the Highlands in the eighteenth and nineteenth centuries see T. M. Devine, *The Scottish Clearances*.
3. Lawrence Buell, *The Environmental Imagination*, p. 145. *Ecocriticism and Narrative Theory* (2018).
4. Devine, *The Scottish Clearances*, pp. 2–3.
5. William Cronon, 'The Trouble with Wilderness'.
6. For a definition and discussion of environmental justice see Buell, *The Future of Environmental Criticism*, pp. 114–17, 141–2.
7. Devine, *The Scottish Clearances*, p. 226.
8. Fredrik Albritton Jonsson, *Enlightenment's Frontier*, p. 199.
9. *United Nations' Sustainable Development Goals*, Goal 8.
10. For ecophobia, see Simon Estok, *The Ecophobia Hypothesis* and 'Theorizing in a Space of Ambivalent Openness'.
11. Susan Oliver, 'Planting the Nation's "Waste Lands"' and 'Sir Walter Scott's Transatlantic Ecology'.
12. Rob Nixon, *Slow Violence and The Environmentalism of the Poor*, pp. 2–10.
13. Walter Scott, *Minstrelsy of the Scottish Border* 2: 349.
14. Susan Oliver, 'The Matter of Landscape'.
15. Scott, *Old Mortality*, pp. 32–3.
16. For examples see Andrew Smith and William Hughes, eds, *EcoGothic*, and *Gothic Nature Journal: New Directions in Ecohorror and EcoGothic*.
17. Scott, *Waverley*, p. 356; Oliver, 'Sir Walter Scott's Transatlantic Ecology', pp. 117–18.
18. Oliver, 'Sir Walter Scott's Transatlantic Ecology', p. 118.
19. Rob White, *Environmental Harm* and 'Green Victimology and Non-human Victims', p. 239.
20. Roland Robertson, 'Glocalization'; Ursula Heise, *Sense of Place and Sense of Planet*.

21. Brian Russell Roberts and Michelle Ann Stephens, *Archipelagic American Studies*, p. 10.
22. George B. Handley, 'Toward an Environmental Phenomenology of Diaspora', p. 656. Cited Roberts and Stephens, *Archipelagic American Studies*, p. 10. See also Paul Giles, 'Afterword: the Archipelagic Accretion', in Roberts and Stephens, *Archipelagic American Studies*, p. 427.
23. Gilles Deleuze and Félix Guattari, *A Thousand Plateaus*, pp. 3–25 (4).
24. Linda Fitzpatrick, *The Real Price of Fish*.
25. Scott, *The Bride of Lammermoor*, p. 50.
26. David Hewitt, in Scott, *The Antiquary*, p. 447.
27. Devine, *The Scottish Clearances*, p. 226.
28. Jonsson, *Enlightenment's Frontier*, pp. 112–16, 202–3.
29. Susan Oliver, 'Trees, Rivers, and Stories', pp. 293–5.
30. Scottish Government, 'Active Salmon Netting Stations that have Submitted Catch Returns'; River Tweed Commission, 'Tweed Angling Code for Salmon and Sea-Trout'.
31. See Paul Crutzen and Eugene Stoermer, 'The "Anthropocene"', p. 17; Crutzen, 'Geology of Mankind'.
32. Donna Haraway, *Staying With the Trouble*, pp. 198–206.
33. Anna Tsing et al., 'Anthropologists are Talking about the Anthropocene'.
34. Examples include John Naismyth, *Observations on the Different Breeds of Sheep*; John Little, *Practical Observations*.
35. Millar, *The Origin of the Distinction of Ranks*.
36. William F. Ruddiman, 'How Did Humans First Alter Global Climate'.
37. See David Hunt, *Early Farming Communities in Scotland*, and Mark L. Anderson, *A History of Scottish Forestry*, I: 6.
38. J. W. H. Conroy et al., 'The History of the Beaver in Scotland and its Future Reintroduction'.
39. These theories remain contested. The draining of many of Scotland's ancient carbon sinks in the form of peat bogs has left limited but significant evidence of CO_2 levels and plant life.
40. Scott, *Letters* 4: 146.
41. The painting was commissioned as one of three to hang in the British Parliament building, the Palace of Westminster. It now hangs in the Scottish National Gallery.
42. Scott, *A Legend of the Wars of Montrose*, p. 172.
43. See Andrew C. Kitchener, 'Extinctions, Introductions and Colonisations', p. 76.
44. Ibid. pp. 76–7.
45. Ibid. p. 76.
46. Sir John Sinclair, *The Statistical Account of Scotland* 1791–1799.
47. See Chris Bambery, *A People's History of Scotland*, pp. 74, 109.
48. Naismyth, *Observations on the Different Breeds of Sheep*; Little, *Practical Observations*.
49. Scott, *A Legend of the Wars of Montrose*, p. 4.

50. Scott, *Journal*, p. 145.
51. Scottish Government, *The Scottish Rural Development Programme 2014–2020*.
52. Thomas Pennant, *Arctic Zoology*, 1: iv.
53. For deforestation and the extinction of wolves, see Roy Robinson, 'State of Afforestation in the Highlands'.
54. Sharon Levy and Peter Cairns, 'The Age of Extinction'.
55. J. H. Alexander, in Scott, *A Legend of the Wars of Montrose*, p. 241.
56. Scott, *A Legend of the Wars of Montrose*, p. 103.
57. Ibid. pp. 99, 101, 103, 131, 149.
58. Ibid. p. 181.

10

Redgauntlet: Speculation in History, Speculation in Nature

Matthew Wickman

When literature emerged in its modern form as imaginative writing over the course of the long eighteenth century, it acquired a special relationship with the otherwise unimaginable. That is the subject of this chapter, one that focuses on Walter Scott less as the writer of historical fiction (in some ways the Great Oxymoron) than of the unthinkable. Where historical fiction exposes and, sometimes, sutures gaps in our understanding of the past, the unimaginable or unthinkable tries to get at what eludes (our understanding of) history altogether, whether that be some invisible hinge on which history turns or some alternative suppressed by the sheer weight of history. How does Scott address not so much what we forget as what never could come to mind in the first place? How is he an author not so much of the historical, political or cultural unconscious as of the unthinkable? These are the questions I will address.

To get at them, consider these observations from some familiar and influential figures in literary theory. Raymond Williams famously explained literature as a response to historical – better said, *material* – conditions. He remarked that the 'practical specialization of work to the wage-labour production of commodities; of "being" to "work" in these terms; of language to the passing of "rational" or "informative" "messages"; [and] of social relations to functions within a systematic economic and political order' collectively instituted a new set of 'pressures and limits' that 'were challenged in the name of a full and liberating "imagination" or "creativity"'.[1] In the generation of possible – literary – worlds yet unrealised, society formulated a response to dehumanising conditions. In a similar vein, Theodor W. Adorno once lauded the 'deliberate digressiveness' of Walter Benjamin's thought for its embrace of a 'promise of happiness. Everything that Benjamin said or wrote sounded as if thought, instead of rejecting the promises of fairy tales and children's books with its usual disgraceful "maturity", took them so literally that real fulfilment itself was now within sight of knowledge.'[2] Even Fredric Jameson, in qualifying the utopian dimensions of literature, acknowledged its formal implications in precisely such aspiration: 'The symbolic act', the literary text, 'begins by generating and producing its own context in the same moment of emergence in which it steps back from it, taking its measure with a view toward its own projects of transformation'.[3]

And so, when Amitav Ghosh more recently observes that 'climate change casts a much smaller shadow within the landscape of literary fiction than it does even in the public sphere', he is radically revising our inherited sense of literary possibility.[4] He foregrounds as much in the title and especially subtitle of his book: *The Great Derangement: Climate Change and the Unthinkable*. It is difficult for writers to represent climate change, certainly with any emotive force, he argues, if the phenomenon itself eludes thought. The reasons for the unthinkability of climate change are (paradoxically) not too hard to fathom. On one hand, climate change presents a challenge to human experience, occurring through a process of what Rob Nixon calls 'slow violence' that is too gradual (if, nonetheless, persistent) to perceive.[5] And on the other hand, climate change upends the learned behaviour of cultural and literary theorists, the tendency to identify and elaborate on differences of race, class, gender, sexual orientation, historical period, language and numerous others. As Dipesh Chakrabarty puts it, 'the figure of the human in the age of the Anthropocene, the era when humans act as a geological force on the planet, changing its climate for millennia to come', alters our focus. Instead of focusing in on anthropological differences, which are the stuff of cultural studies, 'the scientific literature on global warming thinks of humans as constitutively one – a species, a collectivity whose commitment to fossil-fuel based, energy-consuming civilization is now a threat to civilization itself'.[6] Were one to take climate change seriously, Chakrabarty implies, one would effectively eradicate differences between cultures and even historical periods, given the 200-plus-year history of industrialisation; in essence, we would lay waste to the work of cultural studies much as the most dire forecasts of climatological doom predict a similarly grim outcome for numerous species on our planet. But unlike the threat of, say, nuclear holocaust – another prospective agent of destruction – the incursions of climate change will be so incremental that we will barely see them coming: slightly warmer temperatures, then droughts, sea-level rise, poorer crops, and so forth. Like frogs in a heating cauldron, we will be insentient to the early signs of our own demise.

And yet, as horrifying as the implications of climate change and ecocide may be, the phenomenon of the 'unthinkable' to which Ghosh and Chakrabarty refer has become a newly recurrent attraction, and not merely a canonical point of privilege (per Williams, Adorno and Jameson), in recent schools of literary criticism and theory. The trendiness of the unthinkable seems different, to be sure, from the traditionally 'unthought' or overlooked, whether in the Foucaultian sense of human (or post-human) expressive possibilities that fall outside the grid of representation or in the form of historical lacunae in our transmissions of culture (regarding, for example, the absence of women writers from the canon).[7] The unthinkable as I am describing it here, and as Ghosh and Chakrabarty invoke it, refers instead to the kinds of models evoked, for example, in object-oriented ontology and speculative realism.[8] The former, as is well known, refers to a non-relational conception of the reality of things independent of human mediation – an imaginary, Graham Harman contends, that exceeds 'networks, negotiations, relations, interactions, and dynamic fluctuations', all of which reimpose the presence of the human in the object world. (An 'interaction', of course, implies human relation to objects, as does a 'negotiation'; by the same token, a 'network' implies a system as humans imagine it. And so on.) By contrast, Harman argues, an object-oriented ontology corresponds to 'a *weird* realism in which real individual objects resist all forms of causal or cognitive mastery'.[9] Literary studies fashioned after 'OOO' are radically decontextualising, pushing back against 'history' as never historical enough, never sufficiently in touch with the things of the world.

Quentin Meillassoux lends further grist to this mill of inhuman unthinkability, conjuring in speculative realism a 'great outdoors' that challenges philosophy to override its traditional, Kantian tendency to reduce all thought to the thinking subject (guaranteeing that 'reality' is only the measure of human mediation). In its place, philosophy would find itself reckoning with the kinds of empirical data regularly postulated by the sciences, which routinely theorise situations in which no human could possibly be present to think them (for example, at the inception of the earth, even the very universe, billions of years prior to human inception).[10] Such assertions pose 'a great representational challenge to literature', Mark McGurl observes, given that the latter's 'most epic productions' from the depths of memory 'are, matched against deep [geological] time ... cosmically small'. Geological time situates us 'altogether beyond the pale of aesthetic redemption', to direct contemplation of 'the knowledge that reason, too, is sure to be engulfed in a larger darkness. That time' in the unspecifiable but certain future – if only when the sun expends its energy and erupts into a nova that engulfs the earth – 'will be the time not only of our death but of the death of death and the concept of infinity, too'.[11] It will be the apocalypse to end all apocalypses, the eradication of all categories in name and thought, with nobody present to record or even recognise it. Or so we imagine, or fail to imagine, it.

There is an undeniable appeal to such fictions, a kind of *frisson* at the thought of our vulnerability, even our inability to frame that vulnerability properly to ourselves. Such thinking inevitably bears the trace of the literary – of fiction specifically as the effort to think what has never happened. That said, literature within this mode of affect is largely unconcerned with literary history.[12] Instead, it constitutes a kind of *romance* in the Romantic sense, a quality of difference from everyday life, an alternative to (mere) history, an effort to reckon with the unthinkable.[13]

And this brings us to Walter Scott's novel *Redgauntlet*. Published in 1824, *Redgauntlet* was an odd successor to a genre and narrative structure that Scott had perfected over a number of previous works, beginning with *Waverley* a decade earlier (1814). *Waverley* sets the story of an eponymous English soldier against the backdrop of an actual historical event, the Jacobite rebellion of 1745. Subsequent Scott historical novels – *Old Mortality* (1816), *Rob Roy* (1818) and *The Heart of Mid-Lothian* (1818) – would reprise the basic plot structure of *Waverley*, with Henry Morton, Francis Osbaldistone and Jeanie Deans finding themselves swept up by circumstances surrounding the Battle of Bothwell Bridge, the 1715 Jacobite rebellion and the Porteous Riots, respectively. *Redgauntlet* occupies a curious place relative to these precursors. Set in the 1760s, it recounts the adventure of two friends, Darsie Latimer (born Sir Arthur Darsie Redgauntlet) and Alan Fairford, who are unwittingly caught up in a putative third Jacobite rebellion. Latimer, who has been abducted by his uncle (a veteran of the '45 and an instigator of this latest coup), and Fairford, who goes in search of his friend, both encounter Charles Edward Stuart, who has made one last risky voyage into Britain in the hopes of raising an army and instigating one final attempt to retrieve his rightful kingdom. This dream dissolves, however, when the prince's supporters confront the reality of their situation – their sparse numbers, their relative disorganisation and their realisation that the Jacobite cause has devolved into a memory (or, perhaps better said, into the trace of grievances that take the form of political critique rather than outright rebellion). At one point in the story, Latimer's uncle, Hugo Redgauntlet, offers his nephew counsel that eventually condemns his own cause: 'Beware', he says, 'of struggling with a force sufficient to crush you, but abandon yourself to that train of events by which we are both swept along, and which it is impossible that either of us can resist'.[14]

Such ideas about the sweeping tide of history underwrite much of Scott's literary output. However, unlike with *Waverley* and *Rob Roy*, the Jacobite conflict in *Redgauntlet* never happened. At least, it never happened as a historical event. In that respect, *Redgauntlet* is not a romance set against the backdrop of history, but a romance set against the backdrop of still more romance.[15] *Redgauntlet*, groping its way towards a history it cannot name, seems almost more akin to a national tale than a historical novel.[16] And this, in turn, raises the question of the particular brand of romance in this novel, given that it seeks no true dialectical corollary in history. But neither is it fantasy, as Scott lends expression here to residues of an actual culture otherwise unexpressed. In terms we discussed above, we might call this novel a form of speculative realism, though not in Meillassoux's sense of the bifurcation of philosophy from the sciences. Instead, *Redgauntlet* speaks to an 'unthinkable' aspect of Scott's era – whether to a third Jacobite rebellion or simply the residual traces of an incomplete conversion to 'British' modernity – and to the ways such *verboten* ideations manifest themselves in the early decades of the nineteenth century. How Scott brings the 'unthinkable' to consciousness – the narrative techniques whereby he renders the unimaginable more palpable to us – is what I wish to explore.

Much of the plot of *Redgauntlet*, Scott tells us in a later, 1832 introduction, concerns 'Jacobite enthusiasm' and the 'circumstances[,] fascinating to the imagination', that attended and then, more importantly, succeeded the Jacobite rebellion.[17] 'Most Scottish readers who can count the number of sixty years', Scott remarks, 'must recollect many respected acquaintances of their youth, who, as the established phrase gently worded it, had been *out in the Forty-five*. It may be said, that their political principles and plans no longer either gained proselytes or attracted terror, – those who held them had ceased to be the subjects either of fear or opposition.'[18] And yet, Scott continues, the 'love' of these 'old men' for 'past times, their tales of bloody battles fought against romantic odds, were all dear to the imagination, and their little idolatry of locks of hair, pictures, rings, ribbons, and other memorials of the time in which they still seemed to live, was an interesting enthusiasm'.[19] And so, while *Redgauntlet* partly tells about a make-believe Jacobite plot twenty years after the '45, its real subject matter is the vitality of the Jacobite imaginary, conveyed through tunes (which Scott calls 'a kind of free-masonry amongst performers'), or 'a single word' or 'a gripe of the hand' – in short, through some 'private sign' of shared understanding and sympathy.[20] Such communications constitute ethereal, performative correlatives to the 'locks of hair, pictures, rings, ribbons, and other memorials of the time' to which Scott refers in 1832, and in which he personally trafficked (as all who have visited Abbotsford will recognise).[21]

The wealth of scholarship on these tokens and remnants of Jacobite culture in late eighteenth-century Scotland alters and even inverts the picture we sketched above. *Waverley* and *Rob Roy*, we said, are romances set against the backdrop of history. *Redgauntlet*, by contrast, is romance set against romance, but perhaps it would be better to describe it as history rooted in romance, history set against the backdrop of romance.[22] This history, however, is not a product of the novel's characters and their machinations – again, these events never occurred, at least not in the form in which Scott recounts them. Rather, 'history' here embeds itself in the novel's account of a body of shared signifiers, of an atmosphere of romance, of a mood. It speaks to and in the spirit of what Murray Pittock terms the 'environment' in which Jacobite relics and attitudes circulated. While *environment* presents a challenge to thought, per Ghosh and Chakrabarty, 'environment' for Pittock does not designate the air we breathe as much as the milieu in which we dwell. Environment is a kind of language and, like any language, it employs conventions, though not those of mere speech; instead, this language 'lies "between metaphor and object",' and comprises 'not only a semiotic presence' but also a network of discursive associations predicated as much on their own concealment as on their disclosure. Concealment, in fact, becomes a mode of disclosure: one knows something important is conveying itself precisely because one *cannot* see it, because discovery in this context takes the form of 'oblique reference[s]' that cloak 'explicit ... political sympathies ... in privacy and silence'.[23] Signification here operates, Pittock argues, through 'a multifaceted phenomenon of networks, espionage rings, kinship bonds, cant, catch-phrases, tokens, souvenir objects and voluntary associations'.[24]

This 'environmental language', broadly conceived, is operative through much of the novel. It explains, for example, the musical exchange between the captive Darsie and the fiddler, Wandering Willie. In an episode concerning the 'free-masonry amongst performers', Willie, who had earlier disclosed to the still-free Darsie a supernatural folk legend intimating the danger of the Redgauntlet family, now tacitly announces his presence to the captive Darsie by 'play[ing] twice over', from the yard outside Darsie's quarters, 'the beautiful Scottish air called Wandering Willie'.[25] 'Hope', Darsie relates in his journal, 'will catch at the most feeble twig for support in extremity', and he remarks 'that, in a wild, wandering, and disorderly course of life, men, as they become loosened from the ordinary bonds of civil society, hold those of comradeship more closely sacred'. And so, in testament of his plight, Darsie sings 'two or three lines of the 137th Psalm: by Babel's streams we sat and wept'.[26] Willie then replies with a tune 'the words of which instantly occurred to' Darsie: 'Oh whistle and I'll come t'ye, my lad.' Darsie responds by whistling the song 'Come back again and loe me / When a' the lave are gane', to which Darsie replies with the song 'There's my thumb, I'll ne'er beguile thee.' 'I no longer doubted', Darsie informs us, 'that a communication betwixt us was happily established, and that, if I had the opportunity of speaking to the poor musician, I should find him willing to take my letter to the post, to invoke the assistance of some active magistrate . . . to contribute to my liberation'.[27] Towards the end of the novel, prior to this very liberation, a similar exchange occurs between the two characters.

As telling as, if more understated than, the exchange of messages through song is the repeated reference in the novel to tonality, by which I mean the illocutionary effects of utterances – things communicated inferentially rather than directly, meaning conveyed through mood. In the episode I rehearse above, after Darsie sings the lines from the 137th Psalm, he hears '[t]he country people' in the yard with Willie 'whisper together in tones of commiseration', after which Willie, 'in a tone calculated to reach [Darsie's] ears', tells the folk that he knows a series of other airs – the tunes through which he subsequently carries on his secret, melodic correspondence with the captive.[28] What Darsie hears, literally, are the whispers of the crowd and the voice of Willie, but what communicates itself is collective sympathy. It is the tonality that converts the sounds from *noise* to *language* to *environment*.

Some additional context may help explain what we are hearing, or sensing, with Scott's evocation of tone. Modern readers have inherited, even if unconsciously, the definition of tone bequeathed by I. A. Richards as the 'attitude' held by a speaker or writer 'to his listener', a 'recognition' of his 'relation to them . . . of how he stands towards' them.[29] In the eighteenth century, however, tone was a more expansive category. Thomas Sheridan's *A Course of Lectures on Elocution* (1762), for example, defined 'tones' as 'the types and language of the passions, and all internal emotions, in the same way that articulate sounds are the types and language of ideas'. Tone in this context would seem to signify mood, though Sheridan specified that tone modulates between the 'animal' and 'intellectual' faculties, between 'nature' as those feelings are 'impressed . . . on the human frame' and custom as the contrivance of suitable expression for those feelings.[30] Tone for Sheridan was thus a medial category, linking not only diverse human faculties but also the very status of the human to what is uncivilised, inhuman, or at least closest to nature within us. Samuel Johnson did not go quite this far in the definition of tone he proffered in his *Dictionary of the English Language*, but he too connected tone to a sense of the uncanny – to what is recognisably, but strangely, ourselves. For him, tone not only signifies a 'note' or 'sound' (which he listed as the first of five definitions), or a tactile 'elasticity' (the fifth of the five), but also an 'accent' in the voice, a 'particular or affected sound in speaking' and, perhaps most provocatively, 'a mournful cry', evocative of something upsetting and unresolved.[31]

That irresolution may derive partly from tone's designation of diverse corporeal senses. The word tone derives from the Latin *tonus*, meaning 'tension' (with associations to the word *tonare*, or 'thunder'), and from the Greek *tonos*, meaning 'stretching', and implying the elasticity of a band or fibre (and explaining the traditional association of tonality with music, or with the image of a string or chord being plucked and emitting sound). Tone may thus be felt or heard, but it is only seen in the form of a tincture, making it less a thing (an object defined by *res extensa*) than an elusive quality, a sensate no-thing. This helps explain its resonance in the eighteenth-century philosophical discourse of sensibility – in, for example, Francis Hutcheson's assertions of harmony in our judgements of beauty, or in Adam Smith's claims of 'the harmonious and sonorous pronunciation peculiar to the English nation' and the 'certain ringing in [the English] manner of speaking which foreigners can never attain', or in Edmund Burke's theory of the sublime (whose key word for a state of sublime incapacity is 'astonishment', from the Latin *ex tonare*, meaning 'issuing from thunder', or 'of a powerful tone'), among others.[32] Later still in the eighteenth century, Immanuel Kant associated tone with 'the presentiment of that which is absolutely not an object of the senses: that is, the intimation of the supersensible'. For Kant, tone conjured 'a vaulting leap beyond concepts into the unthinkable . . . a suspense-ridden tendering of secrets that is actually the mistuning of heads into exaltation'. He thus deemed tone contradictory, for it purportedly supersedes thought and yet 'contains the hope of a disclosure that is only possible in tasks of reason solved with concepts'. Hence, at once 'animal' and 'intellectual' (in Sheridan's formulation), cognitive and affective, tone represented 'a surrogate of cognition, supernatural communication', and thus 'the death of all philosophy'.[33]

This may help explain tone's appeal in later philosophy, whether in Henri Bergson's explication of the 'divers tones of mental life' that stratify levels of experience or in Martin Heidegger's invocation of tone (by way of *Stimmung*, a term denoting both 'voice' and 'mood') as that which, prior to all cognition, discloses the phenomenon or place of being.[34] In each case, tone represents a limit of cognition, less a thought than an experience of the (literally) unthinkable. As Peter Fenves remarks, and bringing us around again to Pittock's overtures to an 'environmental language', tone implies 'an utterly indeterminate and undefinable "atmosphere"', an orienting feature rather than a formal characteristic or rhetorical flourish, which is why it 'cannot designate an individual "style"'.[35] Instead, as an atmospheric agent, tone suggests a degree of detachment that, Niklas Luhmann observes, 'comes into being each time an object occupies a place and creates an ambience that is neither identical to the object nor able to exist without it'.[36] In other words, tone consists of the tension between a body (including a body of text) and its environment, which is why it features in present-day affect and media studies.[37]

And so, returning to Scott, that may also explain the thematic presence of tone in *Redgauntlet*, a text that dramatises the anticipation and foreboding surrounding the difference between actual and possible worlds. Again, possible worlds here are not the products of fantasy but rather of immanence, and imminence – of something in the air and on the brink of materialising on the ground. Accordingly, the novel's appeal to tonality in the episodes involving Wandering Willie echoes similar references to tone at other important moments in the novel. For example, when Alan Fairford, searching for Darsie, is brought before Father Buonaventure, a supposed Catholic priest, he is struck by the 'tone of authority which reigned in [the Father's] whole manner, and by the 'solemn[ity of] tone' in which the Father speaks.[38] Tonality in this instance signifies an impact of bearing that exists independently of the actual words Buonaventure employs; it forms a complement, the narrator tells us, to 'the cast of seriousness or even sadness' that inflects the priest's 'noble countenance', functioning as an illocutionary equivalent to the white cockade (a Jacobite symbol) attached to his hat.[39] We learn later, of course, that Buonaventure is the returning Stuart, the no-longer-quite-so-bonnie Prince Charlie. Shortly after this exchange, when the female character Lilias Redgauntlet (introduced earlier in the novel as the mysterious 'Green Mantle') tries to communicate to Darsie the secret of his parentage – that he too is a Redgauntlet, and that Lilias is his sister – she communicates 'in a tone partly sorrowful and partly impatient' a message he is at first slow to understand, but whose importance is initially conveyed precisely through the tenor of its recitation.[40] Then, later, at the novel's conclusion, after Sir Edward, the Laird of Redgauntlet, Darsie's uncle and captor, has retired to a convent as Father Hugo, the narrative informs us that he wears around his neck a small silver box containing a lock of hair. Inscribed on this box is the motto *Haud obliviscendum*, 'never to be forgotten', which, we are told, 'seemed to intimate a tone of mundane feeling and recollection of injuries' suggestive of Father Hugo's undying memory of 'the sufferings . . . of the House of Redgauntlet'.[41] In all these instances, tone either substitutes for or else supplements the Jacobite objects that, Pittock argues, conjure a cultural 'environment' that was, if anything, more vital for being ethereal, elusive, atmospheric.

Redgauntlet is thus a novel in which virtually nothing happens but in which climactic (because *climatic*) occurrences seem perpetually on the verge of happening, perpetually in the air. In this respect it is not a historical novel so much as a subjunctive one expressive of states of unreality or divided realities – things true, but not; present, but absent; here, intangibly.[42] Or, perhaps it would be better to call *Redgauntlet* not a subjunctive novel but a *speculative* one. I invoke this term with an eye to speculative realism, a school of thought I mentioned above associated with the work of Quentin Meillassoux.

Speculative realism has recently become an object of attention in Romantic studies. The discussion that follows is intended less to make a case that Scott's work can or should be interpreted through Meillassoux's than that each traces the *unthinkability* of the situations it describes to a similar source. That source, we will see, is David Hume. Getting there will require a detour through philosophical history, but one that reveals Scott at a powerful formal crux of the novel's development at the nexus of actual and possible worlds. In Scott's case, we will see, literature may not fail to rise to the challenge of modern thought, as Ghosh suggests, as much as provide an imaginative origin for precisely that critique.

Let's begin with speculative realism, which is designed to theorise the existence of realities we are not able to accommodate. At least, we are not able to do so in the phenomenological and ontological traditions of post-Kantian philosophy, because these realities occur in domains of which we have no experience, or where we literally do not exist. Meillassoux does not evoke states of being one associates with the unconscious, but instead beguiling moments in deep time whose factuality the sciences can now verify but whose reality excludes our own: 'the date of the origin of the universe (13.5 billion years ago)', of 'the accretion of the earth (4.56 billion years ago)', of the 'origin of life on earth (3.5 billion years ago)' and 'of the origin of humankind (. . . 2 million years ago)'. 'Empirical science today', he reflects, 'is capable of producing statements about events anterior to the advent of life as well as consciousness'.[43] Contrary to the eighteenth-century philosopher George Berkeley, who posited that every object implies a perceiver, science now registers states of existence where no human perceiver was or ever could have been.[44] This means that science circumvents those cognitive habits we have inherited from Kant – habits that conceive of such non-human states as 'the date of the origin of the universe' as 'noumenal' realms to which we have no access. Left to us instead, Kant reasons, are 'phenomenal' realities mediated to us not only through our senses but also our consciousness, our culture, our gender, and all other facets of our identities. Meillassoux calls such convictions of insuperable mediation – a reflex of thought in which we place ourselves at the centre of the universe – 'correlationism'. This reflex whereby we place ourselves at the centre of the universe – the centre of any possible reality – is 'the central notion of modern philosophy',[45] and it extends from Kant and Hegel to phenomenology, psychoanalysis, deconstruction, feminism, cultural studies, postcolonialism, media studies, and multiple other branches of modern thought.[46] But not to Scott, not in *Redgauntlet*. Or so I assert; so I believe we will see.

There is, in fact, a more direct and compelling connection between speculative realism and *Redgauntlet* than a line running from Scott's novel to empirical science. After all, as we have remarked above, much of *Redgauntlet*, less a historical novel or even a romantic history than a romantic romance, defies experience. At the same time, the novel is awash in experience in the form of 'environmental' forces that communicate across cultures and that people recognise even when the traces of their experience seem ethereal. Hence, in the former, 'materialist' sense, the history on which the novel is based never happened; like the gothic fiction of Ann Radcliffe, which ultimately explains away the supernatural instantiations to which its episodes appear to lead, *Redgauntlet*'s portents of revolutionary change (the 'environmental' traces of residual Jacobitism) are at some level ciphers, units of signification without substance. But in the latter, immaterial sense, this insubstantiality is less an indictment of (non-) actuality than an acknowledgement that some realities evade the official records of history. In each case, the tension created between experience and understanding (between 'environment' and 'history'), and by extension the connection between Meillassoux and Scott, does not concern science per se as much as question what counts as real. And that leads us to Meillassoux's critique of Kant that runs through Hume.

The speculative aspects of *Redgauntlet* demand a little intellectual context for us to see them clearly. And for Scott, as for Meillassoux, that context ultimately runs through a chapter of intellectual history involving Hume. One of Hume's most striking philosophical achievements concerned the detachment of ideas about the world from the world itself: 'The memory, senses, and understanding are . . . all of them founded on the imagination, or the vivacity of our ideas.'[47] Ideas, in other words, tell us nothing about the true nature of things, only about our relation to them. This means that we don't really understand the causal nature of reality; all we have is an associative relation to it, a customary relation to it – things seeming to belong together (like light and heat). While Kant appreciated the trenchancy of Hume's arguments – famously claiming that Hume awakened him from his 'dogmatic slumber'[48] – he was dissatisfied with Hume's conclusions. In their place, Kant sought to reconcile Hume's emphasis on the pulsations of experience with the laws of nature, including our own human nature, that explain our experience and reveal the workings of cause and effect. Kant's 'categories', his a priori concepts of the understanding, were born from this union.

But the nineteenth-century Scottish philosopher J. Hutchison Stirling found Kant's solution of the Humean puzzle unsatisfactory. 'Kant has not answered Hume', he declared, for Kant had actually argued in something of a circle. As Cairns Craig summarises Stirling's argument, the causality that Kant's categories purportedly revealed 'could not be effectively imposed on the world by the mind without the phenomena having already suggested to the categories the ways in which "real" causes of causation are to be distinguished from mere regular succession', or association, which had been Hume's contention. In other words, before Kant's 'categories' could *explain* our experience, they first *relied* on it. And, because experience precedes the categories that supposedly explain them, the *categories themselves* effectively became contingent and associative: 'That which is supposed to be supplied only by the categories in constructing the "world" must already be evidenced in the phenomena by the very necessity which only the categories are supposed to provide.'[49]

In essence, Kant's categories do not give us access to *nature* as much as present a hardened associationism. Hence, Stirling turns us to Hume as an explanation of why. But if we are to *speculate* on nature it will only be via the logic of contingency, which is why Meillassoux also turns to Hume. In order to escape the logic of correlationism – that is, in order to evade the mediation of reality through the Kantian categories of understanding; in order to posit the validity of things where those categories cannot reach – Meillassoux asserts 'that thought is not necessary (something can be independently of thought), and that thought can think what there must be when there is no thought' (that is, we can *know* that something can exist independently of thought).[50] This leads him to contingency, a point Hume had underscored in undercutting causality. Contingency 'expresses the fact that physical laws remain indifferent as to whether an event occurs or not', including the 'fact' of thought.[51] Meillassoux inflates contingency into an absolute (or non-contingent) principle,[52] adding that a strong theory of contingency does not lead to chaos:

> For although we maintain that the laws of nature could actually change for no reason, nevertheless, like everyone else, we do not expect them to change *incessantly*. In other words, our claim is that it is possible to sincerely maintain that objects could *actually and for no reason whatsoever* behave in the most erratic fashion, without having to modify our usual everyday relation to things.[53]

This presents a familiar difficulty known, he observes, 'as "Hume's problem"'.[54] This is the 'problem' we observed above that demotes causality to the level of (mere) association, (mere) customary observation – in other words, contingency. This means that for Meillassoux, as for Stirling, Kant has not answered Hume, or has not closed the lid on contingency. And Meillassoux's way of pursuing the implications of Kant's failure leads him to the mathematical ontology of Alain Badiou, the set-theoretical negotiation of contingency, and the speculatively realist conclusion of 'existence outside thought'.[55] This conclusion asserts 'the fact that science does indeed think that *what comes before comes before, and that what came before us came before us*'.[56] And because we can now establish existence outside our own experience, we can evade the prison-house of correlationism.

So goes the path of speculative realism. But rather than following it to Badiou's mathematical ontology, I wish to stay with Hume, for that is where we uncover the link between Scott and speculation, *Redgauntlet* and realism. In undercutting causality, Meillassoux remarks, Hume shifts attention from facts to beliefs: 'Since we cannot demonstrate the necessity of the causal connection . . . we should stop asking ourselves why the laws are necessary and ask instead about the origin of our *belief* in their necessity.' This 'replaces a question about the nature of things with a question about our relation to things', as we observed above.[57] Belief is an important category for Hume inasmuch as it designates a relation that cannot ascend to the level of proven fact even as it marshals a stronger level of emotional and commonsensical assent than mere fiction: a 'belief is nothing but an idea, that is different from a fiction, not in the nature, or the order of its parts, but in the *manner* of its being conceiv'd'.[58] As Ian Duncan recounts it, Hume's point here initiated a new understanding of fiction, including its intensification as belief: 'In the modern era fiction comes to designate a cognitive engagement with reality rather than, as in Platonic or Christian conceptions, the falsification of a reality guaranteed by metaphysical forms of truth.'[59] This would prove instrumental to Scott, whose fiction appealed to

> reading as a mode of reverie, of total imaginative absorption in an illusion of presence that cancels the line between fiction and history, by setting it within a Humean sequence of romantic absorption, disillusioning reflection, and a sentimental return to common life that at once reaffirms its historical necessity and recognizes its fictionality.[60]

Fiction in Scott becomes an exercise in avowed inauthenticity and what Hume calls *custom* even as its 'absorptive' qualities, its creation of worlds through the generative force of its imagination, attest to its realism *on other grounds* or for beings *other than ourselves*.

This makes *Redgauntlet* an exemplary illustration of Scott's historical fiction, despite its outlier status as a novel of tangential, even imaginary, history. It is the contingency of history here, its 'speculative' quality, that allows its readers to address the unthinkable. This is no mean feat for a nineteenth-century novel, as Amitav Ghosh recognises. Novels during this era tend to conceive of 'time as an irresistible, forward movement'; accordingly, they position themselves 'with the avant-garde as it hurtles forward in its impatience to erase every archaic reminder of Man's kinship with the nonhuman'.[61] The novel form thus bears an especially pungent musk of the modern, carrying with it the deep assumptions that impose the human form on the natural world, that devolve interspecies, planetary considerations to the (comparatively) vulgar status of moral dilemmas, that telescope life onto human character at the expense of everything else and thus, as a result, create conditions of unthinkability around precisely those issues about which we most urgently need to think. But in Scott's hands, crucially, every history implies an alternative existence as romance, as an alternative to – itself. *Redgauntlet* makes this process acutely transparent, for it takes romantic speculation as its object of narrative.[62] Yes, the clandestine rebellion rehearsed in the novel ultimately fails, but its success or failure seems almost beside the point; for, as recorded in the chronicles of the era, this rebellion never existed in the first place. This is a novel not about the Jacobite history that *is*, nor even, as in *Waverley* or *Rob Roy*, the history that *might have been*.

Rather, this is about history that *also is* – in song, in mood, in the air. Hence, and contrary to Ghosh's dire dismissals, *Redgauntlet* situates the unthinkable squarely within history. And today, given the material and spiritual crises of the Anthropocene, of institutions across civil society (including universities), of political failures to address racial, economic and other tensions, of the preponderance of trauma and abuse, of hyper-distractedness, and more, this makes Scott, ultimately, an author of hope. For, take what is given, *Redgauntlet* suggests, and define it any way you like; even make it as dire as you fear. Now consider that it might be different, and perhaps better. And even if worse, it might yet be made different again. In all likelihood, and in ways we may imagine as unthinkable, it probably already is.

Notes

1. Raymond Williams, *Marxism and Literature*, p. 50.
2. Theodor Adorno, *Prisms*, p. 230.
3. Frederic Jameson, *The Political Unconscious*, p. 81.
4. Amitav Ghosh, *The Great Derangement*, p. 7.
5. See Rob Nixon, *Slow Violence and the Environmentalism of the Poor*.
6. Dipesh Chakrabarty, 'Postcolonial Studies and the Challenge of Climate Change', p. 2.
7. On literature as a self-reflexive meta-discourse that breaks the logic of representation by representing nothing, no 'real' thing, see Michel Foucault, *The Order of Things*, pp. 299–300.
8. For an example of such speculation within ecocriticism, see Timothy Morton, *Hyperobjects*.
9. Harman, 'The Well-Wrought Broken Hammer', pp. 187–8. For an example of what such 'realism' looks like in the period of Scott, see Evan Gottlieb, *Romantic Realities*, and Chris Washington and Anne C. McCarthy, eds, *Romanticism and Speculative Realism*.
10. See Quentin Meillassoux, *After Finitude*.
11. Mark McGurl, 'The Posthuman Comedy', pp. 538–9.
12. Indeed, this is one of its limitations. See Wai Chee Dimock's response to McGurl in 'Low Epic'.
13. On the idea of romance, see Ian Duncan, *Modern Romance and Transformations of the Novel*.
14. Walter Scott, *Redgauntlet*, p. 168.
15. According to Bruce Beiderwell, the novel's romantic quality may be most on display in its depiction of state authority, which 'is envisioned as most satisfying when it is represented as least active' ('Scott's *Redgauntlet* as a Romance of Power', p. 275). For Yoon Sun Lee, *Redgauntlet* 'demonstrate[es] how the idea of the Scottish nation could be efficaciously

suspended in an imaginary and literally anachronistic void' ('Giants in the North', p. 110). But for Emily Allen, *Redgauntlet* simply furnishes a response to Scott's earlier novel of 1824, the failed *Saint Ronan's Well*, his sole attempt at domestic realism ('Re-Marking Territory').

16. 'Refusing a teleological or deterministic philosophy of history, *Redgauntlet* presents a complex and heterogeneous vision of the past, not as the triumphant linear progression towards the present so dear to Whig historians, but as the interspersion or collision of disparate desires and ambitions.' Rohan Maitzen, '"By No Means an Improbable Fiction"', p. 170.
17. Scott, *Redgauntlet* (Waverley Novels New Edition), p. iv.
18. Ibid. pp. xx–xxi.
19. Ibid. pp. xxi–xxii.
20. Ibid. pp. 201, 306.
21. Ibid. p. xxii. On the psychical and domestic economy of collection at Abbotsford, see Caroline McCracken-Flesher, 'Anxiety in the Archive', and also 'Where We Never Were' in this volume.
22. For James Kerr, the 'contradiction in Scott's fictional ideology' between a suspicion about truths recounted through language and a conviction, nevertheless, that there is a truth to history, 'has a formal corollary in the jarring admixture of romance and realism that runs throughout the Waverley Novels. In *Redgauntlet* this modal mixture has become the definitive proposition of Scott's writing. Scott has set aside any ambition to write a faithful account of the past, and has composed a historical romance about the writing of history.' 'Fiction Against History', p. 237.
23. Murray Pittock, *Material Culture and Sedition, 1688–1760*, p. 16.
24. Ibid. p. 2.
25. Scott, *Redgauntlet*, p. 200.
26. Ibid. p. 201.
27. Ibid. p. 202.
28. Ibid. p. 201.
29. I. A. Richards, *Practical Criticism*, p. 182.
30. Thomas Sheridan, *A Course of Lectures on Elocution*, pp. 129, 121.
31. Samuel Johnson, *A Dictionary of the English Language*.
32. See Hutcheson, *An Inquiry into the Original of our Ideas of Beauty and Virtue*; Adam Smith, *Lectures on Rhetoric and Belles Lettres*, p. 16; and Burke, *A Philosophical Enquiry*, p. 53. I draw here from my essay 'Tonality and the Sense of Place'.
33. Immanuel Kant, 'On a Newly Arisen Superior Tone in Philosophy', pp. 61–2.
34. Henri Bergson, *Matter and Memory*, p. 14; on Heideggerian *Stimmung*, see Giorgio Agamben, 'Vocation and Voice'.
35. See Fenves's 'Introduction: The Topicality of Tone', in Fenves, *Raising the Tone of Philosophy*, pp. 3–4.
36. Niklas Luhmann, *Art as a Social System*, p. 112.
37. I am thinking here, for example, of 'affective tonality', a term Mark Hansen introduces in *New Philosophy for New Media* (2004) and carries into his later

work. It designates a corporeal attunement and represents the interface between the body's own modality and the imprint of its environment.
38. Scott, *Redgauntlet*, pp. 279, 287.
39. Ibid. p. 276.
40. Ibid. p. 296.
41. Ibid. p. 380.
42. This novel, as Marshall Brown observes, creates a kind of stasis: 'In pursuing fidelity to individual experience, Scott's literary version of history spurns both the [*longue*] *durée* and the revolutionary transformation' ('Rethinking the Scale of Literary History', p. 134).
43. Meillassoux, *After Finitude*, p. 9.
44. As Berkeley puts in the mouth of a spokesperson in 'Three Dialogues between Hylas and Philonous' (1713), 'sensible things really do exist: and if they really exist, they are necessarily perceived by an infinite mind: therefore there is an infinite mind, or God' (George (Bishop) Berkeley, *Philosophical Works*, p. 202).
45. Meillasoux, *After Finitude*, p. 5.
46. The irony is that Kant is known for effectuating a 'Copernican turn' in philosophy by displacing attention from *what* we know to *how* we know it – from the knowable to the knower. But then he essentially overrides this Copernican move by situating the knowing subject at the firm, immovable centre of the universe.
47. David Hume, *A Treatise of Human Nature*, p. 313.
48. Werner S. Pluhar contextualises this statement in his 'Translator's Introduction' in Kant's *Critique of Judgment*, p. xxxi.
49. Cairns Craig, *Association and the Literary Imagination*, pp. 49–50.
50. Meillassoux, *After Finitude*, p. 36.
51. Ibid. p. 39.
52. See ibid. p. 79.
53. Ibid. pp. 84–5 (Meillassoux's emphasis).
54. Ibid. p. 85.
55. Ibid. p. 117.
56. Ibid. p. 123 (Meillassoux's emphasis).
57. Ibid. p. 88 (Meillassoux's emphasis).
58. Hume, *A Treatise of Human Nature*, p. 146 (Hume's emphasis).
59. Ian Duncan, *Scott's Shadow*, p. 124.
60. Ibid. p. 138.
61. Amitav Ghosh, *The Great Derangement*, p. 70.
62. Ghosh makes an exception for the genre of science fiction, attending appreciatively to *Frankenstein* as the first iteration of this genre. He finds in Scott an early, similarly attuned admirer: 'Sir Walter Scott wrote an enthusiastic review' of *Frankenstein*, 'and he would say later that he preferred it to his own novels' (*The Great Derangement*, pp. 67–8).

Bibliography

Works by Scott

The Abbot. 1820. Christopher Johnson, ed. Edinburgh: Edinburgh University Press, 2000.

The Antiquary. 1816. David Hewitt, ed. Edinburgh: Edinburgh University Press, 1995.

The Betrothed. 1825. J. B. Ellis, ed. Edinburgh: Edinburgh University Press, 2009.

The Bride of Lammermoor. 1819. J. H. Alexander, ed. Edinburgh: Edinburgh University Press, 1995.

Castle Dangerous. 1831. J. H. Alexander, ed. Edinburgh: Edinburgh University Press, 2006.

Chronicles of the Canongate. 1827. Claire Lamont, ed. Edinburgh: Edinburgh University Press, 2000.

Essays on Chivalry, Romance, and the Drama. 1818. Edinburgh: Cadell, 1834.

The Fortunes of Nigel. 1822. Frank Jordan, ed. Edinburgh: Edinburgh University Press, 2004.

Guy Mannering. 1815. P. D. Garside, ed. Edinburgh: Edinburgh University Press, 1999.

The Heart of Mid-Lothian. 1818. Alison Lumsden and David Hewitt, eds. Edinburgh: Edinburgh University Press, 2004.

Ivanhoe. 1820. Graham Tulloch, ed. Edinburgh: Edinburgh University Press, 1998.

The Journal of Sir Walter Scott. W. E. K. Anderson, ed. London: Canongate, 1998.

Kenilworth: A Romance. 1821. J. H. Alexander, ed. Edinburgh: Edinburgh University Press, 1993.

The Lady of the Lake. Edinburgh: John Ballantyne and Co., 1810.

The Lady of the Lake. 2nd edn. Edinburgh: John Ballantyne and Co., 1810.
The Lay of the Last Minstrel. London: Longman, 1805.
A Legend of the Wars of Montrose. 1819. J. H. Alexander, ed. Edinburgh University Press, 1995.
The Letters of Sir Walter Scott, 1825–6. H. J. G. Grierson, ed. London: Constable, 1935.
The Life of Napoleon Buonaparte, Emperor of the French. With a Preliminary View of the French Revolution. 9 vols. Edinburgh: Longman etc., 1827.
Marmion. 1808. Ainsley McIntosh, ed. Edinburgh: Edinburgh University Press, 2018.
Minstrelsy of the Scottish Border. 2 vols. Kelso: James Ballantyne, 1802.
The Miscellaneous Prose Works of Sir Walter Scott. 6 vols. Edinburgh: Robert Cadell, 1827.
The Monastery. 1820. Penny Fielding, ed. Edinburgh: Edinburgh University Press, 2001.
Old Mortality. 1816. Douglas Mack, ed. Edinburgh: Edinburgh University Press, 1993.
Paul's Letters to his Kinsfolk. Edinburgh: Archibald Constable, 1816.
The Pirate. 1822. Mark Weinstein and Alison Lumsden, eds. Edinburgh: Edinburgh University Press,
Redgauntlet. 1824. G. A. M. Wood, with David Hewitt, ed. Edinburgh: Edinburgh University Press, 1997.
Reliquiae Trotcosienses or the Gabions of the Late Jonathan Oldbuck Esq. of Monkbarns. Gerard Carruthers and Alison Lumsden, eds. Edinburgh: Edinburgh University Press, 2004.
Review. *Tales of My Landlord. The Quarterly Review* 16 (January 1817): 430–80.
Rob Roy. 1818. David Hewitt, ed. Edinburgh: Edinburgh University Press, 2008.
Saint Ronan's Well. 1824. Mark Weinstein, ed. Edinburgh: Edinburgh University Press, 1995.
Tales of the Crusaders. Vol. 1. Edinburgh: Archibald Constable & Co., 1825.
The Talisman. 1825. J. B. Ellis, ed. Edinburgh: Edinburgh University Press, 2009.
The Visionary. P. D. Garside, ed. Cardiff: University College Cardiff Press, 1984.
Waverley; or, 'Tis Sixty Years Since. 1814. P. D. Garside, ed. Edinburgh: Edinburgh University Press, 2007.
Waverley Novels. A New Edition. 48 vols. Edinburgh: Cadell, 1829–33.

Works Cited

Adorno, Theodor W. *Prisms*. Samuel and Shierry Weber, trans. Cambridge, MA: The MIT Press, 1992.

Agamben, Giorgio. 'Vocation and Voice'. *Critical Inquiry* 40 (2014): 492–501.

Alexander, J. H. et al. *Introductions and Notes From The Magnum Opus: Waverley to A Legend of Montrose*. EEWN 25 A and B. Edinburgh: Edinburgh University Press, 2012.

Allen, Emily. 'Re-Marking Territory: *Redgauntlet* and the Restoration of Sir Walter Scott'. *Studies in Romanticism* 37.2 (1998): 163–82.

———. *Theater Figures: The Production of the Nineteenth-Century British Novel*. Columbus: Ohio State University Press, 2003.

Allon, Fiona. 'Everyday Leverage, or Leveraging the Everyday'. *Cultural Studies* 29.5–6 (2015): 687–706.

Alloway, Ross. 'Cadell and the Crash'. *Book History* 11.1 (2008): 125–47.

Anderson, Benedict. *Imagined Communities: Reflections on the Origin and Spread of Nationalism*. London: Verso, 2006.

Anderson, Mark L. *A History of Scottish Forestry*. 2 vols. Charles J. Taylor, ed. London: Thomas Nelson, 1967.

Anderson, W. E. K. *The Journal of Sir Walter Scott*. Edinburgh: Canongate, 1998.

Arata, Stephen. 'Scott's Pageants: The Example of *Kenilworth*'. *Studies in Romanticism* 40.1 (2001): 98–107.

Arrighi, Giovanni. *The Long Twentieth Century: Money, Power, and the Origins of Our Times*. New York: Verso, 1994.

Austen, Jane. *Jane Austen's Letters*. Deidre Le Faye, ed. Oxford: Oxford University Press, 1995.

———. *Persuasion*. 1817. James Kinsley, ed. Oxford: Oxford University Press, 2004.

Baillie, Joanna. *Collected Letters of Joanna Baillie*. 2 vols. Judith Bailey Slagle, ed. Madison, NJ: Fairleigh Dickinson University Press, 1999.

Bal, Mieke. 'Over-Writing as Un-writing: Descriptions, World-Making, and Novelistic Time'. *The Novel*. Vol. 2: *Forms and Themes*. Franco Moretti, ed. Princeton: Princeton University Press, 2016, pp. 571–610.

Balibar, Etienne. 'Politics of the Debt'. *Postmodern Culture* 23.3 (May 2013). Accessed online: doi:10.1353/pmc.2013.0049

Ball, Stephen J. 'Performativity, Commodification and Commitment: An I-Spy Guide to the Neoliberal University'. *British Journal of Educational Studies* 60.1 (2012): 17–28.

Bambery, Chris. *A People's History of Scotland*. London: Verso, 2014.

Barbauld, Anna Letitia. 'Thoughts on the Devotional Taste'. *Prose Works of Anna Letitia Barbauld*. 2 vols. Lucy Aikin, ed. London: Longman, 1825. 2: 232–59.

Bauman, Zygmunt. *Liquid Modernity*. Cambridge: Polity Press, 2000.

Beecher, Catharine E. and Harriet Beecher Stowe. *The American Woman's Home*. New York: J. B. Ford, 1869.

Beiderwell, Bruce. 'Scott's *Redgauntlet* as a Romance of Power'. *Studies in Romanticism* 28.2 (1989): 273–89.

Bell, Barbara. 'The Performance of Victorian Medievalism'. *Beyond Arthurian Romances*. Jennifer Palmgren and Lorretta Holloway, eds. Basingstoke: Palgrave Macmillan, 2005, pp. 191–216.

Bell, Bill, ed. *The Edinburgh History of the Book in Scotland, Vol. 3: Ambition and Industry, 1800–80*. Edinburgh: Edinburgh University Press, 2007.

Bell, David A. *The First Total War*. New York: Houghton Mifflin, 2007.

Berardi, Franco. *The Soul at Work: From Alienation to Autonomy*. Francesca Cadel and Guiseppina Mecchia, trans. Los Angeles: Semiotexte, 2009.

Bergson, Henri. *Matter and Memory*. N. M. Paul and W. S. Palmer, trans. New York: Zone Books, 1991.

Berkeley, George (Bishop). *Philosophical Works, Including the Works on Vision*. Michael R. Ayers, ed. London: Everyman, 1975.

Bewick, William. *Life and Letters of William Bewick (artist)*. 2 vols. Thomas Landseer, ed. London: Hurst and Blackett, 1871.

Blanchot, Maurice. *The Infinite Conversation*. Susan Hanson, trans. Minneapolis: University of Minnesota Press, 1992.

Bloch, Ernst. 'Nonsynchronism and the Obligation to its Dialectics'. Mark Ritter, trans. *New German Critique* 11 (1977): 22–38.

Bold, Valentina. *James Hogg: A Bard of Nature's Making*. Bern: Peter Lang, 2007.

Boltanski, Luc and Eve Chiapello. *The New Spirit of Capitalism*. Gregory Elliott, trans. London: Verso, 2005.

Bolton, Betsy. *Women, Nationalism and the Romantic Stage: Theatre and Politics in Britain, 1780–1800*. Cambridge: Cambridge University Press, 2001.

Booth, Alison. *Homes and Haunts: Touring Writers' Shrines and Countries*. Oxford: Oxford University Press, 2016.

Brown, Bill. 'Thing Theory'. *Critical Inquiry* 28.1 (Autumn 2001): 1–22.

Brown, Marshall. 'Rethinking the Scale of Literary History'. *Neohelicon: Acta Comparationis Litterarum Universarum* 30.1 (2003): 127–36.

Brown, William Wells. *Three Years in Europe*. London: Charles Gilpin, 1852.

Buell, Lawrence. *The Environmental Imagination: Thoreau, Nature Writing and the Formation of American Culture.* Cambridge, MA: Harvard University Press, 1996.

——. *The Future of Environmental Criticism: Environmental Crisis and Literary Imagination.* Malden, MA: Blackwell, 2005.

Burgess, Miranda J. *British Fiction and the Production of Social Order, 1740–1830.* Cambridge: Cambridge University Press, 2000.

——. 'Scott, History, and the Augustan Public Sphere'. *Studies in Romanticism* 40.1 (2001): 123–35.

Burke, Edmund. *A Philosophical Enquiry into the Origin of our Ideas of the Sublime and Beautiful.* 1757. Adam Phillips, ed. Oxford: Oxford University Press, 1990.

——. *Reflections on the Revolution in France and on the Proceedings in Certain Societies in London Relative to that Event.* 1790. Conor Cruise O'Brien, ed. Harmondsworth: Penguin, 1968.

Burstein, Miriam Elizabeth. *Victorian Reformation: Historical Fiction and Religious Controversy, 1820–1904.* Notre Dame: University of Notre Dame Press, 2013.

Butler, Judith. *Notes Towards a Performative Theory of Assembly.* Cambridge, MA: Harvard University Press, 2015.

——. 'Reflections on Trump'. 2017. https://culanth.org/fieldsights/reflections-on-trump

Butler, R. F. 'Maria Edgeworth and Sir Walter Scott: Unpublished Letters, 1823'. *The Review of English Studies* 9.33 (February 1958): 23–40.

Cagidimetrio, Alide. 'A Plea for Fictional Histories and Old-Time "Jewesses"'. *The Invention of Ethnicity.* Werner Sollors, ed. Oxford: Oxford University Press, 1989, pp. 13–43.

Campbell, Tim. *Historical Style: Fashion and the New Mode of History, 1740–1830.* Philadelphia: University of Pennsylvania Press, 2016.

Carlyle, Thomas. 'Review of *Memoirs of the Life of Sir Walter Scott, Baronet.* Vols i–vi. Cadell. Edinburgh, 1837'. *London and Westminster Review* 6.28 (1838): 293–345.

Chakrabarty, Dipesh. 'Postcolonial Studies and the Challenge of Climate Change'. *New Literary History* 43 (2012): 1–18.

Chandler, James. *England in 1819: The Politics of Literary Culture and the Case of Romantic Historicism.* Chicago: University of Chicago Press, 1998.

Clausewitz, Carl von. *On War.* Michael Howard and Peter Paret, trans. and ed. Princeton: Princeton University Press, 1976.

Clover, Joshua. 'Busted: Stories of the Financial Crisis'. *The Nation*, 20 September 2010. www.thenation.com/article/archive/busted-stories-financial-crisis/
——. 'The Rise and Fall of Biopolitics: A Response to Bruno Latour'. *Critical Inquiry* 'In the Moment' blog. 2020. www.critinq.wordpress.com/2020/03/29/the-rise-and-fall-of-biopolitics-a-response-to-bruno-latour/
Conroy, J. W. H., A. C. Kitchener and J. A. Gibson. 'The History of the Beaver in Scotland and its Future Reintroduction'. *Species History in Scotland*. Robert A. Lambert, ed. Edinburgh: Scottish Cultural Press, 1998, pp. 63–92.
Craig, Cairns. *Association and the Literary Imagination: From the Phantasmal Chaos*. Edinburgh: Edinburgh University Press, 2007.
——. *Intending Scotland: Scottish Intellectual Culture since the Enlightenment*. Edinburgh: Edinburgh University Press, 2009.
——. *Out of History: Narrative Paradigms in Scottish and English Culture*. Edinburgh: Polygon, 1996.
——. 'Scott's Staging of the Nation'. *Studies in Romanticism* 40.1 (2001): 13–28.
Crockett, W. S. *Abbotsford*. London: Adam & Charles Black, 1905.
Cronon, William. 'The Trouble with Wilderness; or, Getting Back to the Wrong Nature'. *Uncommon Ground: Rethinking the Human Place in Nature*. William Cronon, ed. New York: Norton, 1995.
Cross, J. W. *Life of George Eliot*. New York: Crowell, n.d.
Crutzen, Paul. 'Geology of Mankind'. *Nature* 415 (3 January 2002): 23.
Crutzen, Paul and Eugene Stoermer. 'The "Anthropocene"'. *Global Change Newsletter* 41 (2000): 17–18.
Currie, Mark. *About Time: Narrative, Fiction and the Philosophy of Time*. Edinburgh: Edinburgh University Press, 2006.
Deleuze, Gilles and Félix Guattari. *A Thousand Plateaus*. Brian Massumi, trans. London and New York: Continuum, 2004.
Derrida, Jacques. *Of Grammatology*. Gayatri Chakravorty Spivak, trans. 1974. Baltimore: Johns Hopkins University Press, 2016.
——. *Of Hospitality*. Stanford: Stanford University Press, 2000.
de Staël, Germaine. *Corinne, or Italy*. Sylvia Raphael, trans. Oxford: Oxford University Press, 1998.
Devine, T. M. *The Scottish Clearances: A History of the Dispossessed, 1600–1900*. London: Penguin, 2019.
——. *The Scottish Nation: 1700–2000*. London: Penguin, 1999.

Dick, Alexander. 'Scott and Political Economy'. *Edinburgh Companion to Sir Walter Scott*. Fiona Robertson, ed. Edinburgh: Edinburgh University Press, 2012, pp. 118–29.

———. 'Walter Scott and the Financial Crash of 1825: Fiction, Speculation, and the Standard of Value'. *Romantic Circles* (2011). https://www.rc.umd.edu/praxis/forgery/HTML/praxis.2011.dick.html

Dimock, Wai Chee. 'Low Epic'. *Critical Inquiry* 39.3 (2013): 614–31.

Doody, Margaret. *Jane Austen's Names: Riddles, Persons, Places*. Chicago: University of Chicago Press, 2015.

Douglas, David. *Familiar Letters of Sir Walter Scott*. 2 vols. Edinburgh: David Douglas, 1894.

Duncan, Ian. 'Death and the Author'. *Taking Liberties with the Author*. Meredith L. McGill, ed. Cambridge, MA: English Institute in collaboration with the ACLS, 2013. ACLS Humanities e-book, pp. 68–101.

———. 'History and the Novel after Lukács'. *Novel: A Forum on Fiction* 50.3 (2017): 388–96.

———. *Human Forms: The Novel in the Age of Evolution*. Princeton: Princeton University Press, 2019.

———. 'Late Scott'. *Edinburgh Companion to Walter Scott*. Fiona Robertson, ed. Edinburgh: Edinburgh University Press, 2012, pp. 130–42.

———. *Modern Romance and Transformations of the Novel: The Gothic, Scott, Dickens*. Cambridge: Cambridge University Press, 1992.

———. *Scott's Shadow: The Novel in Romantic Edinburgh*. Princeton: Princeton University Press, 2007.

———. 'Walter Scott, James Hogg, and Scottish Gothic'. *A New Companion to the Gothic*. David Punter, ed. Oxford: John Wiley and Sons, 2012, pp. 123–34.

Ecocriticism and Narrative Theory. Special Issue. Erin James and Eric Morel, eds. *English Studies* 99.4 (July 2018).

Elliott, Larry. 'Thomas Piketty: The French Economist Bringing Capitalism to Book'. *The Guardian*, 2 May 2014. www.theguardian.com/books/2014/may/02/thomas-piketty-capital-in-the-twenty-first-century-french-economist

Ellis, Sarah Stickney. *The Women of England, their Social Duties and Domestic Habits*. London: Fisher, 1839.

Estok, Simon. *The Ecophobia Hypothesis*. New York: Routledge, 2018.

———. 'Theorizing in a Space of Ambivalent Openness: Ecocriticism and Ecophobia'. *ISLE*, 16.2 (Spring 2009): 203–25.

Favret, Mary A. *War at a Distance: Romanticism and the Making of Modern Wartime*. Princeton: Princeton University Press, 2010.

Fenves, Peter, ed. *Raising the Tone of Philosophy: Late Essays by Immanuel Kant, Transformative Critique by Jacques Derrida.* Peter Fenves, trans. Baltimore: Johns Hopkins University Press, 1993.

Ferguson, Adam. *An Essay on the History of Civil Society.* Fania Oz-Salzberger, ed. Cambridge: Cambridge University Press, 1995.

Ferrier, Susan. *Memoir and Correspondence of Susan Ferrier, 1782–1854.* John A. Doyle, ed. London: John Murray, 1898.

Ferris, Ina. *The Achievement of Literary Authority: Gender, History, and the Waverley Novels.* Ithaca: Cornell University Press, 1991.

——. '"Before Our Eyes": Romantic Historical Fiction and the Apparitions of Reading'. *Representations* 121 (Winter 2013): 60–84.

——. '"On the Borders of Oblivion": Scott's Historical Novel and the Modern Time of the Remnant'. *Modern Language Quarterly* 70.4 (2009): 473–94.

Fielding, Penny. '"That roaming meteor world": James Hogg in Time and Space'. *Studies in Hogg and his World* 27/28 (2019): 3–17.

Fitzpatrick, Linda. *The Real Price of Fish: The Story of Scotland's Fishing Industry and Communities.* Edinburgh: Scottish Fisheries Museum, 2010.

Fleury de Chaboulon, Pierre Alexandre Edouard (Baron). *Memoirs of the Private Life, Return, and Reign of Napoleon in 1815.* Vol. 1. London: John Murray, 1820.

Forbes, Duncan. 'The Rationalism of Walter Scott'. *Cambridge Journal* 7 (1953): 20–35.

Forster, E. M. *Aspects of the Novel.* 1927; Harmondsworth: Penguin, 1976.

Fosbrooke, Thomas Dudley. 'Art. V. *British Monachism: Or, Manners and Customs of the Monks and Nuns of England*'. *The Critical Review, or, Annals of Literature* 38 (1802): 39–44.

Foucault, Michel. *The Order of Things.* New York: Vintage, 1973.

Frey, Anne. *British State Romanticism: Authorship, Agency, and Bureaucratic Nationalism.* Stanford: Stanford University Press, 2009.

Gamer, Michael. 'Authors in Effect: Lewis, Scott, and the Gothic Drama'. *ELH* 66.4 (1999): 831–66.

——. 'Gothic Fiction and Romantic Writing in Britain'. *The Cambridge Companion to Gothic Fiction.* Jerold E. Hogle, ed. Cambridge: Cambridge University Press, 2002, pp. 85–104.

Garside, Peter D. 'Union and *The Bride of Lammermoor*'. *Studies in Scottish Literature* 19 (1984): 72–93.

——. 'Walter Scott and the "Common" Novel'. *Cardiff Corvey: Reading the Romantic Text* 3.2. http://sites.cardiff.ac.uk/romtextv2/files/2013/02/cc03_n02.pdf

———, ed. Walter Scott, *Waverley*. London: Penguin, 2011.
Genette, Gérard. 'Introduction to the Paratext'. *New Literary History* 22.2 (Spring 1991): 261–72.
———. *Narrative Discourse: An Essay in Method*. Jane E. Lewin, trans. Ithaca: Cornell University Press, 1980.
Ghosh, Amitav. *The Great Derangement: Climate Change and the Unthinkable*. Chicago: University of Chicago Press, 2016.
Gibson, John. *Reminiscences of Sir Walter Scott*. Edinburgh: Adam and Charles Black, 1871.
Goodman, Kevis. *Georgic Modernity and British Romanticism: Poetry and the Mediation of History*. Cambridge: Cambridge University Press, 2004.
Gothic Nature Journal: New Directions in Ecohorror and EcoGothic. https://gothicnaturejournal.com
Gottlieb, Evan. *Romantic Realities: Speculative Realism and British Romanticism*. Edinburgh: Edinburgh University Press, 2016.
———. *Walter Scott and Contemporary Theory*. New York: Bloomsbury Academic, 2013.
Gregg, Melissa. 'Getting Things Done: Productivity, Management, and the Order of Things'. *Networked Affect*. Ken Hillis, Susanna Paasonen, Michael Petit, eds. Cambridge, MA: The MIT Press, 2015.
Griffiths, Devin. *The Age of Analogy: Science and Literature between the Darwins*. Baltimore: Johns Hopkins University Press, 2016.
Grossberg, Lawrence. 'Is there a Fan in the House? The Affective Sensibility of Fandom'. *The Adoring Audience: Fan Culture and Popular Media*. Lisa A. Lewis, ed. Abingdon: Taylor and Francis, 1992.
Gumbrecht, Hans Ulrich. 'The Roads of the Novel'. *The Novel*. Vol. 2: *Forms and Themes*. Franco Moretti, ed. Princeton: Princeton University Press, 2006, pp. 611–46.
Gurton-Wachter, Lily. *Watchwords: Romanticism and the Poetics of Attention*. Stanford: Stanford University Press, 2016.
Handley, George B. 'Toward an Environmental Phenomenology of Diaspora'. *Modern Fiction Studies* 55.3 (2009): 649–57.
Handwerk, Gary. 'Romantic Irony'. *The Cambridge History of Literary Criticism*. Vol. V: *Romanticism*. Marshall Brown, ed. Cambridge: Cambridge University Press, 2000.
Hansen, Mark. *New Philosophy for New Media*. Cambridge, MA: The MIT Press, 2004.
Haraway, Donna. *The Companion Species Manifesto: Dogs, People, and Significant Otherness*. Chicago: Prickly Paradigm Press, 2003.

——. *Staying With the Trouble*. Durham, NC: Duke University Press, 2016.
Harman, Graham. 'The Well-Wrought Broken Hammer: Object-Oriented Literary Criticism'. *New Literary History* 43.2 (2012): 183–203.
Harney, Marion. *Place-making for the Imagination: Horace Walpole and Strawberry Hill*. London: Routledge, 2013.
Harris, Jocelyn. *A Revolution Almost Beyond Expression: Jane Austen's Persuasion*. Wilmington: University of Delaware Press, 2007.
Harris, Ron. 'Political Economy, Interest Groups, Legal Institutions, and the Repeal of the Bubble Act, 1825'. *Economic History Society* 50.4 (November 1997): 675–96.
Hawthorne, Nathaniel. *Passages from the English Note-Books of Nathaniel Hawthorne*. Boston, MA: Fields, Osgood, 1870.
Hegel, G. W. F. *Aesthetics: Lectures on Fine Art*. 2 vols. T. M. Knox, trans. Oxford: Oxford University Press, 1975.
Heise, Ursula. *Sense of Place and Sense of Planet: The Environmental Imagination of the Global*. Oxford: Oxford University Press, 2008.
Hesse, Carla. 'Books in Time'. *The Future of the Book*. Geoffrey Nunberg, ed. Turnhout: Brepols, 1996.
Hogg, James. 'The Fords of Callum'. *Friendship's Offering* (1830), pp. 187–96.
Howitt, William. *Homes and Haunts of the Most Eminent British Poets*. 4th edn. London: Routledge, Warne and Routledge, 1863.
Hughes, Gillian. 'Pickling Virgil? Scott's Notes to *The Lay of the Last Minstrel*'. *Scottish Literary Review* 7.2 (Autumn/Winter 2015): 51–62.
Hume, David. *A Treatise of Human Nature*. 1739. Ernest C. Mossner, ed. London: Penguin, 1968.
Hunt, David. *Early Farming Communities in Scotland: Aspects of Economy and Settlement*. British Archeological Reports. BAR British Series 159: i (1987): 10–16.
Hutcheson, Francis. *An Inquiry into the Original of our Ideas of Beauty and Virtue*. 1725. London: J. Darby, 1726.
Ireland, William Henry. *The Napoleon Anecdotes: Illustrating the Mental Energies of the Emperor of France*. Vol. 3. London: C. S. Arnold, 1823.
Jackson-Houlston, C. M. *Gendering Walter Scott: Sex, Violence and Romantic Period Writing*. London: Routledge, 2017.
Jameson, Fredric. *The Antinomies of Realism*. London: Verso, 2013.
——. *Archaeologies of the Future: The Desire Called Utopia and Other Science Fictions*. London: Verso, 2005.
——. *The Political Unconscious: Narrative as a Socially Symbolic Act*. Ithaca: Cornell University Press, 1981.

Jarrells, Anthony. *Britain's Bloodless Revolutions: 1688 and the Romantic Reform of Literature*. Basingstoke: Palgrave, 2005.

[Jeffrey, Francis]. 'Marmion; A Tale of Flodden Field'. *Edinburgh Review* 12 (April 1808): 1–35.

——. 'Waverley – A Novel'. *Edinburgh Review* 24 (November 1814): 208–43.

Jenkins, David and Mark Visocchi. *Mendelssohn in Scotland*. London: Chappell, 1978.

Johnson, Samuel. *A Dictionary of the English Language*. 3rd edn. London: A. Millar, 1766.

Jones, Catherine. *Literary Memory: Scott's Waverley Novels and the Psychology of Narrative*. Lewisburg, PA: Bucknell University Press, 2003.

Jonsson, Fredrik Albritton. *Enlightenment's Frontier: The Scottish Highlands and the Origins of Environmentalism*. New Haven, CT: Yale University Press, 2013.

Joseph, Miranda. *Debt to Society: Accounting for Life under Capitalism*. Minneapolis: University of Minnesota Press, 2014.

——. 'Investing in the Cruel Entrepreneurial University'. *SAQ* 114.3 (July 2015): 491–511.

Kant, Immanuel. *Critique of Judgment*. 1790. Werner S. Pluhar, trans. Indianapolis: Hackett, 1987.

——. 'On a Newly Arisen Superior Tone in Philosophy'. *Raising the Tone of Philosophy: Late Essays by Immanuel Kant, Transformative Critique by Jacques Derrida*. Peter Fenves, trans. and ed. Baltimore: Johns Hopkins University Press, 1993.

Kerr, James. 'Fiction Against History: Scott's *Redgauntlet* and the Power of Romance'. *Texas Studies in Literature and Language* 29.3 (1987): 237–60.

Kitchener Andrew C. 'Extinctions, Introductions and Colonisations of Scottish Mammals and Birds since the Last Ice Age'. *Species History in Scotland*. Robert A. Lambert, ed. Edinburgh: Edinburgh University Press, 1998, pp. 63–92.

Knight, Ellis Cornelia. *Autobiography of Cornelia Knight, Lady Companion to the Princess of Charlotte of Wales*. 2 vols. London: Allen, 1841.

——. *Marcus Flaminius; Or, a View of the Military, Political and Social Life of the Romans; In a Series of Letters from a Patrician to His Friend*. 1792. 2nd edn. 2 vols. London: Cadell and Davies, 1808.

Koselleck, Reinhart. *Futures Past: On the Semantics of Historical Time*. Cambridge, MA: The MIT Press, 1985.

——. *The Practice of Conceptual History: Timing History, Spacing Concepts*. Todd Samuel Presner et al., trans. Stanford: Stanford University Press, 2002.

Krugman, Paul. 'Why We're in a New Gilded Age'. *New York Review of Books* 61.8 (8 May 2014). www.nybooks.com/articles/2014/05/08/thomas-piketty-new-gilded-age/

Laidlaw, William. 'Abbotsford Notanda'. *Gentleman's Magazine* 2 N.S. (1869): 586–95, 680–92.

Lamont, Claire, ed. *Waverley*. Oxford: Oxford University Press, 1986.

Langan, Celeste. 'Understanding Media in 1805: Audiovisual Hallucination in *The Lay of the Last Minstrel*'. *Studies in Romanticism* 40.1 (Spring 2001): 49–70.

Langan, Celeste and Maureen N. McLane. 'The Medium of Romantic Poetry'. *The Cambridge Companion to British Romantic Poetry*. James Chandler and Maureen N. McLane, eds. Cambridge: Cambridge University Press, 2008, pp. 239–63.

Lazzarato, Maurizio. *The Making of Indebted Man*. Joshua David Jordan, trans. Los Angeles: Semiotext(e), 2012.

Leavis, F. R. *The Great Tradition*. 1948. London: Penguin, 1980.

Lee, Yoon Sun. 'Austen's Scale-Making'. *Studies in Romanticism* 52.3 (2013): 171–95.

———. 'Giants in the North: *Douglas*, the Scottish Enlightenment, and Scott's *Redgauntlet*'. *Studies in Romanticism* 40.1 (2001): 109–21.

———. 'Vection, Vertigo, and the Historical Novel'. *Novel: A Forum on Fiction* 52.2 (2019): 179–99.

Leopold, Aldo. *A Sand County Almanac and Sketches Here and There*. New York: Oxford University Press, 1949.

Levy, Sharon and Peter Cairns. 'The Age of Extinction: Scotland's Bogs Reveal a Secret Paradise for Birds and Beetles'. *The Guardian*, 27 November 2019.

Lincoln, Andrew. *Walter Scott and Modernity*. Edinburgh: Edinburgh University Press, 2007.

Little, John. *Practical Observations on the Improvement and Management of Mountain Sheep and Sheep Farms*. Edinburgh: Macredie, Skelley, and Muckersy, 1815.

Liu, Alan. 'Friending the Past: The Sense of History and Social Computing'. *New Literary History* 42.1 (2011): 1–30.

———. *Local Transcendence: Essays on Postmodern Historicism and the Database*. Chicago: University of Chicago Press, 2008.

Livesey, Ruth. *Writing the Stage Coach Nation: Locality on the Move in Nineteenth-Century Britain*. Oxford: Oxford University Press, 2016.

Lockhart, J. G. *Memoirs of the Life of Sir Walter Scott, Bart*. 7 vols. Edinburgh: Robert Cadell, 1837–8.

Lordon, Frédéric. *Willing Slaves of Capital: Spinoza and Marx on Desire*. New York: Verso, 2014.

Lorenz, Chris. '"If You're So Smart, Why Are You Under Surveillance?" Universities, Neoliberalism, and Public Management'. *Critical Inquiry* 38.3 (2012): 599–629.

———. 'Unstuck in Time. Or: The Sudden Presence of the Past'. *Performing the Past: Memory, History, and Identity in Modern Europe*. Karin Tilman et al., eds. Amsterdam: Amsterdam University Press, 2010.

Luhmann, Niklas. *Art as a Social System*. Eva M. Knodt, trans. Stanford: Stanford University Press, 2000.

Lukács, Georg. *The Historical Novel*. 1937. Hannah Mitchell and Stanley Mitchell, trans. London: Merlin Press, 1962.

Lumsden, Alison. 'Towards the Edinburgh Edition of Walter Scott's Poetry'. *Walter Scott: New Interpretations*. Susan Oliver, ed. *The Yearbook of English Studies* 47 (2017): 127–42.

———. *Walter Scott and the Limits of Language*. Edinburgh: Edinburgh University Press, 2010.

Lumsden, Alison and Ainsley McIntosh. 'The Narrative Poems'. *The Edinburgh Companion to Walter Scott*. Fiona Robertson, ed. Edinburgh: Edinburgh University Press, 2012, pp. 35–46.

Lupton, Christina. 'Contingency, Codex, the Eighteenth-Century Novel'. *ELH* 81.4 (2014): 173–92.

Lynch, Andrew. '"Simply to Amuse the Reader": The Humor of Walter Scott's Reformation'. *Postmedieval: A Journal of Medieval Cultural Studies* 5.2 (2014): 169–83.

Lynch, Deidre. 'Austen Extended/Austen for Everyday Use'. *Imagining Selves: Essays in Honor of Patricia Meyer Spacks*. Rivka Swenson and Elise Lauterbach, eds. Newark: University of Delaware Press, 2008, pp. 235–65.

McCracken-Flesher, Caroline. 'Anxiety in the Archive: From the Antiquary to the Absent Author'. *Scottish Literary Review* 7.2 (2015): 102–8.

———. *The Doctor Dissected: A Cultural Autopsy of the Burke and Hare Murders*. Oxford: Oxford University Press, 2012.

———. *Possible Scotlands: Walter Scott and the Story of Tomorrow*. Oxford: Oxford University Press, 2005.

———. 'Walter Scott's Romanticism: A Theory of Performance'. *The Edinburgh Companion to Scottish Romanticism*. Murray Pittock, ed. Edinburgh: Edinburgh University Press, 2011, pp. 139–49.

McGann, Jerome. 'Walter Scott's Romantic Postmodernity'. *Scotland and the Borders of Romanticism*. Leith Davis, Ian Duncan and Janet Sorensen, eds. Cambridge: Cambridge University Press, 2004, pp. 113–29.

McGurl, Mark. 'The Posthuman Comedy'. *Critical Inquiry* 38.3 (2012): 533–53.
McIntosh, Ainsley. 'A Critical Edition of Walter Scott's *Marmion*'. PhD thesis, University of Aberdeen, 2010.
———. '"Land Debateable": The Supernatural in Scott's Narrative Poetry'. *Walter Scott: New Interpretations*. Susan Oliver, ed. *The Yearbook of English Studies* 47 (2017): 143–60.
Mack, Douglas S., ed. *James Hogg, Memoirs of the Author's Life and Familiar Anecdotes of Sir Walter Scott*. Edinburgh: Scottish Academic Press, 1972.
McNeil, Kenneth. 'Ballads and Borders'. *The Edinburgh Companion to Walter Scott*. Fiona Robertson, ed. Edinburgh: Edinburgh University Press, 2012, pp. 22–34.
McWilliam, Erica, Caroline Hatcher et al. 'Developing Professional Identities: Re-making the Academic for Corporate Times'. *Pedagogy, Culture and Society* 7.1 (1999): 55–72.
Maitzen, Rohan. '"By No Means an Improbable Fiction": *Redgauntlet*'s Novel Historicism'. *Studies in the Novel* 25.2 (1993): 170–83.
Manning, Susan. *Fragments of Union: Making Connections in Scottish and American Writing*. Basingstoke: Palgrave, 2002.
———. 'Walter Scott: The Critical Question'. *The Cambridge Quarterly* 26.2 (1997): 177–88.
Marche, Stephen. 'The Literature of the Second Gilded Age'. *Los Angeles Review of Books*, 16 June 2014. https://lareviewofbooks.org/article/literature-second-gilded-age/#
Markovits, Daniel. *The Meritocracy Trap: How America's Foundational Myth Feeds Inequality, Dismantles the Middle Class, and Devours the Elite*. New York: Penguin Press, 2019.
Marx, Karl. *Capital: A Critique of Political Economy*. Vol. 1. Ben Fowkes, trans. New York: Penguin, 1990.
Marx, Karl and Friedrich Engels. *The Communist Manifesto*. New York: Penguin Classics, 2002.
Mayer, Robert. *Walter Scott and Fame: Authors and Readers in the Romantic Age*. Oxford: Oxford University Press, 2017.
Meillassoux, Quentin. *After Finitude: An Essay on the Necessity of Contingency*. Ray Brassier, trans. London: Continuum, 2008.
Mill, John Stuart. Review of Scott's *Life of Napoleon Buonaparte*. *Westminster Review* 9 (April 1828): 251–313.
Millar, John. *The Origin of the Distinction of Ranks*. 1771. John Price, ed. Bristol: Thoemmes, 1990.
Millgate, Jane. '*Persuasion* and the Presence of Scott'. *Persuasions* 15 (1993): 184–9.

———. 'Text and Context: Dating the Events of *The Bride of Lammermoor*'. *The Bibliothek* 9 (1979): 2003–13.

———. *Walter Scott: The Making of the Novelist*. Toronto: University of Toronto Press, 1984.

Monboddo, James Burnett, Lord. *Of the Origins and Progress of Language*. 2nd edn. 2 vols. Edinburgh: Balfour, Cadell, 1774.

Montesquieu, Charles Louis de Secondat de. *The Spirit of the Law*. Anne M. Cohler, Basia Carolyn Miller and Harold Samuel Stone, eds and trans. Cambridge: Cambridge University Press, 1989.

Moody, Jane. *Illegitimate Theatre in London, 1770–1840*. Cambridge: Cambridge University Press, 2007.

Moretti, Franco. 'Serious Century'. *The Novel*. Vol. 1: *History, Geography, and Culture*. Franco Moretti, ed. Princeton: Princeton University Press, 2006.

Morton, Timothy. *Hyperobjects: Philosophy and Ecology after the End of the World*. Minneapolis: University of Minnesota Press, 2013.

Muir, Edwin. *The Complete Poems of Edwin Muir*. Peter Butter, ed. Aberdeen: Association for Scottish Literary Studies, 1991.

———. *Scott and Scotland: The Predicament of the Scottish Writer*. London: G. Routledge, 1936.

Mullen, Mary. 'Anachronistic Aesthetics: Maria Edgeworth and the "Uses" of History'. *Eighteenth-Century Fiction* 26.2 (2013–14): 233–59.

Nairn, Tom. *The Break-up of Britain: Crisis and Neonationalism*. London: NLB, 1977.

———. 'The Three Dreams of Scottish Nationalism'. 1970. Rpt. *A Diverse Assembly: The Debate on the Scottish Parliament*. Lindsay Paterson, ed. Edinburgh: Edinburgh University Press, 1998, pp. 31–9.

Naismyth, John. *Observations on the Different Breeds of Sheep, and the State of Sheep Farming, in the Southern Districts of Scotland: Being the Result of a Tour Through These Parts, Made Under the Direction of The Society for Improvement of British Wool*. Edinburgh: W. Smellie, 1795.

Neal, Larry. 'The Financial Crisis of 1825 and the Restructuring of the British Financial System'. *Federal Reserve Bank of St. Louis* Review (1997): 53–76.

———. *The Rise of Financial Capitalism: International Capital Markets in the Age of Reason*. New York: Cambridge University Press, 1990.

Nichols, John. *The Progresses, and Public Processions, of Queen Elizabeth*. Vol. 1. London: Printer to the Society of Antiquaries, 1788.

Nixon, Rob. *Slow Violence and The Environmentalism of the Poor*. Cambridge, MA: Harvard University Press, 2011.

O'Brien, Karen. *Women and Enlightenment in Eighteenth-Century Britain*. Cambridge: Cambridge University Press, 2009.

Oliver, Susan. 'The Matter of Landscape: Ecologies of Violence for Our Time'. *The Bottle Imp* 16 (2014): 1–5.

———. 'Planting the Nation's "Waste Lands": Walter Scott, Forestry and the Cultivation of Scotland's Wilderness'. *Literature Compass* 6.3 (2009): 585–98.

———. 'Sir Walter Scott's Transatlantic Ecology'. *Wordsworth Circle*, 44.2–3 (2013): 115–20.

———. 'Trees, Rivers, and Stories: Walter Scott Writing the Land'. *Yearbook of English Studies* (2017): 279–99.

'On Reading and Readers'. *New Monthly Magazine* 14 (November 1820): 533–9.

Parker, Hershel. *Herman Melville: A Biography*. Vol. 2. Baltimore: Johns Hopkins University Press, 2002.

Patmore, Coventry. *The Angel in the House*. London: Macmillan, 1863.

Peacock, Thomas Love. 'The Four Ages of Poetry'. *Literary Miscellany*. 1820. *Peacock's Four Ages of Poetry, Shelley's Defence of Poetry, Browning's Essay on Shelley*. H. F. B. Brett-Smith, ed. Boston and New York: Houghton Mifflin Company, 1925, pp. 3–20.

Pearlstein, Steven. '"Capital in the Twenty-First Century" by Thomas Piketty'. *The Washington Post*, 28 March 2014. www.washingtonpost.com/opinions/capital-in-the-twenty-first-century-by-thomas-piketty/2014/03/28/ea75727a-a87a-11e3-8599-ce7295b6851c_story.html?utm_term=.91ad9307e27b

Pennant, Thomas. *Arctic Zoology*. 2 vols. London: Henry Hughes, 1784.

Perkin, Harold. *The Rise of Professional Society: England Since 1880*. London: Routledge, 1989.

Peters, John Durham. *The Marvelous Clouds: Toward a Philosophy of Elemental Media*. Chicago: University of Chicago Press, 2015.

Piketty, Thomas. *Capital and Ideology*. Arthur Goldhammer, trans. Cambridge, MA: Harvard University Press, 2020.

———. *Capital in the Twenty-First Century*. Arthur Goldhammer, trans. Cambridge, MA: Harvard University Press, 2014.

Pittock, Murray. *Material Culture and Sedition, 1688–1760: Treacherous Objects, Secret Places*. New York: Palgrave Macmillan, 2013.

———. *Scottish and Irish Romanticism*. Oxford: Oxford University Press, 2008.

Poot, Luke Terlaak. 'Scott's Momentaneousness: Bad Timing in *The Bride of Lammermoor*'. *Nineteenth-Century Literature* 72.3 (2017): 283–310.

Porter, Jane. *The Scottish Chiefs, A Romance*. 1810. Peterborough, ON: Broadview, 2007.

Price, Fiona. 'National Identities and Regional Affiliations'. *The Cambridge Companion to Women's Writing in the Romantic Period*. Devoney Looser, ed. Cambridge: Cambridge University Press, 2015, pp. 183–97.

———. *Reinventing Liberty: Nation, Commerce, and the Historical Novel from Walpole to Scott*. Edinburgh: Edinburgh University Press, 2016.

Purdy, Jedediah. *After Nature: A Politics for the Anthropocene*. Cambridge, MA: Harvard University Press, 2015.

Quayle, Eric. *The Ruin of Sir Walter Scott*. London: Hart-Davis, 1968.

Ragussis, Michael. *Figures of Conversion: The 'Jewish Question' and English National Identity*. Durham, NC: Duke University Press, 1995.

Rancière, Jacques. 'Good Times, or Pleasure at the Barrière'. *Staging the People: The Proletarian and his Double*. David Fernbach, trans. London: Verso, 2011.

Rangarajan, Padma. 'History's Rank Stew: Scott, Mill, and the Politics of Time'. *Romanticism* 21.1 (2015): 59–71.

Richards, I. A. *Practical Criticism: A Study of Literary Judgment*. New York: Harcourt, Brace and Company, 1930.

Rigney, Ann. *The Afterlives of Walter Scott: Memory on the Move*. Oxford: Oxford University Press, 2012.

River Tweed Commission. 'Tweed Angling Code for Salmon and Sea-Trout'. www.rtc.org.uk/Tweed_Angling_Code_for_Salmon_and_Sea-trout_WORD_Ver_2016.pdf

Roberts, Brian Russell and Michelle Ann Stephens, eds. *Archipelagic American Studies*. Durham, NC: Duke University Press, 2017.

Robertson, Fiona. 'Castle Spectres: Scott, Gothic Drama, and the Search for the Narrator'. *Scott in Carnival*. J. H. Alexander and D. S. Hewitt, eds. Aberdeen: Scottish Academic Press, 1993, pp. 444–58.

———. *Legitimate Histories: Scott, Gothic, and the Authorities of Fiction*. Oxford: Clarendon, 1994.

———. *Lives of the Great Romantics II: Keats, Coleridge & Scott by their Contemporaries*. London: Pickering and Chatto, 1997.

Robertson, Roland. 'Glocalization: Time-Space and Homogeneity-Heterogeneity'. *Global Modernities*. Mike Featherstone, Scott Lash and Roland Robertson, eds. London: Sage, 1995.

Robinson, Roy. 'State of Afforestation in the Highlands'. *Transactions of the Inverness Scientific Society and Field Club* 9 (1918–1925): 313–14.

Robinson, Terry F. '"Life is a Tragicomedy!": Maria Edgeworth's *Belinda* and the Staging of the Realist Novel'. *Nineteenth-Century Literature* 67.2 (2012): 139–76.

Rousseau, Jean-Jacques. *Letter from M. Rousseau of Geneva to M. D'Alembert of Paris Concerning the Effects of Theatrical Entertainments on the Manners of Mankind. Translated from the French.* 1758. London: J. Nourie, 1759.

Rowland, Ann Wierda. 'Romantic Poetry and the Romantic Novel'. *The Cambridge Companion to British Romantic Poetry.* James Chandler and Maureen McLane, eds. Cambridge: Cambridge University Press, 2008, pp. 117–35.

Ruddiman, William F. 'How Did Humans First Alter Global Climate?' *Scientific American,* 292.3 (2005): 46–53.

Said, Edward. *Orientalism.* New York: Vintage, 1979.

Schiefelbein, Michael E. *The Lure of Babylon: Seven Protestant Novelists and Britain's Roman Catholic Revival.* Macon, GA: Mercer University Press, 2001.

Schumpeter, Joseph. *Imperialism and Social Classes.* Cleveland and New York: Meridian Books, 2007.

———. *The Theory of Economic Development.* New York: Routledge, 2017.

Scott, David. 'William Patten and the Authorship of "Robert Laneham's Letter" (1575)'. *English Literary Renaissance* 7 (September 1977): 297–306.

Scottish Government. 'Active salmon netting stations that have submitted catch returns'. www.webarchive.org.uk/wayback/archive/3000/http://www2.gov.scot/topics/marine/publications/msfoieirdisclosures/activesalmonnetting

———. *The Scottish Rural Development Programme 2014–2020.* www2.gov.scot/Topics/farmingrural/SRDP/RuralPriorities/Options/UplandandPeatlandSites/DefinitionsofLandTypes (last accessed 9 October 2020).

Sen, Amartya. 'Merit and Justice'. *Meritocracy and Economic Inequality.* Kenneth Arrow, Samuel Bowles and Steven Durlauf, eds. Princeton: Princeton University Press, 2000.

Serres, Michel. *The Parasite.* Lawrence R. Schehr, trans. Baltimore: Johns Hopkins University Press, 1980.

Shelley, P. B. *The Major Works.* Zachary Leader and Michael O'Neill, eds. Oxford: Oxford University Press, 2003.

Sheridan, Thomas. *A Course of Lectures on Elocution.* 1762. Rpt. Menston: Scolar Press, 1968.

Sider, Justin. '"Modern-Antiques", Ballad Imitation, and the Aesthetics of Anachronism'. *Victorian Poetry* 54.4 (2016): 455–75.

Simpson, David. *Romanticism and the Question of the Stranger.* Chicago: University of Chicago Press, 2013.

Sinclair, Sir John. *The Statistical Account of Scotland 1791–1799.* 20 vols. J. Withrington and Ian R. Grant, gen. eds. East Ardsley: EP Publishing, 1978.

Smiles, Samuel. *Industrial Biography: Iron Workers and Tool Makers*. London: J. Murray, 1863.
Smith, Adam. *An Inquiry into the Nature and Causes of the Wealth of Nations*. 3 vols. London: W. Strahan, 1776.
———. *Lectures on Rhetoric and Belles Lettres*. J. C. Bryce, ed. Indianapolis: Liberty Fund, 1985.
———. *The Theory of Moral Sentiments*. London: A. Millar, 1759.
Smith, Andrew and William Hughes, eds. *EcoGothic*. Manchester: Manchester University Press, 2013.
Smith, Horace. 'A Graybeard's Gossip about his Literary Acquaintances'. *New Monthly Magazine* 82.12 (1848). *Lives of the Great Romantics II: Vol. 3, Scott*. Fiona Robertson, ed. London: Pickering and Chatto, 1997, pp. 290–9.
Sorensen, Janet. *Strange Vernaculars: How Eighteenth-Century Slang, Cant, Provincial Languages, and Nautical Jargon Became English*. Princeton: Princeton University Press, 2017.
Stendhal. *Le Rouge et le Noir*. Paris: A. Levasseur, 1830.
Stewart, Dugald. *Lectures on Political Economy, The Collected Works of Dugald Stewart*. Vol. 8. William Hamilton, ed. Edinburgh: Thomas Constable and Co., 1855.
Stewart, Matthew. 'The 9.9 Percent is the New American Aristocracy'. *The Atlantic* (June 2018). https://www.theatlantic.com/magazine/archive/2018/06/the-birth-of-a-new-american-aristocracy/559130/
Stowe, Harriet Beecher. *Sunny Memories of Foreign Lands*. 2 vols. 1854. Rpt. Carlisle, MA: Applewood, n.d.
Sutherland, John. *The Life of Walter Scott: A Critical Biography*. Malden, MA: Blackwell, 1995.
Sutherland, Kathryn. 'Fictional Economies: Adam Smith, Walter Scott and the Nineteenth-Century Novel'. *ELH* 54.1 (Spring 1987): 97–127.
Tambling, Jeremy. *On Anachronism*. Manchester: Manchester University Press, 2013.
Terada, Rei. 'Two Hundred Years of University Reform and How to Dream It'. *Reclamations* 3 (2010). Web.
Thomas, Julia. *Shakespeare's Shrine: The Bard's Birthplace and the Invention of Stratford-upon-Avon*. Philadelphia: University of Pennsylvania Press, 2012.
Thorne, Christian. 'In Saecula Saeculorum: On How Stories End'. *MLQ* 76.2 (2015): 247–69.
Trumpener, Katie. *Bardic Nationalism: The Romantic Novel and the British Empire*. Princeton: Princeton University Press, 1997.
Tsing, Anna et al. 'Anthropologists are talking about the Anthropocene'. *Ethnos* 81.3 (2016): 535–64.

Twain, Mark [Samuel L. Clemens]. *Life on the Mississippi*. Boston, MA: James R. Osgood, 1883.

Underwood, Ted, Hoyt Long and Richard Jean So. 'Cents and Sensibility'. *Slate*, 10 December 2014. www.slate.com/articles/business/moneybox/2014/12/thomas_piketty_on_literature_balzac_austen_fitzgerald_show_arc_of_money.html

United Nations' Sustainable Development Goals. www.un.org/sustainabledevelopment

Volkova, Olga. 'On *Scott's Russian Shadow*: Historicity in *The Bride of Lammermoor* and *Dead Souls*'. *Studies in Romanticism* 53 (2014): 149–70.

Washington, Chris and Anne C. McCarthy, eds. *Romanticism and Speculative Realism*. New York: Bloomsbury, 2018.

Watson, Alex. *Romantic Marginality: Nation and Empire on the Borders of the Page*. London: Pickering and Chatto, 2012.

Watson, Nicola. *The Literary Tourist*. Houndsmills: Palgrave, 2006.

Weber, Samuel. *Return to Freud: Jacques Lacan's Dislocation of Psychoanalysis*. Cambridge: Cambridge University Press, 1991.

Welsh, Alexander. *The Hero of the Waverley Novels*. Princeton: Princeton University Press, 1992.

West, Jane. *Alicia de Lacy: An Historical Romance*. 4 vols. London: Longman, 1814.

———. *The Refusal*. 3 vols. London: Longman, Hurst, Rees and Orme, 1810.

Westover, Paul 'The Transatlantic Home Network: Discovering Sir Walter Scott in American Authors' Houses'. *Transatlantic Literature and Author Love in the Nineteenth Century*. Paul Westover and Ann Wierda Rowland, eds. London: Palgrave, 2016, pp. 153–74.

White, Rob. *Environmental Harm: An Eco-Justice Perspective*. Bristol: Policy Press, 2014.

———. 'Green Victimology and Non-human Victims'. *International Review of Victimology* 24.2 (2018): 239–55.

Wickman, Matthew. *Literature after Euclid: The Geometric Imagination in the Long Scottish Enlightenment*. Philadelphia: University of Pennsylvania, 2016.

———. *The Ruins of Experience: Scotland's "Romantick" Highlands and the Birth of the Modern Witness*. Philadelphia: University of Pennsylvania Press, 2007.

———. 'Tonality and the Sense of Place in Fergusson's "Elegy, on the Death of Scots Music"'. *Heaven-Taught Fergusson: Robert Burns's Favourite Poet*. Robert Crawford, ed. East Linton: Tuckwell Press, 2003.

[Wilkins, John]. *Letters Hitherto Unpublished, Written by Members of Sir Walter Scott's Family to their Old Governess*. London: E. Grant Richards, 1905.

Williams, Raymond. *Keywords: A Vocabulary of Culture and Society*. Rev. edn. London: Fontana, 1983.
——. *Marxism and Literature*. New York: Oxford University Press, 1977.
Wollstonecraft, Mary. *The Works of Mary Wollstonecraft*. 7 vols. Janet Todd and Marilyn Butler, eds. London: Pickering, 1989.
Woolf, Virginia. *Between the Acts*. Mark Hussey, ed. New York: Harcourt, 2008.
——. 'Sir Walter Scott I. Gas at Abbotsford'. *The Moment and Other Essays*. London: Hogarth Press, 1947.
Wordsworth, William. *The Excursion: Being a Portion of The Recluse, a Poem*. London: Longman, Hurst, Rees, Orme, and Brown, 1814.
——. *William Wordsworth: The Major Works*. Stephen Gill, ed. Oxford: Oxford University Press, 2008.
Worrall, David. *The Politics of Romantic Theatricality, 1787–1832: The Road to the Stage*. Basingstoke: Palgrave, 2007.
——. *Theatric Revolution: Drama, Censorship, and Romantic Period Subcultures 1773–1832*. Oxford: Oxford University Press, 2008.
Worth, Christopher. '"A Very Nice Theatre at Edinr.": Sir Walter Scott and Control of the Theatre Royal'. *Theatre Research International* 17.2 (1992): 86–95.

Index

Abbotsford, 8, 9, 100–1, 117, 131, 142–57
  domestics, 151
  'foreigners', 155, 157
  gas lighting, 5
  as a home, 152
  as a homosocial space, 145–7
  as a museum, 143
  as a national home, 144
  operations of, 151
  as a place of memory, 144
  residents (women), 9, 143–4, 148, 149–50, 152–6
  tourism, 143, 146–51
  visitor books, 143, 147, 157
  visitors to, 8–9, 143, 148, 149, 151
  visitors to (women), 144, 150–1
Aberdeenshire, 169
Absentee landlordism, 31
Abu Abdullah Muhammad XII, 59
Acts of Union, 30, 48
Adorno, Theodor W., 181, 183
Agricultural revolution, 68
Alcott, Bronson, 146
Alcott, Louisa May, 146
Allan, William, 145
anachronism, 46, 50, 51, 52, 53, 55, 56, 57, 60, 61

ancien régime, 127, 129, 134
Anderson, Benedict, 48
Anglo-Saxons, 17
Anthropocene period, 9, 165, 166, 170, 171, 182, 195
Anthropocene studies, 167, 170
antiquarianism, 38, 39, 40
anti-Semitism, 59
archipelagic theory, 167, 168–9
Arrighi, Giovanni, 90
Austen, Jane, 46, 47, 49, 61, 62, 65, 66, 67, 69, 77, 79
  opinions of Scott, 46–7
  Persuasion, 46, 47, 48, 49, 61, 77
  Sense and Sensibility, 65

Babbage, Charles, 92
Badiou, Alain, 193
Baillie, Joanna, 143, 144, 148
Balibar, Etienne, 86
Ballantyne, James, 86, 94, 98
Balzac, Honoré de, 65, 66, 67, 71, 72, 77, 79
  Père Goriot, 66, 67, 71
Bambery, Chris, 174
Bank of Scotland, 88, 94
Bauman, Zygmunt, 22, 23
beaver in Scotland, 172, 175
Belshazzar's Feast, 96

Benjamin, Walter, 181
Berardi, Franco, 99
Bergson, Henri, 188
Berkeley, George, 191
Bildungsroman, 11, 20
biodiversity, 169–77
biotic community, 162, 163, 170, 175
Blanchot, Maurice, 8
Bloch, Ernst, 49
Boltanski, Luc, 98
Bolton, Betsy, 125
Bonaparte, Napoleon, 7, 47, 88, 91, 92, 95, 100–1, 102
  as an entrepreneur, 89, 101–2, 103, 105
  Moscow campaign, 92
Booth, Alison, 145
Bothwell Bridge, Battle of, 184
Bramah, Joseph, 93
Brecht, Bertolt, 71
Brontë, Charlotte, 15, 143
  Jane Eyre, 15
Brown, William Wells, 149–50
Buell, Lawrence, 162
Burgess, Miranda, 69, 130
Burke, Edmund, 126, 134, 188
  Reflections on the Revolution in France, 126, 134
Burke, William, and William Hare, 5
Burns, Robert, 2, 148
Butler, Judith, 125, 127, 138
Byron, George Gordon Lord, 46, 47, 115–16, 144
  annotation, 114–16
Byron, Lady, 152

Cadell, Robert, 94, 107n, 116
Cagidemetrio, Alide, 59
Campbell, Thomas, 142, 157n
Campbell, Timothy, 14–15

capital, 65, 69, 71, 72, 78, 79
capitalism, 66–7, 73, 85, 86, 89, 98–100, 105, 165
  agro-capitalism, 170
  print capitalism, 103
  software capitalism, 22
Capitalocene, 170
carbon dioxide, 172
carbon sink, 172, 176
Carlyle, Thomas, 2, 103,
Catholicism, 8, 59, 117, 126–37
Caulshields Loch, 152
Chakrabarty, Dipesh, 182, 183
Chandler, James, 44n, 49–50, 51, 58
Chiapello, Eve, 98
Christianity, 58–9, 128
clearances, 161–77, 178n
Clemens, Samuel, 147
climate change, 5, 161, 165, 172, 182–3
coaches, 22, 23–4, 27
colonialism, 1, 168
Constable, Archibald, 7, 87, 88, 90, 91, 92, 94, 102, 103, 106n, 107n, 157n
  Miscellany, 87, 90–1, 94
contingency, 11, 53, 77, 192, 193, 194
Cooper, James Fenimore, 147, 158n
correlationism, 191, 192–3
Covenanters, 33, 166
Crabbe, George, 15, 157n
Craig, Cairns, 2, 126, 192
credit collapse (1825), 89
Cronon, William, 162
Crutzen, Paul, 170
Culloden, Battle of, 114, 166, 176
Currie, Mark, 13

Dalgleish, William (butler), 151
Dalkeith, Harriet Countess of, 113
Davy, Humphrey, 145, 157n
De Quincey, Thomas, 23
de Staël, Germaine, 128
debt, 7, 81–105
Deleuze, Gilles, 168, 177
Derrida, Jacques, 4, 118, 142, 144, 147, 151, 155
Devine, T. M., 68, 162, 163, 169
Dick, Alexander, 66
dilation, 16, 17
disaggregation, 16
Don Quixote, 11
Dryburgh Abbey, 152
Duncan, Ian, 3, 6, 34, 73, 83–4, 194

ecocriticism, 162–3, 167, 176, 177
ecogothic, 166, 175, 176
ecological engineering, 163, 167, 175
ecological violence, 161, 167, 175
Edgeworth, Maria, 48, 69, 144, 148
  Ennui, 48
Edinburgh Weekly Journal, 28
Eliot, George, 2, 3
Ellis, Sarah Stickney, 144
English Studies, 162
Enlightenment, 54, 60, 111, 113, 120
Enlightenment historiography, 29, 36, 55
environmental justice, 161, 164, 165, 170, 176
Everett, Edward, 142
extinction, 162, 164, 172, 174, 176

Faed, Thomas, 144
Falls of Clyde, 154
fashion, 14, 69
Fenves, Peter, 189
Ferdinand & Isabella, 59
Ferguson, Adam, 54

Ferrier, Susan, 69, 143, 144, 149, 155
Ferris, Ina, 3, 5, 6, 29, 57
Fielding, Penny, 6
Financial crash (1825–6), 67, 86, 107n, 152
fishing, 169, 170
fishing industry, 165, 169, 171
food production and security, 164
Forbes, Duncan, 66
forestry, 151, 161, 164, 171–2, 173, 176–7
Forster, E. M., 2
Fosbrooke, Thomas, 131
Foucault, Michel, 183
frame narrators, 28, 36, 40, 41, 67, 117
French Revolution, 5, 90, 95, 124, 125, 126, 127
Frey, Anne, 48
Fugitive Slave Act, 150
future anterior, 6, 29, 36, 37, 38, 40, 41, 42, 43, 44, 45n

Garrick, David, 142, 146
Garside, Peter, 51
Gaza Strip, 178n
gender
  femininity, 127, 128, 130, 133, 134, 138
  masculinity, 128, 131, 132, 133, 134, 136, 137, 138
  performativity, 125, 129, 130, 133, 138
Genette, Gérard, 18, 51, 116
George IV: visit to Edinburgh, 2, 8, 126, 137
'Getting Things Done', 98
Ghosh, Amitav, 9, 182, 183
Gibson, Jack, 172
Gibson, John, 107n

glaciation, 171, 172
Glencoe, 173
Glocal theory, 167, 168
Goethe, Johann Wolfgang von, 129
Gogol, Nikolai, 29
Goodman, Kevis, 12
Graham, Helen, 146
Griffiths, Devin, 14, 15
Guattari, Félix, 168, 177
Gumbrecht, Hans Ulrich, 11, 12, 20
Gurton-Wachter, Lily, 21

habitat disruption, 162
Hall, Sir James, 142
Handley, George B., 168
Haraway, Donna, 170, 172
Harman, Graham, 183
Hartstonge, Matthew Weld, 130
Hawthorne, Nathaniel, 147, 148, 156
Hegel, George Friedrich, 50, 52, 53, 56, 60, 191
Hegelianism, 53, 58, 60
Heidegger, Martin, 188–9
Heise, Ursula, 168, 177
Hewitt, David, 118, 169
highlandism, 50, 120
Highlands, 162, 163, 167
historical distance, 32
historical fiction, 11, 14, 48, 125, 181
historicism, 53, 56, 60
history, 49, 51, 52, 59, 60
Hogg, James, 40, 43, 144, 145, 146
　narrators, 40, 42
　temporality, 40, 41, 42
　'The Fords of Callum', 40, 43
Hughes, Gillian, 111, 114, 121
Hume, David, 192, 193, 194
Hutcheson, Francis, 188

imagined community, 60
imperialism, 54, 86, 88, 100, 168
Industrial Revolution, 9
inequality, 66, 78
inheritance, 7, 65, 66, 70, 73, 77–8, 79
insolvency, 84, 85
Irving, Washington, 142, 155
Islam, 59

Jackson-Houlston, C. M., 134
Jacobinism, 8, 127, 130
Jacobite Rebellion, 176, 184
Jacobitism, 75, 76, 130, 185, 186, 189, 190, 191, 194
James V, 115
James VI and I, 31
Jameson, Fredric, 50–1, 72–3, 182, 183
Jarrells, Anthony, 6–7, 136
Jeffrey, Francis, 17, 119, 157n
Johnson, Samuel, 188
Jones, Claire, 3
Jonsson, Fredrik Albritton, 163, 169–70
Jordan, country of, 178n
Judaism, 58–60

Kafka, Franz, 128
Kant, Immanuel, 183, 188, 190–3
Kitchener, Andrew, 172
Knight, Ellis Cornelia, 8, 124, 125
　Marcus Flaminius, 124, 127
Knox, John, 133
Knox, Robert, 5
Koselleck, Reinhart, 22, 49

Lacan, Jacques, 45n
Laidlaw, William, 145, 152, 159n
　'Abbotsford Notanda', 152
land ethics, 161

land management, 161, 164, 171
Langan, Celeste, 6, 7, 112, 119
Langham Letter, 137
Largs battlefield, 152
Lazzarato, Maurizio, 84, 86
Leavis, F. R., 2
Lee, Yoon Sun, 19, 49
Leopold I, as Prince Leopold, 153
Leopold, Aldo, 162
Lincoln, Andrew, 3, 73, 130
Liu, Alan, 14, 25
Livesey, Ruth, 24
Lockhart, John Gibson, 2, 117, 144, 145, 146, 147, 152, 153
  Memoirs of the Life of Sir Walter Scott, 2, 144
Lordon, Frédéric, 105
Lorenz, Chris, 12
Lowlands, 163, 175
Luhman, Niklas, 189
Lukács, Georg, 2, 12, 35, 50, 52, 53, 58, 60, 67, 163
Lumsden, Alison, 3, 7, 154
Lupton, Christina, 13
Lynch, Andrew, 133
Lynch, Deidre, 49, 61

McCracken-Flesher, Caroline, 3, 8, 196n
McCrie, Reverend Thomas, 133
McGann, Jerome, 3, 116, 122n
McGurl, Mark, 183
Mcintosh, Ainsley, 121, 122n
Mackenzie, Henry, 145
McLane, Maureen, 112, 119
McNiel, Kenneth, 111
Macpherson, James, 119
Malthus, Thomas, 74
Manning, Susan, 119
marginalisation, 9, 125, 163, 178
Markovits, Daniel, 78

Martin, John, 114, 115
Marx, Karl, 79, 87, 106n
Mayer, Robert, 3
Meillassoux, Quentin, 183, 190, 191, 193
Melrose, 154, 166
Melrose Abbey, 147, 155
Melville, Herman, 146–7
Melville, Robert Dundas, 2nd Viscount, Lord, 130
Mendelssohn, Felix, 147, 148
Menzies, William, 96
mercantilism, 73
meritocracy, 66, 67, 70, 73, 77, 78, 79, 80
migrants, 60
Mill, John Stuart, 94–5
Millar, Margaret (family governess), 152, 153
Millgate, Jane, 57
modernisation, 72, 170
modernity, 32, 34, 36, 48, 49, 126, 130, 138, 143
monarchy, 126
Moniteur, 87, 91
Montagu, Lord, 130
Montesquieu, 32, 33
Moody, Jane, 125
Morayshire, 169
Moretti, Franco, 18
Muir, Edwin, 2
Mullen, Mary, 52

Nairn, Tom, 2
Napoleonic Wars, 48, 87, 88, 89, 90
narration, 51, 62
narrative deceleration, 17, 18
Nasrid dynasty, 59
national history, 60
national language, 16

national tales, 14
Neolithic period, 165, 170, 172
Nixon, Rob, 165, 177
Norman Conquest, 17
Normans, 16, 58
novel of manners, 14

object-oriented ontology, 183
Oliver, Susan, 9
orientalism, 2
overfishing, 170

Palestine, 178n
Patmore, Coventry, 144
Peacock, Thomas Love, 119
Pennant, Thomas, 176
performance, 8, 126, 138
performance, political, 123, 126, 130, 132, 135, 137, 138
performance, theatre, 130
performance, violence, 135, 137
Perkin, Harold, 69–70
persona standi in judicio, 92
Peterloo Massacre, 28, 130
Peters, John Durham, 13
Piketty, Thomas, 65–9, 71, 72–3, 77, 78–9, 80n
Pittock, Murray, 112, 186, 189, 190
Plantationocene, 170–1, 175
Poot, Luke Terlak, 29
Pope, Alexander, 59
Porteous Riots, 184
Porter, Jane, 8, 125, 128, 129
predator animals, 164, 168, 173, 175
Price, Dr Richard, 126
Price, Fiona, 8, 69
progress, 1, 22, 28, 29, 34, 52–7, 60, 70, 72, 83, 120, 125
propriety, 127, 137, 144

Protestantism, 128, 130–8
Purdie, Tom, 145, 151

Quarterly Review, 133

Radcliffe, Anne, 191
Rancière, Jacques, 124
Reconquista, 59
'Revolution in Manners', 68
Roberts, Brian, 168
Robertson, Fiona, 3
Robertson, Roland, 168
romance, 47, 48, 51, 60, 85
Romantic period, 125
Romantic poetry, 119
romanticism, 56
Rose, Hugh, 164
Rousseau, Jean-Jacques, 54, 56, 127
Rowland, Ann, 114
royalists, 33
Ruddiman, William, 171
Russell, James, 175

Said, Edward, 2
Saxons, 16, 58
Schlegel, Friedrich, 51, 52
Schumpeter, Joseph, 100
Scott, Anne (daughter), 143, 144, 146, 152, 155, 156
Scott, Charles (son), 143, 155
Scott, Charlotte (spouse), 110, 143, 144, 145–6, 152, 153, 154, 155, 158n
Scott, Charlotte Hope (granddaughter), 149, 150, 158n
Scott, Major Walter (son), 143
Scott, Michael, 4
Scott, Sophia (daughter), 143, 145, 149, 152, 153, 154–5

Scott, Walter
  and anachronism, 6
  and antiquarianism, 117–18
  as 'Author of *Waverley*', 83, 85, 92, 93, 94, 95, 96, 104, 117
  and authorship, 4
  and Catholicism, 126
  and colonialism, 58
  and daughters, 154, 156
  and Edinburgh Oil Gas Light Company, 5, 92
  and environmentalism, 9, 161, 169, 175, 178
  family, 152, 155
  finances, 1, 2, 67, 84, 86, 87, 88, 94, 100
  as founder of the River Tweed Commissioners, 170
  and gender, 3
  and gender performativity, 8, 133, 134
  and genre mixing, 119
  and Gothic, 3, 56, 126, 166
  and historical fiction, 6, 12, 25, 163
  and historicism, 54
  and history, 4, 17, 34, 34, 35, 38, 42, 48
  and home, 142, 143
  and hospitality, 142–5, 148, 152, 153, 155
  and hunting, 176
  and imperialism, 100
  laird of Abbotsford, 71, 77
  as landowner, 5
  Magnum Opus Edition, 14, 17, 30, 69, 109
  and memory, 3, 4
  and modernity, 3, 126
  and monarchy, 32
  and nation, 126
  as national spokesperson, 5
  and performativity, 129, 130, 136
  as poet, 109
  and the press, 3
  and printing, 5
  and prophecy, 37
  and Protestantism, 126
  reputation, 1, 2, 3
  and Royal Society of Edinburgh, 5
  and Scotland, 2, 112, 114
  and space, 12, 13, 15, 18, 22, 23, 31
  and temporality, 22, 24, 25, 28, 29, 30, 31, 33, 35, 36, 37, 38, 126
  and theatre, 126, 129
  and wife Charlotte Scott, 154, 156
  WORKS
  The Abbot, 8, 126, 130, 131, 132, 135, 137
  The Antiquary, 20, 21, 117, 120, 130, 131, 155, 169
  The Betrothed, 4, 86
  The Bride of Lammermoor, 6, 28–34, 35, 37–40, 42, 43, 57, 60, 169
  Castle Dangerous, 4
  The Chronicles of the Canongate, 7, 67
  The Doom of Devorgoil, 130
  'Essay on the Drama', 132, 133
  The Fortunes of Nigel, 4
  Guy Mannering, 72, 77, 130, 168, 170
  The Heart of Mid-Lothian, 4, 23, 24, 77, 164, 184
  The House of Aspen, 129
  Ivanhoe, 6, 15, 16, 57, 58, 59, 60, 130
  Journal, 84, 85, 88, 89, 97, 99, 102, 104

Scott, Walter (*cont.*)
   Kenilworth: A Romance, 8, 126, 130, 131, 135, 137, 138
   The Lady of the Lake, 1, 8, 110, 114, 120, 173
   The Lay of the Last Minstrel, 4, 111, 113, 121, 145
   A Legend of the Wars of Montrose, 168, 172, 173, 174, 176
   The Life of Napoleon Buonaparte, 7, 84, 86, 87, 88, 90, 91, 92, 94, 97–104
   The Lord of the Isles, 142
   Marmion, 119, 121, 122n
   Minstrelsy of the Scottish Border, 4, 8, 46, 111, 113–16, 166, 171
   The Monastery, 131, 166
   The Pirate, 169, 170
   Redgauntlet, 9, 86, 169, 170, 184–6, 189–90, 191, 193, 194, 195
   Reliquiae Trotcosienses, 116, 117, 118
   Rob Roy, 6, 17, 46, 56, 57, 60, 73–7, 184–6, 194
   Saint Ronan's Well, 7, 68–9, 70, 72, 76, 77
   The Tale of Old Mortality, 57, 60, 133, 153, 166, 184
   Tales of my Landlord, 4, 174
   Tales of the Crusaders, 92–3, 94, 95
   The Visionary, 28
   Waverley, 1, 14–20, 23, 25, 47–51, 53, 54–5, 56, 58, 60, 62, 73, 129, 130, 142, 166, 167, 184–6, 194
   Waverley Novels, The, 3, 38, 43, 72, 86, 92, 109, 117, 126, 128, 130, 145, 161
Scottish Borders, 5, 9, 142, 162, 163, 169, 174
Scottish Enlightenment, 29, 48, 125
Scottish Romanticism, 111, 119
Scottish Rural Development Programme, 175
Selkirk, 153
Sen, Amartya, 78
Shakespeare, William, 142
sheep, 162, 164, 166, 167, 171, 174
sheep frontier, 163, 169
Shelley, Percy, 28
Sheridan, Thomas, 187–8
Sider, Justin, 51, 52
Sinclair, Sir John, 174
slavery, 73–4
slow violence, 165, 166
Smith, Adam, 73, 78, 188
Smith, Charlotte, 69
Smith, Horace, 143–4
Smith, Sarah, 142, 143
Sorensen, Janet, 17
Southey, Robert, 114
species loss, 9, 162, 165, 167, 172
species reintroduction, 174
species removal, 171, 175
stadial history, 125, 127, 171
Stendhal, 11
Stephens, Michelle, 168
Stewart, Dugald, 66
Stewart, Matthew, 78
Stirling, J. Hutchison, 192, 193
Stoermer, Eugene, 170
Stowe, Harriet Beecher, 143, 150–1
Stuart, Charles Edward, 114, 120, 184
Stuart dynasty, 34
surplusage, 118, 120
sustainable development goals, 164
Sutherland, 163, 164, 169
Sutherland, Countess of, 169

Tambling, Jeremy, 52
teleology, 50, 52
temporality, 12, 13, 14, 17, 19, 40, 41, 49, 50, 51, 52
Terry, Daniel, 130
Theatre Royal, 125, 126, 129
theatricality, 124–8, 130, 131, 135, 137, 138
Thorne, Christian, 16
tone, 188, 189
Tory, 28, 33, 57
translation, 15
Trump, President Donald, 138
Trumpener, Katie, 111
Tsing, Anna, 170
Twain, Mark *see* Clemens, Samuel

unclosing, 15, 16
United Nations, 164
unthinkability, 182, 183, 185, 195

vermin, 168
Volkova, Olga, 29

Walpole, Horace, 51, 142
Watson, Alex, 116, 118, 121
Watt, James, 161, 170
wealth, 65, 66, 69
Welsh, Alexander, 72
West, Jane, 8, 125, 127–8, 130, 131, 133, 137
West Bank, 178n
Whig, 28, 33, 57
White, Rob, 167
Wickman, Matthew, 9, 50, 120
wilderness, 162, 173
Williams, Raymond, 181, 183
Wollaston, Dr William Hyde, 145
Wollstonecraft, Mary, 127, 132, 137
wolves in Scotland, 175–6
Wordsworth, William, 21, 73
Worrall, David, 125, 120
Worth, Christopher, 129

EU representative:
Easy Access System Europe
Mustamäe tee 50, 10621 Tallinn, Estonia
Gpsr.requests@easproject.com

www.ingramcontent.com/pod-product-compliance
Lightning Source LLC
Chambersburg PA
CBHW070348240426
43671CB00013BA/2443